Railways Restored

Guide to Railway Preservation 1992/93

Edited by Alan C. Butcher

Happy 40th.
Lorraine David
Jonathan & Chloe.

01. 9. 94.

IAN ALLAN Publishing

Editor's Notes

On the following pages will be found a guide to the major preserved railways, railway museums and preservation centres in the British Isles. Information for visitors has been set out in tabular form for easy reference, together with a locomotive stocklist for most centres.

Many preservation centres and operating lines provide facilities for other groups and organisations to restore locomotives and equipment on their premises. It has not been possible to include full details of these groups, but organisations which own locomotives are shown under the centres at which they operate. In addition a full list of member societies of the ARPS is given elsewhere. In the case of most operating lines their length is given but there is no guarantee that services are operated over the entire length.

Within the heading to each entry a heading block has been incorporated for easy reference as to what each site offers in the way of passenger service to visitors. These are as follows:

Railways providing a passenger service between two or more stations with public access; eg Mid-Hants Railway.

SC A railway or preservation site offering a passenger service on a short length of line, on a regular basis, with public access at only one point; eg Lavender Line.

M A museum or site that does not offer a passenger service on a regular basis, if at all; eg Science Museum, London. Some sites may however offer rides on miniature railways.

As well as a guide as to what to expect on each site, this years *Railways Restored* shows what, if any, particular professional body the Companies or Societies belong to, these are:

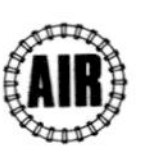

Indicates that the organisation is a member of the Association of Independent Railways (AIR).

Indicates that the organisation is a member of the Association of Railway Preservation Societies (ARPS).

Indicates that the organisation is a member of the Transport Trust (TT).

Membership of the ARPS and TT is open to both organisations and private individuals. Private members are able to take advantage of concessions offered to them by the organisations that subscribe to these two bodies.

The concessions range from a discount on the admission price to free entry. The TT's Travel Back leaflet provides details.

Details given under **Access by public transport** should be checked beforehand to ensure services shown are operating.

Visitors wishing to see specific items of rolling stock or locomotives are advised to check before their visit that the exhibit is available for inspection. It should be stressed that not all items are usually available for inspection due to restoration, operating or other restrictions.

Alan C. Butcher

Right:
Railway preservation is not just about steam. The interest in diesel preservation continues to increase and the Midland Railway Centre has held a number of Steam & Diesel Weekends. Here 'Deltic' No 55015 *Tulyar* accelerates the first train of the day towards Swanwick on 21 April 1991. *Robin Stewart-Smith*

Front Cover:
Southern Railway-built 'Schools' class 4-4-0 No 30926 *Repton* is seen leaving Quorn with the 10.45 ex-Loughborough on 13 October 1991. The locomotive is on loan from the North Yorkshire Moors Railway. *W. A. Sharman*

First published 1992

ISBN 0 7110 2033 7

Published by Ian Allan Ltd, Shepperton, Surrey and printed by Ian Allan Printing Ltd at their works at Coombelands in Runnymede, England

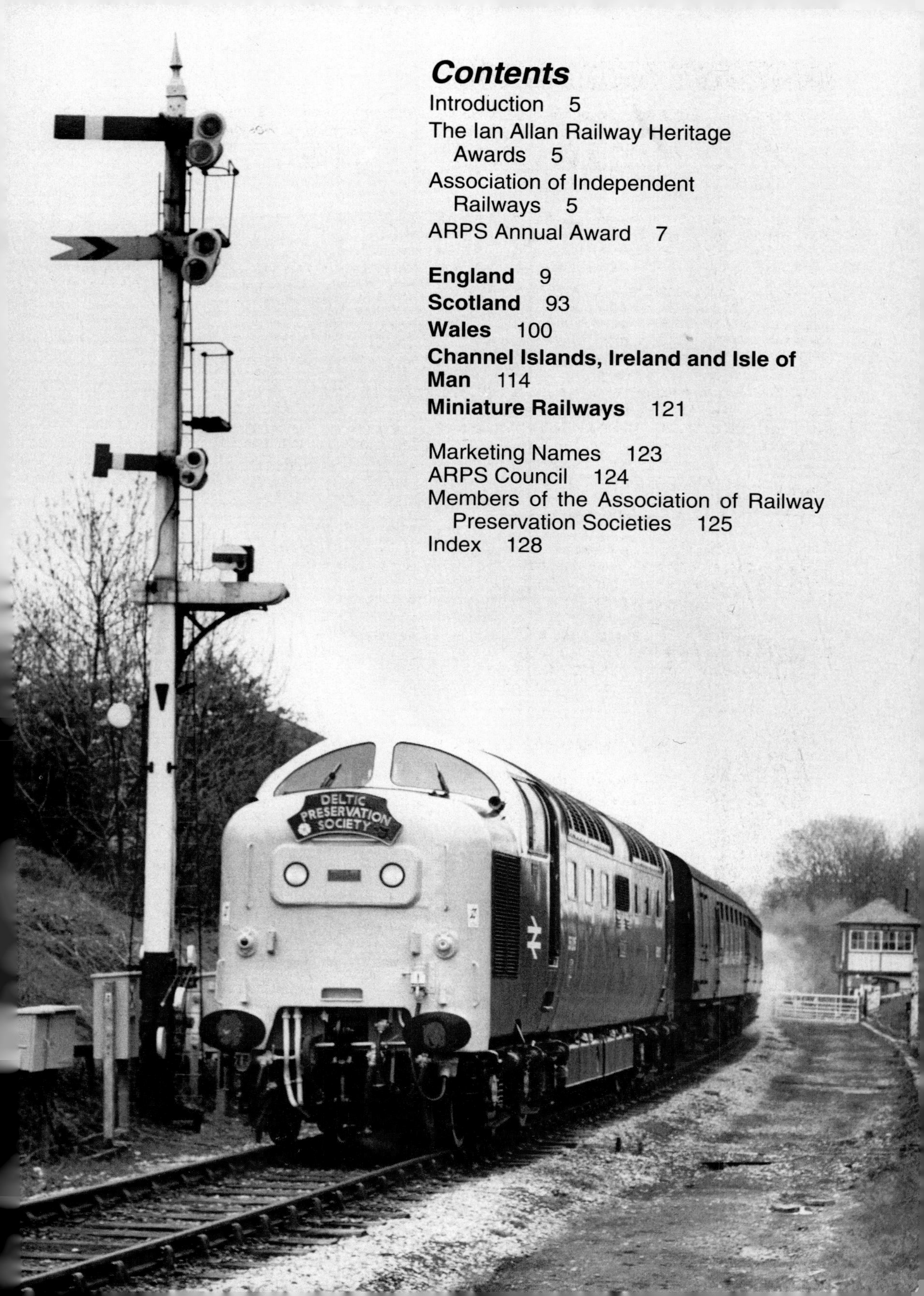

Contents

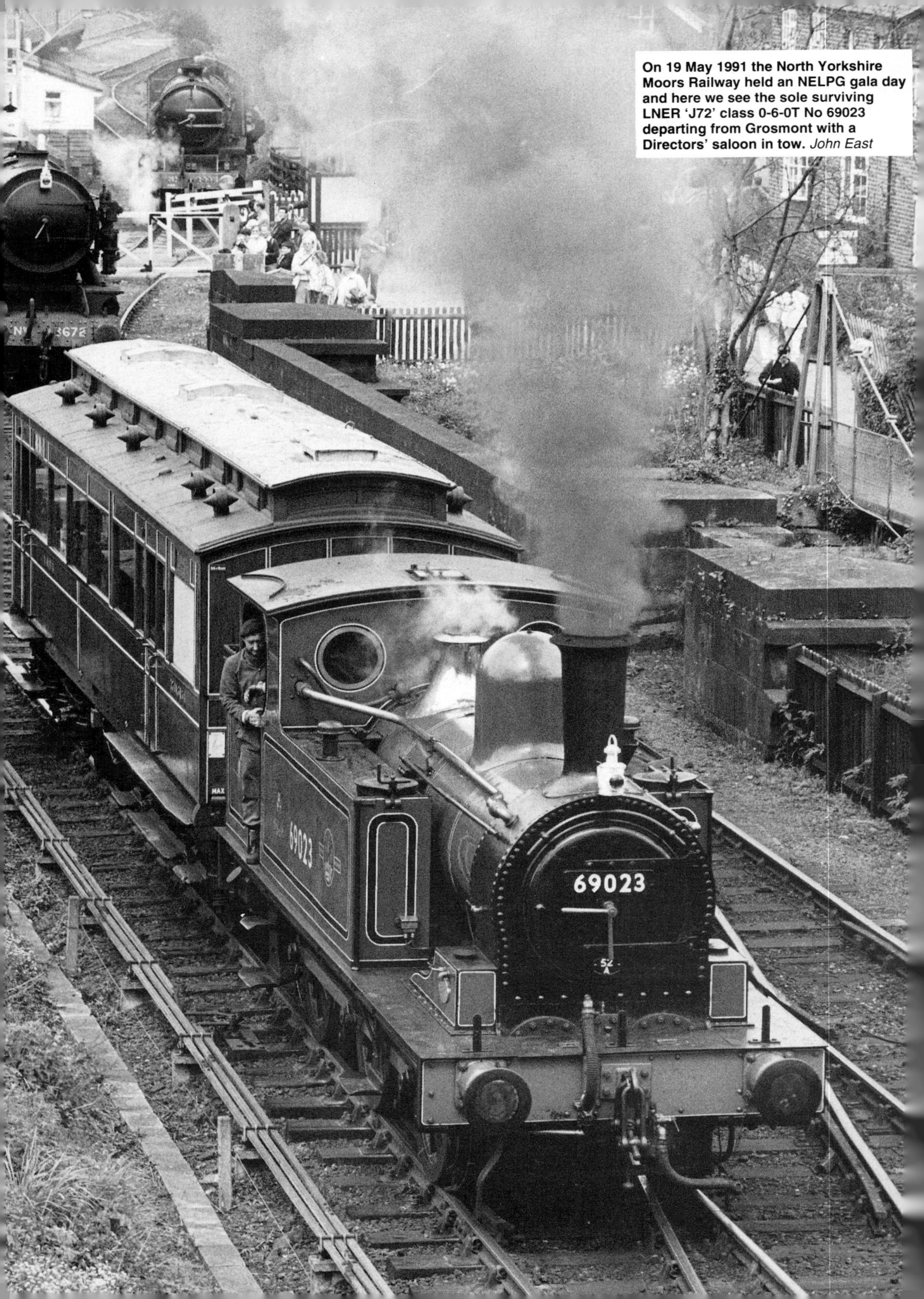

On 19 May 1991 the North Yorkshire Moors Railway held an NELPG gala day and here we see the sole surviving LNER 'J72' class 0-6-0T No 69023 departing from Grosmont with a Directors' saloon in tow. *John East*

Introduction

This year in honour of Ian Allan's 50th Jubilee, we have given a fresh look at this Jubilee Edition. The Jonahs who have been predicting that the 'preservation bubble will burst' have finally been confounded in the face of recession.

In fact, 1991, a year of recession, has been enhanced by firm evidence of the increase value of our volunteer force, as witnessed in the management 'shake up' on the Swanage Railway.

The public's love of steam is even more evident — witness the purchase of ten Finnish 5ft gauge locomotives as an entirely commercial venture. Not for preservation but to satisfy the lust of 'steam punters' at theme parks eager for live experience of a large steam locomotive.

Another extraordinary event was the success of our Railway Workshop Seminar at Swindon in November — attended by a strong force of preservation engineers — many of whom were attending an ARPS seminar for the first time. We were all somewhat confounded by the presentations on regulations made by our friendly Inspecting Officers of Railways who were themselves kind enough to admit that they themselves had had the same problem! They would be only too glad to help steer us through the jungle — a trail that has already been blazed in the past by Major Peter Olver who appropriately was the final speaker. The ARPS and Ian Allan have grown up together over the years and David Allan has already declared the proud claim for his father's firm — 'Enthusiasts publishing for enthusiasts' when opening his 'Great Southern Railways' marketing venture in 1991

The Association wishes them continuing success over the next half century.

The Ian Allan Railway Heritage awards

The awards have been made annually since 1979 with the object of encouraging high standards of structural restoration and environmental care, thereby promoting public recognition and awareness of historic railway structures and their place in the environment. We aim to promote careful design and quality workmanship in restoration, modernisation and maintenance, after taking full account of all relevant factors, particularly, of course, manpower and finance. In this way, we encourage both public and private railways to present their operational premises as an attractive 'shop window' while occupiers of former railway buildings now used for other purposes are similarly encouraged to retain as much as possible of the original character.

The organisers are the Association of Railway Preservation Societies and the main sponsors are Ian Allan Ltd, together with British Rail through their Community Unit and the Railway Heritage Trust. Judging is done from the beginning of May through to the end of August and the results are notified at the beginning of October. The awards are presented in late November at a prestigious location by a well-known public figure, with full media coverage.

1992 sees the inclusion of Ireland in the Awards initially with the addition of a special Premier Award and up to three certificates of Commendation in each sector.

WHAT IS ELIGIBLE

1 Any present or former railway structure such as, for instance a station, warehouse, bridge, viaduct, tunnel or signalling installation, that has been sympathetically restored for whatever purpose.

2 A replica structure intended to re-create or augment some aspect of the railway heritage.

3 A new structure designed in traditional style in order to blend with or complement the local environment.

WHO CAN ENTER?

Any group in Great Britain and Ireland involved in railway preservation, whether as a private railway company or as a less formal organisation. British Rail, Irish Rail, Northern Ireland Railways (NIR). Other public or commercial organisation. Private individuals.

The scheme is divided into:

(a) The Volunteer Sector for organisations run wholly or largely by volunteers.

(b) The Public & Commercial Sector. In cases of doubt, the awards committee decides which sector is appropriate.

For application forms apply to:

Arthur Harding,
6 Ullswater Grove
Alresford, Hants
SO24 9NP
Tel: 0826 22018.

Association of Independent Railways

The Association of Minor Railways (AMR) was formed at the time when railways were fighting for a 'Square Deal' with road competition, and those not parties to the Railway Companies Association formed the AMR in 1938. Its scope and objects were defined then and have remained primarily as a means of combined direct representation to Government departments, as well as discussing matters of mutual interest. It was recognised by the Ministry of Transport in 1939.

Meetings became very infrequent during the war and many of its members were nationalised, and meetings virtually ceased.

In 1944 its membership was limited to those railways operating under the Acts or Light Railway Orders.

During the 1960s the managers of the longer established railways felt that it would be useful if they could meet more formally from time to time to discuss matters of common interest and the AMR was revived in 1970.

INVERNESS
Strathspey
Craignure I.O.Mull
Caledonian Rly (Brechin)
Lochty
Summerlee
GLASGOW Museum
Bo'ness
EDINBURGH
Scottish Mining Museum
NORTH SEA
Scottish Ind.Rly Museum Dalmellington
North Tyneside (North Shields)
CARLISLE
Bowes
Tanfield
Beamish
South Tynedale
Shanes Castle
Rly Pres. Society of Ireland
Ulster Folk & Transport Museum
BELFAST
Downpatrick
Darlington
NYMR (Grosmont)
Snaefell Mountain
Ramsey Electric
Groudle Glen
Manx Electric
DOUGLAS
I.O.M Railway
Ravenglass & Eskdale
Lakeside & Haverthwaite
Steamtown
Lightwater Valley (Ripon)
Embsay
Keighley & Worth Valley
W.Yorks Bradford
LEEDS
Middleton Ind. Museum
National Rly Mus. YORK
Mus.of Army Transport (Beverley)
IRISH SEA
Blackpool
West Lancs
East Lancs (Bury)
Southport
Liverpool Mus
MANCHESTER Museum Cheadle
Cleethorpes Light Rly
DUBLIN
Great Orme
Penrhyn Castle
Llanberis
Snowdon Mountain
Conwy Valley
Crich (Nat. Tramway)
Peak Rail
Midland Rly
Cheddleton
Crewe
Foxfield
Wells & Walsingham
North Norfolk Rly
Irish Steam Pres. Society
Ffestiniog/NGRC
Welsh Highland
Llangollen
Cambrian Rlys (Oswestry)
Chatterley Whitfield (Tunstall)
Chasewater
Great Central
Leicester Mus.
Rutland Rly Mus.
PETERBOROUGH
Bure Valley
County School
Bala
Corris
Fairbourne
Talyllyn
Welshpool & Llanfair
Telford
Ironbridge
Battlefield (Shackerstone)
Cadeby
BIRMINGHAM
Museum S.I. Railway Museum
Nene Valley Rly
East Anglia Transport
Bressingham
Severn Valley
Northampton Steam
Colne Valley
Vale of Rheidol
Coventry - or Airfield Line
Northampton Ironstone
Irchester
East Anglian Rly
Audley End
Bulmer
Leighton Buzzard
Gllouc. & Warks. Rly
Winchcombe
Buckinghamshire
Teifi
Gwili
Pontypool & Blaenavon
Tuam - Westrail 20m NE of Galway
Brecon
Dean Forest
Swindon & Cricklade
Cholsey & Wallingford
Didcot
Ruislip Lido
N.Woolwich
North Downs (Dartford)
LONDON
London Transport
Science Museum
Southall
Caerphilly
Bristol Ind.
Avon Valley
Swindon GWR Mus.
Great Cockcrow
Sittingbourne
Wales Rly Centre
Swansea Maritime & Ind
East Somerset
Mid-Hants
Bluebell Rly
K&ESR
RH&DR
West Somerset
Hollycombe
Hampshire NGR
Lavender Line
Amberley
Tiverton
Bicton
Moors Valley (Ringwood)
Launceston
Seaton
Swanage
Isle of Wight
South Devon
Bodmin
Plymouth
Plym Valley
Paignton & Dartmouth
Alderney
ENGLISH CHANNEL

Since then it has grown in status with considerably rger attendances at twice yearly general meetings hen principal directors and officers take the opportuity of discussing matters of mutual interest and on eciding matters of general policy.

The Association's day to day management is in the ands of a committee of six elected representatives, a ecretary and Treasurer. In April 1988 it became a company limited by guarantee and the name changed to the Association of Independent Railways Ltd.

The objective of representing the industry to Government and other bodies remains unchanged as does the intention to encourage mutual co-operation — not at the expense of fair and healthy competition — between its member companies.

The ARPS Annual Award

his, the premier award made by ARPS, is made to a roup or organisation making an outstanding contribuon to railway preservation during the year of the ward.

The Award takes the form of a Royal Train Headoard from the London, Brighton & South Coast Railay, which is on loan to ARPS from the National Railay Museum. The award is held for one year and the winning group also receives a commemorative plaque. The Award is announced and presented at the Association's Annual General Meeting which is held on the last weekend of January each year.

The APRS Annual Award for 1991 is made to the Isle of Wight Railway Co Ltd, for reopening the line from Havenstreet to a new interchange with British Rail at Smallbrook, noting the effort this had demanded from volunteers and the willing support of Network South-East, Wightlink Ferries, the Island's three local authorities, the English Tourist Board and other official bodies.

Abbreviations

EC	Associated Equipment Co
EG	Allgemeine Eletricitaets Gesellschaft
/Porter	Aveling & Porter Ltd
/Whitworth	Armstrong Whitworth
/Drewry	Baguley/Drewry
/Peacock	Beyer Peacock & Co
/Hawthorn	Black, Hawthorn & Co
TH	British Thomson Houston
/Metcalfe	Davies & Metcalfe
/Electric	English Electric Ltd
/Jennings	Fletcher Jennings & Co
/Walker	Fox Walker
/England	George England & Co
/Clarke	Hudswell Clarke & Co Ltd
/Leslie	Hawthorn Leslie & Co
/Hunslet	Hudson Hunslet
/Stuart	Kerr Stuart & Co Ltd
/Rail	Motor Rail Ltd
/Vick	Metrovick (Metropolitan-Vickers)
/Wardle	Manning Wardle & Co Ltd
/British	North British Locomotive Co Ltd
/Wilson	Nasmyth Wilson & Co Ltd
&K	Orenstein & Koppel
SH	Robert Stephenson & Hawthorn Ltd
/Hornsby	Ruston Hornsby
/Proctor	Ruston Proctor
YEC	Yorkshire Engine Co
DB	German Federal Railways
DSB	Danish State Railways
JZ	Jugoslovenske Zeleznice
MoS	Ministry of Supply
NSB	Norwegian State Railways
RR	Rhodesian Railways
SJ	Swedish Railways
SAR	South African Railways
SNCF	French National Railways
USA TC	United States Army Transportation Corps
WD	War Department
BE	Battery electric
DE	Diesel-electric
DH	Diesel-hydraulic
DM	Diesel-mechanical
E	Overhead electric
F	Fireless
G	Geared
PM	Petrol-mechanical
ParM	Paraffin-mechanical
PT	Pannier tank
R	Railcar
ST	Saddle tank
T	Side tank
VB	Vertical boiler
WT	Well tank
4w	4-wheel

This tender first view of No 7828 *Odney Manor* shows what sparse accommodation was supplied for the crews of some locomotive classes, though in bad weather a tender/cab sheet was often resorted to. No 7828 is seen on 27 April 1991 leaving Rawtenstall on the East Lancashire Railway.
Les Nixon

England

Airfield Line SC

he railway is the only preserved tandard gauge line in Varwickshire and has been onstructed on a 'greenfield' site, by nembers of The 1857 Society, since 983. Originally known as the Coventry Steam Railway Centre, the ublic were first admitted in 1988, fter which time the marketing ame — Airfield Line — was dopted. Development continues nd the site now houses ex-MR ittle Bowden Junction signalbox, nd the rebuilt 112-year old LNWR North Kilworth station building, to e renamed Thistledown Halt on ompletion. Work is on going to onvert the six acre site to an uthentic railway setting.
ocation: Within the boundary of Coventry Airport, south of the city. Easily reached via Rowley Road, unction with A45/A46, Coventry astern by-pass — M6/M69/M1 link oad. Follow Coventry Airport lirection signs — entrance is via Emergency Exit Gate 2

Industrial locomotives

Name	*No*	*Builder*	*Type*	*Built*
—	N2	H/Clarke (1857)	0-6-0T	1952
—	1	A/Barclay (1772)	0-4-0F	1922
Southam	—	H/Clarke(D604)	0-4-0DM	1936
Mazda	—	R/Hornsby (268881)	0-4-0DE	1950
—	L7	R/Hornsby (349038)	4wDM	1954
C.P.May	—	Hibberd (2895)	4wPM	1944

Rolling stock
1 BR Mk 1 Res/buffet (TSO conversion), 2 cranes, 1 fitted van, 1 LNER brake van

OS reference: SP 349750
Access by public transport: BR Coventry, West Midlands bus route 20/21 from City Centre to Toll Bar end
Operating Society/organisation: Coventry Steam Railway Centre Ltd, 18 Lochmore Close, Hinckley, Leics LE10 0TY in conjunction with Carrick Wardale Steam Crane Group and The 1857 Society
Telephone: Hinckley (0455) 634373/635440 evenings only and/or answerphone
On site facilities: Buffet car, souvenir sales shop and picnic area
Catering facilities: Buffet
Length of line: 1,320yds (under construction)
Public opening: Every Sunday and bank holiday from Easter to October, 11.00-17.00, static display. See press for operating days and special events. Other times and party visits by prior arrangement
Car park: On site, access off Rowley Road
Facilities for disabled: Site relatively flat. Members willing to assist, no access to buffet coach, no toilets
Note: The site is not accessible at other times

Amberley Chalk Pits Museum SC

Narrow Gauge and Industrial Railway Collection (incorporating the Brockham Museum of Narrow Gauge Railways)

The NG&IR Collection is part of an open air industrial museum set in 36 acres of the former Pepper & Co

Locomotives
(2ft or 60cm unless otherwise indicated)

Name	*No*	*Builder*	*Type*	*Built*
Polar Bear	—	Bagnall (1781)	2-4-0T	1905
Peter	—	Bagnall (2067)	0-4-0ST	1918
Lion	—	Baldwin (44656)	4-6-0T	1917
Townsend Hook	4	F/Jennings (172L)	0-4-0T (3ft 2¼in gauge)	1880
Scaldwell	—	Peckett (1316)	0-6-0ST (3ft 0in gauge)	1913
—	23†	Spence	0-4-0T (1ft 10in gauge)	1921

chalk pits. A 2ft gauge line has been constructed and this is used for carrying passengers in genuine workmen's vehicles

Museum Director: Robert Taylor

Location: Houghton Bridge, Amberley, West Sussex (3 miles north of Arundel). On B2139. Adjacent to Amberley BR(SR) station

OS reference: TQ 031122

Operating society/organisation: Southern Industrial History Centre Trust, Amberley Chalk Pits Museum, Houghton Bridge, Amberley, Arundel, West Sussex BN18 9LT

Telephone: Bury (0798) 831370 (Museum office)

Car park: Adjacent to Amberley Station

On site facilities: Shop, light refreshments, audio-visual show

Public opening: Wednesday to Sunday (inclusive) each week, and Bank Holiday Mondays, (open all week in school summer holidays) 10.00-last entry 17.00, 1 April-1 November

Special events: Please see press for details

Special Notes: The NG&IR Collection is part of an open air industrial museum set in 36 acres of the former Pepper & Co chalk pits. Displays include working potter, blacksmith, boatbuilder and printer, stationary engines, historic radio collection and newly completed vintage Southdown garage and

Name	*No*	*Builder*	*Type*	*Built*
—		Decauville (1126)	0-4-0T	19[illegible]
Monty	(6)	O&K (7269)	4wDM	1936 (3ft 2¼in gauge)
The Major	(7)	O&K (7741)	4wDM	1937
—	2	Ransomes & Rapier (80)	4wDM	1937
—	—	Hudson-Hunslet (3097)	4wDM	1944
—	2	R/Hornsby (166024)	4wDM	1933
—	(3041) (1320)	M/Rail (Simplex) (ex-PM)	4wDM	1918
—	3101	M/Rail (Simplex) (1381) Armoured	4wPM	1918
Peldon	—	John Fowler (21295)	4wDM	1936
Redland	—	O&K (6193)	4wDM	1937
—	—	Lister (35421)	4wPM	1949
—	(LR 2593)	M/Rail (Simplex) (872)	4wPM	1918
—	27	M/Rail (Simplex) (5863)	4wDM	1934
—	—	M/Rail (Simplex)	4wDM	1949 (10161) (2ft 11in gauge)
Ibstock	—	M/Rail (Simplex) (11001)	4wDM	1951
CCSW	—	Hibberd (1980)	4wDM	1936
Thakeham Tiles	No 3	Hudson-Hunslet (2208)	4wDM	1941
Thakeham Tiles	No 4	Hudson-Hunslet (3653)	4wDM	1948
—	—	H/Clarke (DM686)	0-4-0DM	1948
Star Construction	—	Hudson-Hunslet	4wDm	c1941
—	18	R/Hornsby (187081)	4wDM	1937
—	—	Hudson-Hunslet (2536)	4wDM	1941
—	—	Lister (33937)	4wDM	1949
—	—	R/Hornsby (172892)	4wDm	1934
—	WD 904	Wickham (3403)	2w 2PMR	1943
—	2	Wingrove & Rogers (5031)	4wBE	1953
—	—	Wingrove & Rogers (5034)	4wBE	1953
—	—	Wingrove & Rogers (4998)	4wBE	1953
—	—	Wingrove & Rogers (T8033)	0-4-0BE	1979

†Includes hoist and 'haulage truck' for conversion to 5ft 3in gauge

Below:
Decauville of France built large quantities of narrow gauge equipment for use at home and in their colonies. This example, a 2ft gauge 0-4-0T is preserved at Amberley. *Alan C. Butcher*

uses. A 2ft 0in gauge industrial
ailway system is demonstrated
vhen possible, and a 3ft 2¼in gauge
ine is under construction. In
ddition a 2ft 0in gauge 'main line'
as been constructed and this is
sed for carrying passengers in
enuine workmen's vehicles. The
00yd line, was officially opened by
IRH Prince Michael of Kent on 5
une 1984. The railway is operated
very day the museum is open
subject to mechanical availability),
vith steam locomotive haulage on
ertain days — for details contact
the museum office. Wheelchairs can normally be accommodated on the train. A Narrow Gauge Industrial Railway Introductory Exhibition sets the scene for these and other set-piece display areas

Stock
2 Penrhyn Quarry Railway 4-wheel coaches (2ft gauge, ex-1ft 10¾in gauge); RAF Fauld bogie coach (1940) (2ft gauge); Rye & Camber Tramway bogie (incomplete) (1895) (3ft gauge); 2 Groudle Glen Railway 4-wheel coaches (1896 and 1905) (2ft gauge); 60 other varied pieces of rolling stock of 12 different gauges ranging from 1ft 6in to 3ft 2¼in plus numerous miscellaneous exhibits including track, signals etc

Membership details: Friends of the Amberley Chalk Pits Museum, c/o above address
Membership journal: *Extracts* — twice a year

Avon Valley Railway SC

'ormerly the Bristol Suburban
Railway, services re-commenced
ver the Bitton-School Road Halt
ection in August 1983
Marketing Manager: Ken Goodway
Headquarters: Bitton Railway Co
Ltd, Bitton Station, Bristol, Avon
Main station: Bitton
OS reference: ST 670705
Car park: Bitton
Access by public transport:
Badgerline service No 332 (Bristol-
Bath), No 558 (Bristol-North
Common) or 632 (Bristol-Bath)
Catering facilities: Refreshment
oom is able to supply hot snacks.
Restaurant coach is available for
rivate party catering
On site facilities: Toilets, snack bar
Length of line: 1½ miles
Public opening: Please contact for
etails, available on pre-recorded
message on Bitton (0272) 327296.
992 operating dates are —
7-20 April; 3/4, 24/25 May, 7 June;
, 12, 19, 26 July; 2, 9, 16, 23,
0/31 August; 6, 27 September;
October, plus Santa Specials
Special events: 7 June and
September — Friends of Thomas;
July, 2 August and 4 October —
Heavy Horse Days; 19 July — Teddy
Bear's Picnic; 31 August —
Railways on Canvas; 27 September
– Steaming for Barnado's;
8/29 November, 5/6, 12/13, 19/20,
3 December — Santa Specials;
6/27 December, 1 January 1993 —
Mince Pie Specials
Facilities for disabled: Coach
onverted to disabled vehicle

Locomotives

Name	*No*	*Origin*	*Class*	*Type*	*Built*
Sir Frederick Pile	34058	SR	BB	4-6-2	1947
—	44123	LMS	4F	0-6-0	1925
—	45379	LMS	5MT	4-6-0	1937
—	47324	LMS	3F	0-6-0T	1926
—	48173	LMS	8F	2-8-0	1943
—	80104	BR	4MT	2-6-4T	1955

Locomotive notes: All locomotives undergoing restoration.

Industrial locomotives

Name	*No*	*Builder*	*Type*	*Built*
Edwin Hulse	2	Avonside (1798)	0-6-0ST	1918
Littleton No 5	—	M/Wardle (2018)	0-6-0ST	1922
Fonmon	—	Peckett (1936)	0-6-0ST	1924
—	—	RSH (7151)	0-6-0T	1944
—	—	R/Hornsby (235519)	4wDM	1945
—	—	Baguley/Drewry (2153)	0-4-0	1941
—	2	Bagnall (2842)	0-4-0ST	1946
General Lord Robertson	610	Sentinel (10143)	0-8-0DH	1961
Kingswood	—	Barclay (446)	0-4-0DM	1959
—	10128	Sentinel (10128)	0-4-0DM	1963

Locomotive notes: R/Hornsby (235519) and Bagnall (2842) undergoing restoration.

Stock
16 ex-BR Mk1 coaches (9 stored off-site); 1 ex-BR Mk 1 Restaurant Coach; 1 ex-BR Mk 1 sleeper; 1 ex-LMS 'Royal Scot' corridor 3rd; 1 ex-LMS brake composite corridor; 3 open wagons; 3 box vans; 3 refrigerated box vans; 1 ex-GWR Fruit 'C'; 1 ex-GCR box van; 1 ex-BR Lowmac; 1 ex-BR ballast wagon; 1 ex-LMS 12-ton box van; 1 ex-LMS 5 ½-ton handcrane and runner

Owners
44123 and 47324 (the London Midland Society)
80104 (the Port Line Project)

Membership details: Mrs V. Baldwin, 18 Gays Road, Hanham, Bristol
Membership journal: *Semaphore* — quarterly

The Battlefield Steam Railway

A quiet country railway operated by members of the Shackerstone Railway Society Ltd, who are undertaking the extension of the line to Shenton and the battlefield of Bosworth
Headquarters: Market Bosworth Light Railway, Shackerstone station, near Market Bosworth, Leicestershire
Telephone: (0827) 715790 (weekends only); (0827) 880754 (weekdays and weekends only)
Main station: Shackerstone
Other public station: Market Bosworth, Shenton*
OS reference: SK 379066
Car park: Shackerstone
Access by public transport: Leicester City Bus, service 153 (tel: 0533 536544). Leicester to Market Bosworth (square) weekdays and Sundays
Refreshment facilities: Shackerstone cafe on station. Licensed bar on train
Souvenir shop: Shackerstone
Museum: Shackerstone
Depot: Shackerstone
Length of line: 4¼ miles*
Passenger trains: Shackerstone-Market Bosworth-Shenton*
Period of public operation: Passenger steam service will operate: Sundays and bank holiday Mondays 5 April-25 October. Station and museum only are open Sundays throughout the year
Special events: 3/4 May — Teddy Bears Picnic; 23-25 May — Friends of Thomas the Tank; 21 June — Father's Day; 22-26 June — Schools Week; 28 June — Postman Pat; 19 July — Treasure Hunt; 23 August — Battlefield Special; 29-31 August — Friends of Thomas the Tank; 13 September — Battlefield Special; 20 September — Grand Parents Day

Locomotives

Name	*No*	*Origin*	*Class*	*Type*	*Built*
—	D2245	BR	04	0-6-0DM	1956

Industrial locomotives

Name	*No*	*Builder*	*Type*	*Built*
Linda	—	Bagnall (2648)	0-4-0ST	1941
The King	—	Borrows (48)	0-4-0WT	1906
Waleswood	—	H/Clarke (750)	0-4-0ST	1906
—	11	Hunslet (1493)	0-4-0ST	1925
Dunlop No 7	—	Peckett (2130)	0-4-0ST	1951
—	3	RSH (7537)	0-6-0T	1949
—	4	RSH (7684)	0-6-0T	1951
Lamport No 3	—	Bagnall (2670)	0-6-0ST	1942
Florence	2	Bagnall (3059)	0-6-0ST	1953
—	—*	R/Hornsby (235513)	4wDM	1945
—	—	R/Hornsby (263001)	4wDM	1949
The 1211 Squadron	—	R/Hornsby (347747)	0-6-0DM	1957
—	—	R/Hornsby (393304)	4wDM	1956
—	—	R/Hornsby (423657)	4wDM	1958
—	—	S/Crossley (7697)	0-6-0DM	1953

*Converted to steam power 1983

Stock
6 ex-BR Mk 1 coaches; 2 ex-BR converted DMU coaches; 4 parcels vans; 2 rail mounted steam cranes; 2 rail mounted diesel crane; Small number of wagons; ex-BR Griddle car; SR brake van; MR brake van

***Special notes:** An extension of the line from Market Bosworth to Shenton and the battlefield of Bosworth is being undertaken and will open in April 1992, subject to HM Railway Inspectorate approval
Operating Manager: A. G. Briggs
Operating Company/Preservation Society contact: A. G. Briggs, 40 Newstead Avenue, Burbage, Hinckley, Leics LE10 2JB
Membership journal: *Shackerstone News* — 3/4 times/year
Marketing name: The Battlefield Line

Right:
Looking uncannily like one of those 'opening day' official photos, this new building at Shackerstone on the Battlefield Steam Railway is a tribute to the volunteers. The building was carefully modelled on photographs to give it that authentic look. 1 April 1991.
Melvyn Hopwood

Beamish SC

'he railway station, signalbox and oods shed have been completely ecreated along with the other xhibits to show a way of life long ast. There are some very old ocomotives in the collection.
Museum Director: Peter Lewis
ocation: The North of England)pen Air Museum, Beamish, ;ounty Durham DH9 0RG.
)S reference: NZ217547
'elephone: Stanley (0207) 231811
;ar park: At museum
ccess by public transport: Bus ervice from Worswick Street, Iewcastle upon Tyne; Bus service Ios 775 and 778 from Sunderland ia Chester-le-Street; Bus service 20 from Milburngate, Durham City
)n site facilities: 200-acre open air ıuseum vividly recreates life in the Iorth of England around the turn of ıe century. The Town with entists's home and surgery, olicitor's office, the Sun Inn public ouse, Co-operative shops and rinter's workshop. The railway tation with country station, goods ard, signalbox and rolling stock nd locomotives often in steam. The ;olliery Village with furnished pit ottages, 'drift' mine and colliery uildings. Home Farm with farm ouse, livestock and exhibitions. 'ea Room, souvenir shop and icnic areas

Locomotives

Name	No	Origin	Class	Type	Built
—	876	NER	C1	0-6-0	1889
Locomotion	1*	—	—	0-4-0	1975

*Replica, and may be out on long-term loan

Industrial locomotives

Name	No	Builder	Type	Built
Twizell	3	Stephenson (2730)	0-6-0T	1891
—	14	H/Leslie (3056)	0-4-0ST	1914
South Durham Malleable*	No 5	Stockton Ironworks	0-4-0ST	c1880
Coffee Pot	—	Head Wrightson	0-4-0VB	1871
—*	E1	Black, Hawthorn (897)	2-4-0CT	1883
Hetton Loco	—	G. Stephenson (1)	0-4-0	1822
—	—	R/Hornsby (476140)	0-4-0DM	1963
Jacob	680	McEwan Pratt	0-4-0P	1916

*In store for long-term restoration

Owner
Hetton Loco (on loan from National Railway Museum)
Locomotion (the Locomotion Trust)

Note
Not all exhibits on display

Public opening: April-October (inclusive) daily 10.00-18.00. November-March (inclusive) daily except Mondays 10.00-17.00. Last admission is always 4pm. Please check for Christmas opening times. Locomotives do not steam, and some areas are closed in winter months

Special events: A full programme of events is planned for 1992
Length of line: Approx ½-mile single line connecting rebuilt NER station to colliery sidings. No through passenger trains
Facilities for disabled: Not ideal for wheelchairs. Rolling stock not converted. Advanced notice for parties to Bookings Officer preferred

Bicton Woodland Railway SC

passenger-carrying line of 18in auge with stock mainly from the Voolwich Arsenal Railway and of Vorld War 1 vintage
ocation: Bicton Park, near idmouth
)S reference: SY 074862
)perating society/organisation: icton Woodland Railway, Bicton ;ardens, East Budleigh, Budleigh alterton, Devon
'elephone: Colaton Raleigh (0395) 8465
;ar park: On site
ccess by public transport: Buses ass half-hourly from Exeter, ;xmouth, Sidmouth in season

Locomotives

Name	No	Builder	Type	Built
Woolwich	1	Avonside (1748)	0-4-0T	1916
Bicton	2	R/Hornsby (213839)	4wDM	1942
Carnegie	3	Hunslet (4524)	0-4-4-0DM	1954
Clinton	4	H/Hunslet (2290)	0-4-0	1941
*Budley**	—	R/Hornsby (235624)	4wDM	1945

*Static exhibit

Stock
4 open bogie coaches; 5 closed bogie coaches

On site facilities: Refreshments, shop, one museum, toilets, 18in gauge railway
Length of line: 3,250yd

Public opening: Please contact for details
Facilities for disabled: Toilets, wheelchairs available. Special carriage for wheelchairs

Birmingham Museum of Science & Industry — M

Location: Newhall Street, Birmingham B3 1RZ
OS reference: SP 064874
Organisation: Birmingham City Council
Telephone: 021-236 1022
Car park: Public multi-storey nearby in Newhall Street
Access by public transport: Birmingham New Street or Snow Hill stations, then short walk following signs
Facilities: Shop, refreshments
Opening times: Monday-Saturday 09.30-17.00; Sunday 14.00-17.00

Locomotives

Name	*No*	*Origin*	*Class*	*Type*	*Buil*
City of Birmingham	46235	LMS	8P	4-6-2	193

Industrial locomotives

Name	*No*	*Builder*	*Type*	*Built*
Secundus	—	B/Seekings	0-6-0WT	1874
Leonard	1	Bagnall (2087)	0-4-0ST	1919
Lorna Doone	56	K/Stuart (4250)	0-4-0ST	1922

*2ft 8in gauge
†2ft gauge

Special notes: Facilities for the disabled (toilets and lifts). Special parking facility

Birmingham Railway Museum — SC

Location: 670 Warwick Road (A41), Tyseley, Birmingham B11 2HL
OS reference: SP 105841
Operating society/organisation: Birmingham Railway Museum Trust telephone: 021-707-4696
Car park: Site
Access by public transport: West Midlands Travel bus routes Nos 37, 44 from city centre. BR service to Tyseley station (no Sunday service)
On site facilities: The Museum is on the site of a former GWR/BR steam shed and has been equipped with much specialised railway engineering machinery. Souvenir shop, restaurant, passenger demonstration line and station, viewing gallery, schools education service
Refreshment facilities: Available in 'Chuffs' restaurant
Length of line: ⅓-mile
Public opening: Static display daily 10.00-17.00 except Christmas and New Year. Steam days most Sundays and Bank Holidays, Easter-October
Special events: Santa and Halloween (see press for details)
Special notes: Tyseley is a centre for 'Steam on BR' railtours over the BR lines to Stratford upon Avon and Didcot (via Oxford). In 1983 an Education Service for schools began

Locomotives

Name	*No*	*Origin*	*Class*	*Type*	*Buil*
Albert Hall	4983	GWR	'Hall'	4-6-0	193
Earl of Mount Edgcumbe	5043	GWR	'Castle	4-6-0	193
Defiant†	5080	GWR	'Castle'	4-6-0	193
Thornbury Castle	7027	GWR	'Castle'	4-6-0	194
*Clun Castle**	7029	GWR	'Castle'	4-6-0	195
—†	7752	GWR	5700	0-6-0PT	193
—	7760	GWR	5700	0-6-0PT	193
—	9600	GWR	5700	0-6-0PT	194
*Kolhapur**	5593	LMS	'Jubilee'	4-6-0	193
Scots Guardsman	6115	LMS	'Royal Scot'	4-6-0	192
—	13029	BR	08	0-6-0DE	195
—	40118	BR	40	1Co-Co1	196

*On loan to the Great Central Railway
†On loan to Gloucestershire Warwickshire Railway

Locomotive notes: 4983 is undergoing restoration, 9600 is dismantled

Industrial locomotives

Name	*No*	*Builder*	*Type*	*Buil*
Rocket	—	Peckett (1722)	0-4-0ST	192
—	1	Peckett (2004)	0-4-0ST	194
—	—	Baguley (800)	0-4-0PE	192
Henry	—	H/Leslie (2491)	0-4-0ST	190
Count Louis†	—	B/Lowke (32)	4-4-2	192

†15in gauge — on static display

Stock

1 Pullman bar car*; 1 Gresley buffet car; 1 LNWR semi-Royal Saloon*; 1 GWR VIP Saloon; 1 30-ton steam crane and sundry goods vehicles; 1 GWR Inspection Saloon; 1 Tourist 3rd open coach; 2 TPO vehicles (1 LNWR, 1908; 1 LMS 1950); 1 GWR brake 3rd corridor coach; 1 BR Mk 1 BFK coach; 1 LMS 50ft parcels van; 1 LNWR 6-wheel guard's van; 1 GWR 'Toad' guard's van; 1 SR PMV; 1 GWR 6-wheel Mess Tool van; Plus varied goods vehicles
*In store

NB Some static display locomotives and stock were offered for sale late in 1991

perating, providing a service of isits to schools in the Midlands nd party visits from schools to the museum. Membership is available o the public providing free entry to site events, magazines, members' evenings, etc.
Membership details: From the museum office

Note: All attractions and facilities are advertised subject to availability

Blackpool & Fleetwood Tramway

Operating organisation: Blackpool Transport Services Ltd, Rigby Road, Blackpool, Lancashire FY1 5DD
Telephone: (0253) 23931
Length of line: 11½ miles, standard gauge
Period of public operation: Daily throughout the year
Number of trams: 86 double- and single-deck trams the Blackpool & Fleetwood Tramway is the sole surviving street tramway system in the United Kingdom and attracts visitors from all over the country. During the autumn the streets are illuminated and several specially decorated trams are used
Managing Director: Anthony Depledge
Traffic Manager: David Eaves

Bluebell Railway

This famous steam railway was the first standard gauge passenger line to be taken over by enthusiasts. It derives its name from bluebells which proliferate in the woodlands adjoining the line. A strong Victorian atmosphere pervades this branch line which has a large collection of Southern and pre-Grouping locomotives and coaches.
Operations Manager: Mr M. S. Millar
Headquarters: Bluebell Railway Preservation Society, Sheffield Park Station, Uckfield, East Sussex TN22 3QL
Telephone: Newick (082 572) 2370 for travel information (24hr talking timetable); Newick 3777 for bookings etc during office hours
Main station: Sheffield Park
Other public stations: Horsted Keynes
Car parks: Sheffield Park, Horsted Keynes
OS reference: Sheffield Park TQ 403238, Horsted Keynes TQ 372293
Access by public transport: Haywards Heath BR and bus to Horsted Keynes village weekdays, or direct to Sheffield Park on summer and winter Sundays. Additional bus services on certain days, timetable brochure available by sending sae

Locomotives

Name	*No*	*Origin*	*Class*	*Type*	*Built*
	—27	SECR	P	0-6-0T	1910
Stepney	55	LBSCR	A1X	0-6-0T	1875
Fenchurch	72	LBSCR	A1X	0-6-0T	1872
Pioneer I	1178	SECR	P	0-6-0T	1910
Bluebell	323	SECR	P	0-6-0T	1910
—	263	SECR	H	0-4-4T	1905
Birch Grove	473	LBSCR	E4	0-6-2T	1898
—	488	LSWR	0415	4-4-2T	1885
—	592	SECR	C	0-6-0	1901
—	58850	NLR	2F	0-6-0T	1880
Earl of Berkeley	3217	GWR	9000	4-4-0	1938
—	30064	SR	USA	0-6-0T	1943
—	541	SR	Q	0-6-0	1939
—	830*	SR	S15	4-6-0	1927
—	847	SR	S15	4-6-0	1937
Stowe	928	SR	V	4-4-0	1934
—	1618	SR	U	2-6-0	1928
—	1638	SR	U	2-6-0	1931
—	96	LSWR	B4	0-4-0T	1905
—	C1	SR	Q1	0-6-0	1942
Sir Archibald Sinclair	34059	SR	BB	4-6-2	1947
Port Line	35027	SR	MN	4-6-2	1948
Camelot	73082	BR	5MT	4-6-0	1955
—	75027	BR	4MT	4-6-0	1954
—	78059†	BR	2MT	2-6-0	1956
—	80064	BR	4MT	2-6-4T	1953
—	80100	BR	4MT	2-6-4T	1954
—	92240	BR	9F	2-10-0	1959
Blackmore Vale	21C123	SR	WC	4-6-2	1946

Industrial locomotives

Name	*No*	*Builder*	*Type*	*Built*
Blue Circle	—	A/Porter (9449)	2-2-0TG	1926
Baxter	—	F/Jennings (158)	0-4-0T	1877
Stamford—	—	Avonside (1972)	0-6-0ST	1927
Sharpthorn	—	M/Wardle (641)	0-6-0ST	1877

*Purchased without tender
†Purchased without tender, for conversion to tank engine

Right:
Ex-SECR 0-6-0T No 323 *Bluebell* waits at Horstead Keynes station on the Bluebell Railway with the first northern shuttle train of the day on 19 May 1991.
Dennis C. Pope

Refreshment facilities: Sheffield Park, Horsted Keynes (licensed bars at both stations). The 'Regency Belle' wine and dine train runs on certain dates and is also available for private charter
Souvenir shops: Sheffield Park, Horsted Keynes
Museum: Sheffield Park
Depots: Sheffield Park (locomotives), Horsted Keynes (stock)
Length of line: 5 miles — plus first section of extension of route to East Grinstead, see timetable for services over this section
Passenger trains: Sheffield Park-Horsted Keynes
Period of public operation: Sundays in January, February and December, also Boxing and New Year's Day. Saturdays and Sundays in March, April and November. Wednesdays, Saturdays and Sundays in May and October. Daily June-September inclusive. Daily for October schools half term week. Museum and locomotive sheds at Sheffield Park open daily except Christmas Day
Special events: Extensive programme of events held during the year and detailed in advance (send SAE for details)

Stock
Substantial collection of pre-Nationalisation coaches including SECR, LSWR, Bulleid, Maunsell and Chesham vehicles. Also freight stock and engineers' vehicles plus 45ton steam crane

Owners
592 (the Wainwright C Class Preservation Society)
541, 830, 847 and 1618 (the Maunsell Locomotive Society Ltd)
96 and 21C123 (the Bulleid Society Ltd)
263 (the H Class Trust)
73082 (the Camelot Locomotive Society)
C1 (on loan from the National Railway Museum)
928 (on loan from Montagu Venturers Ltd)
80064 (80064 Group)
35027, 1178 (the *Port Line* Project)

Facilities for disabled: All station facilities are on the level and ramps available for placing wheelchair visitors into trains. Special toilet in Buffet at Sheffield Park

Membership details: Membership Secretary c/o above address
Membership journal: *Bluebell News* — quarterly

Bodmin Steam Railway

The Bodmin Steam Railway typifies the bygone branch railways of Cornwall. The terminus, close to Bodmin town centre, has an interesting collection of small standard gauge locomotives and rolling stock; and the operating line winds down to a junction with British Rail at Bodmin Parkway. From the track there are scenic views across the beautiful valley of the River Fowey. Most trains are steam-hauled except Saturday
Location: Bodmin General station, on B3268
General Manager: Mr W. K. Searle

Locomotives

Name	*No*	*Origin*	*Class*	*Type*	*Built*
—	3802	GWR	2884	2-8-0	1938
—	5552	GWR	4575	2-6-2T	1928
Western Lady	D1048	BR	52	C-C	1962
—	W79976	BR (AC Cars)	—	4wDM	1958
—	D3452	BR	10	0-6-0DE	1957
—	D3559	BR	08	0-6-0DE	1958

Industrial locomotives

Name	*No*	*Builder*	*Type*	*Built*
—	19	Bagnall (2962)	0-4-0ST	1950
Alfred	—	Bagnall (3058)	0-4-0ST	1953
—	—	Bagnall (3121)	0-4-0F	1957
Peter	—	Fowler (22928)	0-4-0DM	1940
Progress	—	Fowler (4000001)	0-4-0DM	1945
Swiftsure	—	Hunslet (2857)	0-6-0ST	1943
Progress	—	Peckett (1611)	0-4-0ST	1923
Corrall	—	R/Hornsby (304470)	4wDM	1946
Lec	—	R/Hornsby (443642)	4wDM	1960
Ugly	62	RSH (7673)	0-6-0ST	1950

perating society/organisation: odmin & Wenford Railway, odmin General Station, Bodmin, ornwall PL31 1AQ
elephone: All enquiries (0208) 3666
ar park: Bodmin General only, no arking permitted at BR's Bodmin arkway station
ccess by public transport: ıterchange with BR at Bodmin arkway (arrivals by BR train only). ocal bus services to Bodmin
efreshment facilities: Light efreshments only
n site facilities: Souvenir shop, mited display of historic artefacts, oilets
ength of line: 3½ miles General-arkway (track to Boscarne is in situ ut not usable)
assenger trains: 17-22, 26, 29 pril; 3/4, 6, 10, 13, 17, 20, 24-29, 1 May; 1-30 June (except aturdays); 1-3, 5-10, 12-17, 9-31 July; daily in August and eptember; 4, 11, 18, 25 October, /6, 12/13, 19-24, 27 December
acilities for disabled: Yes
Iembership details: Mr S. ightfoot, Bodmin Railway reservation Society, c/o above ddress
Iembership journal: *Bodmin & Venford News* — 3 issues/year

Stock
8 BR Mk 1 coaches; 3 GWR coaches; 1 GWR Siphon G; Various freight wagons

Owners
D1048 (the Western Lady Ltd)
3802 (GW 3802 Ltd)

Below:
A view over the platform at Bodmin General. 1951-built Bagnall 0-4-0ST No 19 waits with the 11.00am to Parkway. In the background is the running/restoration shed with ample evidence of work in hand.
Melvyn Hopwood

Bowes Railway SC

The railway includes the only preserved rope-hauled standard gauge inclines, whose operation requires considerable skill and sleight of hand. You should not miss the opportunity of inspecting the inclines and cable house and haulage engine when you can
Chairman: Phillip Dawe
Location: Bowes Railway, Springwell Village, near Gateshead, Tyne & Wear (on B1288)
OS reference: NZ 285589
Operating society/organisation: Bowes Railway Co Ltd
Telephone: Tyneside (091) 4161847 (Answerphone)
Car park: Springwell
Access by public transport: Northern Buses services Nos 184 Washington/Birtley, 187/188

Industrial locomotives

Name	*No*	*Builder*	*Type*	*Built*
WST	—	Barclay (2361)	0-4-0ST	1954
—	22	Barclay (2274)	0-4-0ST	1949
—	20/110/709	Barclay (613)	0-6-0DH	1977
—	—	Hunslet (6263)	0-4-0DH	1964
Norwood	77	RSH (7412)	0-6-0ST	1948
—	101	Planet (3922)	4wDM	1959
—	—	Smith (18773)	4wCT	1948

Owners
22 (On loan from Thomas Ness Ltd)
WST (On loan from British Gypsum Ltd)
Norwood (On loan from National Smokeless Fuels)
Barclay 0-6-0DH (On loan from Mr P. Dawe)
Hunslet (On loan from Coal Products Ltd)
Planet and Smith (Bowes Railway Co Ltd)

Stock
20 Ordinary 10-ton wooden hopper wagons (Springwell built); 16 other wooden hopper wagons (of various pedigrees); 3 steel 14-ton hopper wagons; 5 steel 21-ton hopper wagons; 1 reel bogie (for rope replacement); 1 drift bogie (for shunting by rope); 1 loco coal wagon; 7 material wagons; 1 tool van; 3 brake vans; 2 flat wagons; 1 17-ton wooden hopper (ex-NER); 1 18-ton wooden hopper (ex-Ashington); 1

Gateshead Metro/Sunderland, 189 Washington (Brady Sq)-Gateshead 638 Ryton/Sunderland
On site facilities: Exhibition of Railway's history, wagon exhibition, workshop displays. On operating days — shop, refreshments and guided tours. Steam hauled brake van rides. Rope haulage demonstration trains
Public opening: Bank Holidays, also first and third Sundays in each month, Easter-September. Santa specials week prior to Christmas. Disabled Children's Day — mid July. (Tel: 091-416 6956 for confirmation of dates.). Guided tours midweek/out of season can be accommodated with prior notice (not trains)
Length of line: 1¼ miles total length; 1¼ miles of rope haulage; ¾-mile used for passenger trains

21-ton wooden hopper (ex-Seaham); 2 steel ballast Hopper Wagons; 1 tank wagon

Stationary haulage
Met-Vick/Wild, 300bhp electric (Blackham's Hill) 1950
BTH/Robey, 500bhp electric (Black Fell) 1950
Clarke Chapman, 22hp electric (Springwell Yard)
14ft Diam, Gravity Dilly Wheel (Springwell)

Special notes: Preserved section of the Pontop & Jarrow Railway; designed G. Stephenson; opened 1826; the only standard gauge rope-hauled incline railway in the world; Railway's own historic workshops preserved, with examples of all of the Railway's wagon types
Facilities for disabled: Toilet only
Membership details: Management Committee Secretary, c/o above address or telephone number

Membership journal: *The Incline* - quarterly
Disclaimer: The Bowes Railway C[illegible] Ltd wish to point out that all advertised facilities are subject to alteration without prior notice. Th[illegible] company can therefore not be held responsible for any loss or expense incurred

Bressingham Steam Museum SC

Five miles of various gauges of railway running through extensive gardens and a collection of well maintained and impressive main line locomotives. All the fun of the fair, with something for everyone including the mother who never wants to see another steam engine
Location: Two miles west of Diss on the A1066
OS reference: TM 080806
Operating society/organisation: Bressingham Steam Preservation Co Ltd, Bressingham Hall, Diss, Norfolk IP22 2AB
Telephone: Bressingham (037 988) 386 and 382
Car park: Steam Centre (free)
Access by public transport: Diss BR station (3 miles)
On site facilities: 9½/15/24in and standard gauge lines, totalling nearly 5 miles. Museum, steam roundabout, fire museum, souvenir shop and restaurant, extensive gardens and plant centre

Right:
Complete with face, this *Toby the Tram* look alike has been built in the workshops at Bressingham. Constructed on a Motor Rail chassis it is seen alongside Hunslet-built 0-4-0ST *George Sholto.*

locomotives

Name	*No*	*Origin*	*Class*	*Type*	*Buil*
Martello	662	LBSCR	A1X	0-6-0T	187
Thundersley	80	LTSR	3P	4-4-2T	190
Granville	102	LSWR	B4	0-4-0T	189
—	490	GER	E4	2-4-0	189
—	2500	LMS	4P	2-6-4T	193
Royal Scot	6100	LMS	7P	4-6-0	192
Duchess of Sutherland	6233	LMS	8P	4-6-2	193
Oliver Cromwell	70013	BR	7MT	4-6-2	195
Peer Gynt	5865	NSB	52	2-10-0	194
Tom Paine	141R73	SNCF	141R	2-8-2	194
King Haakon VII	377	NSB	21c	2-6-0	191

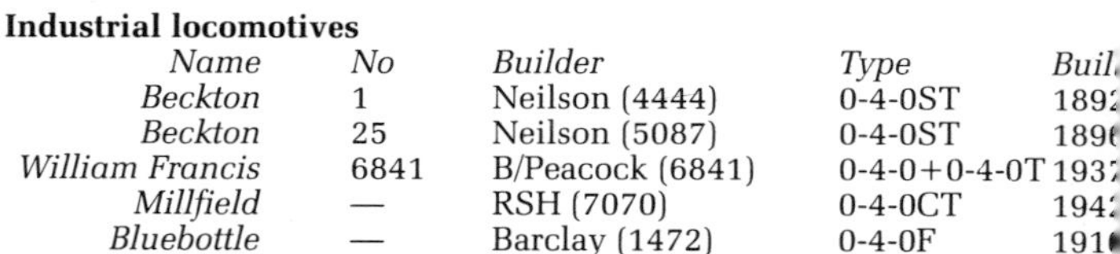

Industrial locomotives

Name	*No*	*Builder*	*Type*	*Buil*
Beckton	1	Neilson (4444)	0-4-0ST	189
Beckton	25	Neilson (5087)	0-4-0ST	189
William Francis	6841	B/Peacock (6841)	0-4-0+0-4-0T	193
Millfield	—	RSH (7070)	0-4-0CT	194
Bluebottle	—	Barclay (1472)	0-4-0F	191

ublic opening: Open daily from April to 31 October. Special steam ays every Sunday and Thursday, lus Wednesdays in July and ugust, and bank holiday Mondays, 0.00-17.30. Christmas at ressingham 29 November-0 December
pecial events: 5th Annual Fire ally 2 August
acilities for disabled: Toilets, heelchairs available. Able to take heelchairs on Nursery Line ailway
pecial notes: Reduced rates for oach parties. Prices on application

Narrow gauge locomotives

Name	No	Builder	Type	Built
Gwynedd	—	Hunslet (316)	0-4-0ST	1883
George Sholto	—	Hunslet (994)	0-4-0ST	1909
Bronllwyd	—	H/Clarke (1643)	0-6-0WT	1930
Eigiau	—	O&K (5668)	0-4-0WT	1912
—	—	M/Rail (22120)	4wDM	1964

15in gauge locomotives

Name	No	Builder	Type	Built
Rosenkavalier	—	Krupp (1662)	4-6-2	1937
Mannertreu	—	Krupp (1663)	4-6-2	1937
Flying Scotsman	4472	W. Stewart (4472)	4-6-2	1976
Alan Bloom	—	Diss (1)	0-4-0DM	1992

9½in gauge locomotives

Name	No	Builder	Type	Built
Princess	—	Motor Gear & Engine Co	4-6-2	1947

Owners
80, 490, 2500, 70013 (on loan from the National Railway Museum)

Bristol Industrial Museum — SC

he Museum houses machinery and ehicles associated with Bristol's ndustrial past, from horse-drawn ehicles to aircraft
ocation: Princes Wharf, Bristol
S reference: ST 585722
perating society/organisation: ristol Industrial Museum, Princes Vharf, Bristol, Avon BS1 4RN
elephone: Bristol (0272) 251470
ar parks: Available nearby
ccess by public transport: Buses centre of town
n site facilities: Shop

Industrial locomotives

Name	No	Builder	Type	Built
Portbury	S3	Avonside (1764)	0-6-0ST	1917
Henbury	S9	Peckett (1940)	0-6-0ST	1937
—	3	F/Walker (242)	0-6-0ST	1874
—	—	R/Hornsby (418792)	0-4-0DM	1958

Length of line: ½-mile
Public opening: Saturday-Wednesday 10.00-13.00; 14.00-17.00
Facilities for disabled: Reasonable access
Special notes: Operation of railway on advertised weekends only, 12.00-18.00
Membership details: Officer in charge D. Martin, Bristol Harbour Railway c/o above address

Buckinghamshire Railway Centre — SC

ormerly known as Quainton Road, ne name of the station, the Centre as been improved considerably uring recent years. Its true otential could, however, be ealised by an enlightened approach llowing operation of steam trains to nd from Marylebone
ocation: Adjacent to BR goods only ne to Aylesbury. Turn off A41 at Vaddesdon 6 miles NW of ylesbury, Bucks
S reference: SP 738190
perating society/organisation: uainton Railway Society Ltd, The ailway Station, Quainton, near ylesbury, Bucks HP22 4BY

Locomotives

Name	No	Origin	Class	Type	Built
—	1	Met Rly	E	0-4-4T	1898
—	0314	LSWR	0298	2-4-0WT	1874
Wightwick Hall	6989	GWR	'Hall'	4-6-0	1948
—	7200	GWR	7200	2-8-2T	1934
—	7715	GWR	5700	0-6-0PT	1930
—	9466	GWR	9400	0-6-0PT	1952
—	41298	LMS	2MT	2-6-2T	1951
—	41313	LMS	2MT	2-6-2T	1952
—	46447	LMS	2MT	2-6-0	1950
—	D2298	BR	04	0-6-0DM	1960
—	3405*	SAR	25NC	4-8-4	1958

*3ft 6in gauge

Industrial locomotives

Name	No	Builder	Type	Built
Sydenham	—	A/Porter (3567)	4wTG	1895
Scott	—	Bagnall (2469)	0-4-0ST	1932
—	—	Baguley (2161)	0-4-0DM	1941
Swanscombe	—	Barclay (699)	0-4-0ST	1891

Telephone: Quainton (029675) 450
Car park: Quainton Road — Free parking
Access by public transport: BR Aylesbury station. Special bus on Bank Holidays connects Centre with BR trains
On site facilities: Souvenir bookshop, light refreshments, toilets, steam-hauled train rides. Museum of small relics, secondhand bookshop, miniature railway
Catering facilities: Victorian Tea specials. Afternoon tea in LNWR dining car, write for details to catering manager. Lunches and afternoon teas by arrangement
Length of line: Two ½-mile demonstration lines
Public opening: Sundays and Bank Holidays: Easter-end October. Wednesdays in June, July and August. Limited opening (no engines in steam) Saturdays, June to September
Special events: Santa Specials in December (please write for details), others throughout the year. Write for details
Facilities for disabled: Access to most of site, but not toilets. No advance notice required
Special notes: One of the largest collection of standard gauge locomotives, together with a most interesting collection of vintage coaching stock, much of which was built in the last century

Name	*No*	*Builder*	*Type*	*Built*
—	—	GF3 Barclay (1477)	0-4-0F	1916
Tom Parry	—	Barclay (2015)	0-4-0ST	1935
—	—	Barclay (2243)	0-4-0F	1948
Osram	—	Fowler (20067)	0-4-0DM	1933
—	—	3 H/Leslie (3717)	0-4-0ST	1928
Sir Thomas	—	H/Clarke (1334)	0-6-0T	1918
—	—	H/Clarke (1742)	0-4-0ST	1946
—	—	Hunslet (2067)	0-4-0DM	1940
Arthur	—	Hunslet (3782)	0-6-0ST	1953
Juno	—	Hunslet (3850)	0-6-0ST	1958
—	65	Hunslet (3889)	0-6-0ST	1964
—	66	Hunslet (3890)	0-6-0ST	1964
—	26	Hunslet (7016)	0-6-0DH	1971
Redland	—	K/Stuart (K4428)	0-4-0DM	1929
Coventry No 1	—	NBL (24564)	0-6-0ST	1939
—	—	Peckett (1900)	0-4-0T	1936
Gibraltar	—	Peckett (2087)	0-4-0ST	1948
—	—	Peckett (2104)	0-4-0ST	1948
—	—	Peckett (2105)	0-4-0ST	1948
—	T1	Hibberd (2102)	4wD	1937
Tarmac	—	Hibberd (3765)	0-4-0DM	1955
—	—	Sentinel (6515)	4wVBTG	1926
—	11	Sentinel (9366)	4wVBTG	1945
—	7	Sentinel (9376)	4wVBTG	1947
—	—	Sentinel (9537)	4wVBTG	1947
Chislet	9	Yorkshire (2498)	0-6-0ST	1951

Stock: *coaches* —
1 LCDR 1st Class 4 wheeler; 1 MSLR 3rd Class 6 wheeler; 4 LNWR coach bodies; 2 GNR 6 wheelers; 3 LNWR; 3 LMSR; 1 BR(W) Hawksworth brake 3rd; 2 BR Mk 1; 1 BR Mk 2; 1 BR Suburban brake; 3 LNER; 1 LNWR full brake 6 wheeler; 1 LMSR passenger brake van; 1 GWR passenger brake van
Wagons —
1 LNWR combination truck; 1 LSWR ventilated fruit van; 1 SR PMV; 1 BR(W) 'Siphon G'; 1 BR horse box; 1 BR CCT

3 ex-London Underground coaches
1 2ft gauge post office mailbag car 803
Sentinel/Cammell 3-car steam railcar unit 5208 (ex-Egyptian National)
Numerous goods vehicles/wagons/vans

Owners
41298, 41313 and 46447, Juno (the Ivatt Locomotive Trust)
9466 (the 9466 Group)

Bulmer Railway Centre — SC

The Centre, opened in 1968, is principally a standard gauge museum and home of two main line express locomotives *King George V* and *Princess Elizabeth*. Both are normally maintained in full working order and, as such, can be absent on main line operations elsewhere. The centre also houses a collection of other locomotives, including

Locomotives

Name	*No*	*Origin*	*Class*	*Type*	*Built*
King George V	6000	GWR	'King'	4-6-0	1927*
—	5786	GWR	5700	0-6-0PT	1930
Princess Elizabeth	6201	LMS	7P	4-6-2	1933*
Cider Queen	2 (D2758)	Hunslet (6999)	05	0-6-0DH	1955

*Telephone to check presence on site

Industrial locomotives

Name	*No*	*Builder*	*Type*	*Built*
Pectin	—	Peckett (1579)	0-4-0ST	1921
Carnarvon	47	Kitson (5474)	0-6-0ST	1934
—	1254	H/Clarke (D1254)	0-6-0	1962

dustrial, as well as various items
' rolling stock.
ocation: H. P. Bulmer Ltd (Cider
akers), Whitecross Road,
ereford. The site is ½-mile from
ty centre on A438 Hereford-
recon road
S reference: SO 505402
perating society: The 6000
ocomotive Association in
njunction with the Princess
izabeth Locomotive Society and
e Worcester Locomotive Society,
behalf of H. P. Bulmer Ltd
elephone: Hereford (0432) 274378
r enquiries
ar park: Free parking on site
ccess by public transport:
idland Red bus services and local
ivate bus services. Hereford (BR)
ation (1 mile)
n site facilities: Souvenir/book
all. Light refreshment facilities
nerally available
ngth of line: About ¾-mile
iblic opening: Weekends and
nk holidays Easter/April-
eptember inclusive. Static display
4.00-17.00). Steam-operated brake
n trips, on specified Sundays and
nk holidays (11.00-17.00).

Locomotive notes: During 1992, *King George V* may be absent while No 6201 will probably be away on main line operations during part of the year. No 5786 and *Pectin* will carry out the official steaming requirements at the Centre.

Stock
Gresley Buffet coach; Several ex-BR Mk 1 coaches; Pullman car from ex-SR 6-PUL electric unit; Small number of freight vehicles including GWR tank wagon and BR Conflat

Owners
6201 (the Princess Elizabeth Locomotive Society)
6000 (on loan from the National Railway Museum)
5786 and 47 (the Worcester Locomotive Society)
Pectin and 1254 (the 6000 Locomotive Association)
2 (D2758) (H. P. Bulmer Ltd)

Telephone for details. Closed on normal weekdays (Mon-Fri)
Special events: Steam open days Easter Sunday and Monday and last Sunday in September. Santa Specials in December (enquire for details)
Special notes: Centre for steam events and servicing depot for main line steam operations in the area
Facilities for disabled: Wheelchair access to most of the site, train rides need assistance (available), no special toilet facilities
General secretary: 6000 Locomotive Association: Mr E. T. Taylor, 18 Merestone Road, Redhill, Hereford HR2 7PS
Membership details: 6000 Locomotive Association, 8 Chancel View, Abbots Mead, Hereford HR2 7XD
Membership journal: *Steam in Hereford* — quarterly

Please note that No 6000 King George V *has been transferred to Swindon GWR Museum.*

Bure Valley Railway

eadquarters: Bure Valley Railway
d, Aylsham Station, Norwich
oad, Aylsham, Norwich NR11
3W
eneral Manager: G. C. Fowler
elephone: (0263) 733858
ax: (0263) 733814
ain public station: Aylsham
Norwich Road); Wroxham
Coltishall Road)
ther public stations: Coltishall,
rampton and Buxton
ar parks: 150 spaces at Aylsham,
) spaces at Wroxham
S reference: Aylsham —
G619540326456; Wroxham —
G630300318646
ccess by public transport: BR
oveton & Wroxham station (200yd)
efreshment facilities: Aylsham
nd Wroxham
ouvenir shops: Aylsham and
'roxham
urney time: Approximately 46min
ach way with 30min turnround
ength of line: 9 miles; 15in gauge
pening times: Daily Easter-end
ctober; Weekends —
ovember/December

Locomotives

Name	*No*	*Class*	*Type*	*Built*
Sydney	—	Guest (18)	2-4-2	1963
Sandy River	24	FLW	2-6-2	1989
—	—	BVR	4w-4wDM	1989
—	5	G&S/Winson	2-6-4T	1992

Stock
19 fully enclosed saloons, 1 fully enclosed brake saloon, 2 guards van, miscellaneous wagons

Passenger trains: Frequency depends on time of year, maximum frequency one hour
Period of public operation: Daily 17-26 April; 2-7 May then Mondays-Thursdays and Sundays to 1 July, then daily 1 July-24 October *except* 8/9, 15/16 October
Facilities for disabled: Toilets at Aylsham and Wroxham, no special rolling stock but each train can carry one wheelchair, advanced notice required
Special events: 24 May — Enthusiasts' Day; 3/4 October — Steam Gala Weekend; Santa Specials, weekends in December
Special notes: Special parties and private charter trains by arrangement
Membership details: Friends of the Bure Valley Railway, Membership Secretary, c/o above address

Cadeby Light Railway SC

A new museum was opened in 1990, 'The Boston Collection', encompassing the lifetime collection of Teddy Boston and his family. The narrow gauge railway running in the grounds of the old rectory has been saved by Teddy Boston's enterprising widow and a small band of dedicated supporters in the face of considerable odds. Echoes of the *Titfield Thunderbolt* and Ancient and Modern. Their endeavours deserve your support

Location: One mile south of Market Bosworth on A447

OS reference: SK 426024

Operating society/organisation: Mrs J. A. Boston, The Old Rectory, Cadeby, Nuneaton, Warwicks CU13 0AS

Telephone: Market Bosworth (0455) 290462

Car park: In local side roads

Access by public transport: Leicester City, 178 from Hinckley, Leicester Corp/Gibson Bros (Comfort Coaches) from Leicester to Market Bosworth (1¼-miles away)

Locomotives

Name	*No*	*Builder*	*Type*	*Bui*
Pixie	—	Bagnall (2090)	0-4-0ST	191
—	2	O&K (7529)	0-4-0WT	191
—	—	Baguley (1695)	0-4-0PM	192
New Star	—	Lister (4088)	4wPM	193
—	20	M/Rail (8748)	4wDM	194
—	42	M/Rail (7710)	4wDM	193
—	87004	M/Rail (2197)	4wDM	192
—	87009	M/Rail (4572)	4wDM	192
—	—	M/Rail (5853)	4wDM	193
—	—	H/Clarke (D558)	4wDM	193
—	87008	R/Hornsby (179870)	4wDM	193
—	87051	R/Hornsby (404967)	4wDM	195
Standard gauge				
—	—	Peckett (2012)	0-4-0ST	194

Stock

Penrhyn Quarrymans coach; 2 flat trucks; 7 open trucks; 2 platelayers trolleys

On site facilities: 2ft gauge railway, also traction engines and a model railway. Brass rubbing centre in church with over 70 replica brasses

Refreshment facilities: Light refreshments available

Public opening: 2nd Saturday of every month, plus 1st Saturday in November and Boxing Day (from 13.30) or by arrangement

Special events: Bonfire Night Steaming 2 November; Santa Special 14 and 26 December

Special notes: Party bookings by prior arrangement

Cambrian Railways Society SC

Location: Oswestry station yard, Oswald Road, Oswestry, Shropshire

OS reference: SJ 294297

Operating society/organisation: Cambrian Railways Society Ltd, C. W. Mottram, 'Delamere', Old Chirk Road, Gobowen, Oswestry, Shropshire SY11 3LH

Industrial locomotives

Name	*No*	*Builder*	*Type*	*Bui*
—	1872	B/Peacock (1827)	0-4-0ST	187
—	1	H/Clarke (D843)	0-4-0DM	195
Adam	1	Peckett (1430)	0-4-0ST	191
—	3	Hunslet (D3526)	0-6-0DM	195
—	6	Peckett (2131)	0-4-0ST	195

Right:
A view inside the goods shed museum at the Cambrian Railways Society headquarters at Oswestry on 1 September 1991 showing a Peckett locomotive, some wheel patterns and a collection of headboards.
Alan C. Butcher

-lephone: (0691) 661648
-r park: In Society's depot
-ngth of line: 400yd, opening 1992 -ubject to obtaining Light Railway -rder)
-blic opening: Daily 10.00-16.00
-ecial notes: The Oswestry Bicycle -useum has moved onto the site -th over 50 cycles on display

Name	No	Builder	Type	Built
—	8	Barclay (885)	0-6-0ST	1900
—	322	Planet (3541)	4wDM	1952
Norma	3770	Hunslet (3770)	0-6-0ST	1952
—	—	Sentinel (9374)	4wVBT	1947
—	—	Hibberd (3057)	4wDM	1946
—	—	Planet	4wDM	1960

Stock
1 GWR auto-trailer; 1 LMS brakevan; 2 tank wagons; 1 open wagon

Chasewater Light Railway SC

-unded in 1959 as the Railway -eservation Society (West -idlands District) the Group -lebrated 30 years of existence in -89. Activities now centre on -mile of track in Chasewater -easure Park
-cation: Chasewater Pleasure Park, -ownhills, West Midlands
-S reference: SK 034070
-perating society/organisation: -hasewater Light Railway & -useum Co
-lephone: (0543) 452623
-r park: Pleasure park
-ccess by public transport: -MPTE 155 from Birmingham, 345 -d 394 from Walsall. Midland Red -d Chase Coaches 154 and 156 -om Birmingham and Cannock
-n site facilities: Refreshments -uffet coach), museum and -uvenir shop. Extensive small -lics collection. Lakeside walk
-tering facilities: Hot and cold -uffet

Industrial locomotives

Name	No	Builder	Type	Built
—	—	Peckett (917)	0-4-0ST	1902
Invicta	8	Barclay (2220)	0-4-0ST	1946
—	3	Barclay (1223)	0-4-0ST	1911
Lion	—	Peckett (1351)	0-4-0ST	1914
Alfred Paget	11	Neilson (2937)	0-4-0ST	1882
—	S100	H/Clarke (1822)	0-6-0T	1949
—	15	H/Clarke (431)	0-6-0ST	1895
Asbestos	4	H/Leslie (2780)	0-4-0ST	1909
—	21	Kent Cont (1612)	4wDM	1929
—	7	R/Hornsby (548641)	0-4-0DE	1961
—	—	Smiths	4wD crane	1951
—	59632	Sentinel (9632)	4wVBT	1957
—	1	M/Rail (1947)	4wPM	1919
—	61/50011	Fowler (4220015)	0-4-0DM	1962

Stock
Passenger services provided with ex-BR DMU trailer cars.
A selection of freight vehicles is also housed at the site, also several pre-Grouping coaches.

Length of line: 1-mile, extension to 1¾ miles under construction
Public opening: Site open 11.00-dusk, Sundays only throughout the year. Trains 12.00-17.30 (or dusk, which ever earlier) every 20min
Special events: Please contact for details
Facilities for disabled: Access to station only, no steps, car park adjacent
Membership details: Brownhills West Station, Hednesford Road, Brownhills West, Walsall WS8 7LT

Chatterley Whitfield Mining Museum M

-cation: Tunstall, Stoke-on-Trent
-urator: Mark Tweedy
-perating society/organisation: -hatterley Whitfield Mining -useum Trust, Tunstall, Stoke-on- -rent, North Staffordshire ST6 8UN
-elephone: (0782) 813337

Locomotives

Name	No	Origin	Class	Type	Built
—	2	NSR	L	0-6-2T	1923

Industrial locomotives

Name	No	Builder	Type	Built
8	6	Robert Heath	0-4-0ST	1886
The Welshman	—	M/Wardle (1207)	0-6-0ST	1890
Joseph	—	Hunslet (3163)	0-6-0ST	1944
—	9	YEC (2521)	0-6-0ST	1952
Hem Heath	3D	Bagnall (3119)	0-6-0DM	1956

Car parks: Main car park has capacity for up to 50 coaches; other overflow car parks are also available
Access by public transport: Nearest British Rail station, Longport. By bus, PMT Services operate regular (10min intervals Monday to Saturday) routes between Hanley
Refreshment facilities: Pit Canteen, 100-seat capacity, open 10.00 to 16.30, seven days a week
Other on-site facilities: Underground tours, British Coal's National Collection, film shows, restored winding engines, toilets, museum shop, education services, mining picture gallery
Length of line: ½-mile; currently non-passenger carrying; operated as a colliery railway siding

Name	*No*	*Builder*	*Type*	*Buil*
—	—	NBL (27876)	0-4-0DM	195
—	LO52	YEC (2745)	0-6-0DE	196
—	13D	T/Hill (181V)	6wDH	196

Stock
3 2ft 6in gauge underground manrider trains; 2 2ft 4in gauge underground manrider trains; 1 2ft gauge underground manrider train; 1 Taylor & Hubbard steam crane; 1 25-ton brake van; Various coal wagons

Public opening: *High season* — 1 March-31 October: site open 10.00-17.00, pit tours 10.00-16.00 (last tour). *Low season* — 1 November-28 February — weekdays — site open 10.00-17.00, pit tours 10.00-15.00 (last tour); Weekends — site open 10.00-17.00, pit tours 10.00-16.00 (lsst tour)

Period of public operation: Locomotive in steam on most opening days
Special events: Various througho the year including annual Steam Carnival
Facilities for disabled: Disabled toilet, surface collection building

Cheddleton Railway Centre SC

A Victorian country station set in the attractive Staffordshire moorlands, situated adjacent to the River Churnet. Pleasant walks can be taken alongside the Caldon Canal, and the Flint Mill Museum is only ⅔-mile away
Location: Cheddleton station, near Leek, Staffordshire
OS reference: SJ 983519
Operating society/organisation: North Staffordshire Railway Company (1978) Ltd
Telephone: Churnetside (0538) 360522
Car park: Riverside car park and picnic area opposite the station
Access by public transport: BR Stoke-on-trent (10 miles). A regular bus service operated by Proctors, PMT and Stevensons from Hanley, Longton and Leek to Cheddleton village
On site facilities: The station contains a refreshment room, souvenir shop and small relics museum. On open days visitors are allowed to visit the yard, signalbox and new locomotive display hall. Modern toilets are also on site
Length of line: 400yd
Public opening: Easter-September inclusive — Sundays and bank holiday Mondays, 11.00-17.30 June, July and August. Sundays October-March 12.00-17.00

Locomotives

Name	*No*	*Origin*	*Class*	*Type*	*Bui*
—	4422	LMS	4F	0-6-0	192
—	80136	BR	4MT	2-6-4T	195
—	D3420	BR	08	0-6-0DE	195
Tamworth Castle	D7672	BR	25	Bo-Bo	196

Industrial locomotives

Name	*No*	*Builder*	*Type*	*Bui*
Josiah Wedgwood	52	Hunslet (3777)	0-6-0ST	195

Locomotive notes: '4F' 4422 was returned to steam in 1991 and is expected to see service on special days in 1992. New to Cheddleton in 1991 was *Tamworth Castle*, purchased by the NSRDG. The diesel group also celebrated the return to traffic of '08' D3420 in 19602 BR livery

Owners
4422 (the 4422 Locomotive Fund)
D3420 and D7672 (the NSR Diesel Group)

Stock
2 ex-BR Mk 1 CK coaches; 2ex- BR Mk 1 BSO coaches; 1 ex-BR Mk 1 SC coach; 1 ex-BR Mk 1 TSO coach; 2 ex-BR brake suburban coaches; 1 ex-NSR coach body; 1 ex-LMS 6-wheel full brake; 1 ex-LMS goods brake van; 2 ex-LMS box vans; 2 ex-BR box vans; 2 ex-LMS 5-plank wagons; 1 ex-LMS hopper wagon; 1 Esso tank wagon; 1 7-ton diesel rail-mounted crane

Special events: 7 June — Model Railway Day; 10 May, 19 July, 30/31 August — Friends of Thomas the Tank Engine Day; 20 September — Transport Day; 13, 20 December — Santa Specials
Facilities for disabled: Access to most of the site is possible by wheelchair. Train rides by arrangement
Membership details: Richard Waterhouse c/o above address

Special notes: Coach parties cater for by prior arrangement. Guided tours available for parties on request. The Railway Centre is adjacent to a BR freight line whic is now mothballed pending a decision on its future. The NSR C would like to re-open the line to passenger trains as the 'Churnet Valley Railway'

Chinnor & Princes Risborough Railway SC

ıe Chinnor & Princes Risborough
ıilway Association was formed in
89 with a view to preserving the
sused line from Princes
sborough to Chinnor, part of the
atlington branch. At the time of
ıblication no on site facilities are
ailable and no public access can
permitted without prior
tification. Anyone requiring up-
-date information is advised to
ntact Peter Harris (address below)
r further details.
cation: Private sidings in
ıinnor, Oxon
S reference:
perating society/organisation:
ıinnor & Princes Risborough
ıilway Association, c/o Peter
ırris, 20 Dalesford Road,
ylesbury, Bucks HP21 9XD
elephone: 0296 433795
cess by public transport: BR
inces Risborough

Locomotives

Name	No	Origin	Class	Type	Built
—	D8568	BR	17	Bo-Bo	1963

Industrial locomotives

Name	No	Builder	Type	Built
—	—	Sentinel (6515)	4wVBTG	1926
Boris	1	Baguley	0-4-0	1952
Iris	420	R/Hornsby (459515)	0-6-0DH	1952

Stock - coaches
1 LMS Inspection Saloon, 1 LNWR Mess coach, 1 BR Mk 1 NDV

Stock - wagons
6 various, 1 Coles self-propelled crane

Length of line: 4 miles, first 3 miles expected to open 1992/93
Public opening: See railway press for details

Cholsey & Wallingford Railway SC

cation: Hithercroft Industrial
state, Wallingford, Oxfordshire
raffic Manager: David
oodenough
perating Society: Cholsey &
'allingford Railway Preservation
ociety, PO Box 16, Wallingford,
xon OX10 0NF
elephone: 0491 35067 (weekends
ıd Bank Holidays only)
ar park: Habitat adjacent to
'allingford station
ccess by public transport: South
idland Bus Company, BR Didcot
ırkway or Cholsey
ublic Opening: Every Sunday
ıster-end September 11.00-17.00.
rains run first and third Sunday
ıd bank holidays 13.00-16.30
ength of line: 1¼ miles
urney time: Approximately 20min
n site facilities: Souvenir and
offee shops. Museum, model
ilway. Children's mini railway
pecial events: 19/20 April —
ıster Bunny; 2 May — Cholsey

Locomotives

Name	No	Origin	Class	Type	Built
—	4247	GWR	4200	2-8-0T	1916
George Mason	08123	BR	08	0-6-0	1955

Industrial locomotives

Name	No	Builder	Type	Built
Walrus	3271	Planet (3271)	0-4-0	1949
—	304470	R/Hornsby	0-4-0	1951
Thames	3	Barclay (2315)	0-4-0ST	1951

May Day; 24/25 May — Spring Fair; 19 July — Teddy Bears' Picnic; 8 August — Cholsey Flower Festival; 30/31 August — Friends of Thomas; 6 December — Cholsey Santa; 13/20 December — Wallingford Santa
Special notes: Light Railway Order now granted and work is proceeding to return to Cholsey (BR) bay platform
Membership details: Bob Morrison, at above address
Membership details: *The Bunk* — 3 issues/year

Cleethorpes Coast Light Railway

Taken over by new management at the beginning of the 1991 season. The first year saw much reconstruction work and improvement, the most noticeable are the new station buildings and locomotive sheds as part of a phased improvement programme. The new operators are committed to regauge to 15in and the introduction of steam is a major goal of future plans. The railway is fortunate to be assisted by the Cleethorpes Coast Light Railway Supporters Association who provide the majority of operating staff.
Operating society/organisation: Cleethorpes Coast Light Railway Ltd, Kingsway Station, Kings Road, Cleethorpes, Lincs DN35 0BY

Industrial locomotives

Name	*No*	*Builder*	*Type*	*Bu*
—	278	S/Lamb (7217)	2-8-0T GH	19
—	800	S/Lamb (15578)	2-8-0GH	19
—	—†	Hibberd (2163)	4wDM	19

All locomotives are 15in gauge
†To be rebuilt as Kerr Stuart-type locomotive

Telephone: 0472-601405 or 601871
Access by public transport: BR Cleethorpes, bus service 17 from pier, Kings Road is on main promenade access
On site facilities: Large car park, station shop, local refreshments lakeside amenity area with boating lake and nature house and good beach
Period of public opening: Daily 17 April-mid September, then Sundays until 20 December. Railway open from 10.00
Special events: 19/20 April — Easter Egg Specials; 3/4, 24/25 Ma and 30/31 August — Lollipop Express; 2-4 May — Model Railwa Exhibition; 12/13 September — Cleethorpes Festival of Transport; 13, 20 December — Santa Special

Colne Valley Railway **SC**

An immaculate country station surrounded by green fields, the railway offers much to entertain as well as to educate. A well-deserved reputation for good food
Location: Castle Hedingham station, Yeldham Road, Castle Hedingham, Halstead, Essex CO9 3DZ
OS reference: TL 774362
Operating society/organisation: Colne Valley Railway Preservation Society
Telephone: Hedingham (0787) 61174 — railway; (0787) 62254 — restaurant
Car park: At the site (access from A604 road) between Castle Hedingham and Gt Yeldham
Access by public transport: Eastern National bus services No 88 Colchester-Halstead, 89 Halstead-Hedingham and Hedingham & District Nos 4 Braintree-Hedingham, 5 Sudbury-Hedingham. Nearest BR station — Braintree
On site facilities: Depot, museum, souvenir shop and restaurant, 4-acre riverside wooded picnic area, toilets, video carriage
Catering facilities: Restaurant carriage open daily 10.00-17.00 and 19.00-22.00 except 22 December-1 March and Mondays out of peak season. Pullman on train service on steam days for Sunday lunch, private hire and evening wine and dine also Sunday lunches and Saturday evening wine and dine Pullman service. All must be prebooked. Buffet carriage open most steam days also
Length of line: ¾-mile

Locomotives

Name	*No*	*Origin*	*Class*	*Type*	*Bui*
—	45163	LMS	5	4-6-0	193
—	D2041	BR	03	0-6-0DM	195
—	03063	BR	03	0-6-0DM	195
—	D2184	BR	03	0-6-0DM	196
—	E79978	BR	—	AC Cars Railbus	195

Industrial locomotives

Name	*No*	*Builder*	*Type*	*Buil*
—	—	Barclay (349)	0-4-0DM	194
Victory	—	Barclay (2199)	0-4-0ST	194
—	190	Hunslet (3790)	0-6-0ST	195
—	72	Vulcan (5309)	0-6-0ST	194
Jupiter	—	RSH (7671)	0-6-0ST	195
—	40	RSH (7765)	0-6-0T	195
Barrington	—	Avonside (1875)	0-4-0ST	192
—	1	H/Leslie (3715)	0-4-0ST	192
—	YD43	R/Hornsby (221639)	0-4-0DM	194
—	—	Hibbard (3147)	0-4-0DM	194

Stock
11 ex-BR Mk 1 coaches; 1 ex-Norwegian State Railway Class B 65 18803 (built 1926) Balcony; Open Second (teak); 2 ex-Pullman cars, *Aquila* and *Hermione;* 1 ex-BR Mk 1 (BG) exhibition carriage; 1 ex-LNER BTO 4357 bar saloon; 1 ex-LNER BG 41975; 1 ex-GWR Engineers Observation Saloon; Steam crane DRG 80103; Sundry items of freight stock

ıblic opening: Daily for static
splays except Christmas, New
ear and January. Locomotives in
eam most Sundays of the month
tween Easter and October
clusive, also Wednesdays 29 July-
September and every Bank
oliday and preceeding Sunday
cept Christmas and New Year.
hools' steam operation most
eekdays in June and Santa
ecials in December

Special events: Playgroup Specials, Rising Five Specials, Victorian Specials, Santa Specials, please telephone for details
Facilities for disabled: To look and ride only
Special notes: The railway has been completely rebuilt on part of the original Colne Valley line track-bed. The railway offers much of educational value specialising in school party visits by appointment at any time of the year. Catering approved by Egon Ronay 'Just-a-bite' guide, also new conference Pullman train now open for evening meals, Tuesdays-Fridays (static, pre-booked only)
Membership details: P. Lemon, 78 Mountbatten Road, Braintree, Essex CM7 6TP

County School SC

preserved station on the former
eat Eastern Railway line at the
rthern end of the Dereham
anch
erating society/organisation:
kenham & Dereham Railway Co
d, County School Station, North
mham, Dereham, Norfolk
lephone: 0362 668181
5 reference: TF 990227
anager: Trevor Cleaver
ı site facilities: Refreshments and
uvenir shop. Picnic area and
untry walks
ıblic opening: Weekends and mid-
eek in summer — free entry

Industrial locomotives

Name	*No*	*Builder*	*Type*	*Built*
Pony	—	H/Leslie (2918)	0-4-0ST	1912
—	—	R/Hornsby (497753)	0-4-0DH	1963
—	—	RSH (8368)	0-4-0DH	1963

Stock - coaches
2 BR Mk 2s

Length of line: ¼-mile at weekends
Membership details: Mid-Norfolk Railway Society, Mr W. George, Swanton Drive, Dereham, Norfolk NR20 4DW (tel: 0362 693841)
Membership journal: *Blastpipe*

Crewe Heritage Centre SC

ocation: Crewe Heritage Centre,
ernon Way, Crewe
S reference: SJ 709552
perating society/organisation:
ewe Heritage Centre
ust/Railside Ltd
lephone: (0270) 212130
ır park: Town Centre, Forge
reet, Oak Street
ccess by public transport: BR
ewe
efreshment facilities: Cafe in APT
n-site facilities: Souvenir shop,
llector's corner
ıblic opening: Limited opening
ıring 1992 due to building work,
ease see press for details or
lephone above number
ıcilities for disabled: Toilets
embership details: Heritage
entre Supporters Association, c/o
oove address
otes: Steam locomotives passed for
se over BR tracks are often stabled between duties on the North Wales Coast Line

Locomotives

Name	*No*	*Origin*	*Class*	*Type*	*Built*
—	D120	BR	45	1Co-Co1	1961
—	D1842	BR	47	Co-Co	1965
—	D5233	BR	25	Bo-Bo	1963
—	D7523	BR	25	Bo-Bo	1965

Industrial locomotives

Name	*No*	*Builder*	*Type*	*Built*
—	—	K/Stuart (4388)	0-4-0ST	1926
Robert	—	H/Clarke (1752)	0-6-0T	1943
Joseph	—	Hunslet (3163)	0-6-0T	1944

Rolling stock
APT vehicle Nos 48103, 48106, 48602, 48603, 48606, 49002, 49002 in use as cafe; 1 BR Mk 1 BSK; 2 BR brake vans

Darlington Railway Centre and Museum

M

Located on the original 1825 route of the Stockton & Darlington Railway, the restored North Road station, dating from 1842, is now a museum which forms the centrepiece of an area devoted to railway history and preservation.

The Museum is administered by Darlington Borough Council. The collection includes locomotives, rolling stock and many small exhibits. The site also includes two other historic buildings of the S&DR — the former Goods Shed and the Hopetown Carriage Works. Steam train rides over a short length of line are available on selected dates, and there are plans for future extension of the line.

British Rail's 'Heritage Line' provides a link to Darlington's main line station and to Shildon, for the Timothy Hackworth Museum

Museum Curator: Steven Dyke
Location: North Road station, Darlington, County Durham DL3 6ST. Approximately ¾-mile north of town centre, off North Road (A167)
OS reference: NZ 289157
Telephone: 0325 460532
Car park: At museum site
Access by public transport: BR services to Darlington North Road station. Local bus services along North Road
Catering facilities: Confectionery and drinks. Party catering by arrangement
On site facilities: Souvenir and book shop. Toilets
Public opening: Daily throughout the year 09.30-17.00 (except Christmas/New Year holidays). Last admission 16.30 (days and times may be subject to amendment)
Special events: Steam days and Railway Carnival (contact for details)
Facilities for disabled: Access to main museum building for wheelchairs. Disabled persons toilet
Membership details: Friends of Darlington Railway Museum and Darlington Railway Preservation Society, both c/o above address
Note: Some locomotives are located in the former goods shed, where restoration work is being undertaken by the Darlington Railway Preservation Society (limited opening to visitors — times vary; groups by arrangement)

Locomotives

Name	No	Origin	Class	Type	Built
Locomotion	1	S&DR	—	0-4-0	1825
Derwent	25	S&DR	—	0-6-0	1845
—	1463	NER	1463	2-4-0	1885
—	910	NER	901	2-4-0	1875

Industrial locomotives

Name	No	Builder	Type	Built
Met	—	H/Leslie (2800)	0-4-0ST	1909
—	17	Head Wrightson (33)	0-4-0VB	1873
—	—	Bagnall (2898)	0-4-0F	1948
—	39	RSH (6947)	0-6-0T	1938

Stock
1 Stockton & Darlington Rly passenger coach (1846)
1 North Eastern Railway Coach body (c1860)
1 NER 20-ton mineral wagon
1 Chaldron wagon

Owners
Locomotion, Derwent, 1463 and 910 are all on loan from the National Railway Museum
Met is on loan from Messrs D. & R. Branch

Darlington Railway Preservation Society

Locomotives

Name	No	Origin	Class	Type	Built
—	78018	BR	2MT	2-6-0	1954

Industrial locomotives

Name	No	Builder	Type	Built
—	2	RSH (7925)	0-4-0DM	1959
—	1	Peckett (2142)	0-4-0ST	1953
David Payne	185	Fowler (4110006)	0-4-0DM	1950
Smiths Dock Co Ltd	—	Fowler (4200018)	0-4-0DM	1947
—	—	GEC	4wE	1928
—	—	R/Hornsby (279591)	0-4-0DM	1949
—	—	R/Hornsby*	4wDM	
—	—	R/Hornsby*	4wDM	
—	—	R/Hornsby*	4wDM	

*1ft 6in gauge

Stock
Various wagons, steam and diesel cranes

Dean Forest Railway

SC

Steam train rides previously operating alongside the Lydney to Parkend line have been extended southwards to Lydney Lakeside
Location: Norchard Steam Centre on the B4234, ¾-mile off A48 at Lydney, Glos
OS reference: SO 629044
Operations Manager: Trevor Radway
Operating society/organisation: Dean Forest Railway Society in conjunction with owning company, Forest of Dean Railway Ltd
Telephone: Dean (0594) 843423
Car park: Adequate for cars and coaches — no charge
Access by public transport: None
On site facilities: A shop and refreshments are available at Norchard along with a museum, photographic display, riverside walk, forest trail and picnic area
Catering facilities: Hot and cold snacks, ploughman's lunches etc on steam days. Parties catered for by appointment
Length of line: 1¼ miles
Public opening: Daily for static display — shop, museum, refreshments open every Saturday and Sunday 11.00-17.00 and weekdays Easter to October. Steam days: Good Friday and all Bank Holiday Saturdays, Sundays and Mondays (Christmas/New Year excepted). All Sundays April-September. Wednesdays in June and July, and every Tuesday, Wednesday and Thursday in August
Special events: Thomas the Tank Engine's Friends 20/21 June, 19/20 September; Preservation Rally 18 October; Santa Specials 29 November, 5/6, 12/13, 19/20 December; Mince Pie Specials 27 December, 1 January
Facilities for disabled: Access to museum, toilets and train rides
Membership details: Mr P. Brammell, 4 Pool Gardens, Higham, Gloucester
Membership jurnal: *Forest Venturer* – quarterly
Marketing name: The Friendly Forest Line

Locomotives

Name	No	Origin	Class	Type	Built
—	4121	GWR	5101	2-6-2T	1937
Pitchford Hall	4953	GWR	'Hall'	4-6-0	1928
—	5521	GWR	4575	2-6-2T	1928
—	5541	GWR	4575	2-6-2T	1928
—	9681	GWR	5700	0-6-0PT	1949
—	03062	BR	03	0-6-0DM	1958
—	03119	BR	03	0-6-0DM	1958
—	08377	BR	08	0-6-0DE	1957

Industrial locomotives

Name	No	Buyilder	Type	Built
—	—	Barclay (2221)	0-4-0ST	1946
Jessie	—	Hunslet (1873)	0-6-0ST	1937
Uskmouth No 1	—	Peckett (2147)	0-4-0ST	1952
Wilbert	—	Hunslet (3806)	0-6-0ST	1953
Warrior	—	Hunslet (3823)	0-6-0ST	1954
—	—	Hunslet (2145)	0-4-0DM	1940
—	—	Fowler (4210101)	0-4-0DM	1955
—	—	Fowler (4210127)	0-4-0DM	1957
—	—	Hibberd (3947)	4wPM	1960
Cabot	39	R/Royce (10218)	0-6-0DH	1965
Lord Marshall of Goring	392	A/Barclay (392)	0-4-0DM	1954

Stock

8 ex-GWR coaches; 16 ex-BR coaches; 3 Wickham trolleys; 1 steam crane Thos Smith (Rodley) TS 5027 (10 ton); 1 45 ton steam crane (Cowans Sheldon) ADRC 95222; 50 + wagons

Below:
1991 saw a special visitor to the Dean Forest Railway in the shape of GWR 4-4-0 No 3440 *City of Truro*. This was for the opening of the line through to Lydney Lakeside. No 3440 is seen here returning from Lakeside heading north towards Norchard on 8 September 1991. *Hugh Ballantyne*

Didcot Railway Centre

SC

Based around the GWR engine shed and depot, the Centre now has a typical GWR small country station with signalbox (from Radstock), re-creation of Brunel's broad gauge railway, two demonstration lines, and a small relics museum
General Manager: Michael Dean
Location: Adjacent to BR station, Didcot, Oxfordshire. Access via station subway
OS reference: SU 525907
Operating society/organisation: Great Western Society Ltd, Didcot Railway Centre, Didcot, Oxon OX11 7NJ
Telephone: Didcot (0235) 817200
Car park: Didcot BR station
access by public transport: Didcot Parkway BR station
Refreshment facilities: Refreshment room open all days centre is open (lunches, snacks)
On site facilities: GWR locomotive depot, replica GWR station, museum and broad gauge demonstration. Souvenir sales. Rides are available on the demonstration lines on steamdays
Length of line: 1,000yd
Public opening: Saturdays and Sundays all year (except 26 Dec). Daily 4 April-27 September. Steamdays first and last Sunday each month from March, Bank Holidays, all Sundays June-August and all Wednesdays 5 August-2 September. Open 11.00-17.00 (dusk in winter)
Train rides: On Steamdays there is normally continuous operation of the passenger train, interrupted by freight train demonstrations and turning of the locomotives on some days
Special events: 20 June — Midsummer Steaming (to 10pm); 5 July — Steam Day for Disabled; 12 July — Teddy Bears' Picnic; 26/27 September — Autumn Steam Gala; 31 October — Photographers Evening (to 9pm); Sundays 29 November-20 December — Santa Steamings; 27/28 December, 1-3 January 1993 — New Year Steamings
Facilities for disabled: Steps at access from BR subway may cause problems but assistance can normally be provided (advance notification is useful)
Membership details: Brian Phillips, at above address
Membership journals: *Great Western Echo* — quarterly; *National Newsletter* — eight times annually

Locomotives

Name	No	Origin	Class/builder	Type	Built
—	22	GWR	Diesel Railcar	1A-A1	1940
—	1338	GWR (Cardiff Rly)	Kitson (3799)	0-4-0ST	1898
Trojan	1340	GWR	Avonside (1380)	0-4-0ST	1897
—	1363	GWR	1361	0-6-0ST	1910
—	1466	GWR	1400	0-4-2T	1936
—	3650	GWR	5700	0-6-0PT	1939
—	3738	GWR	5700	0-6-0PT	1937
—	3822	GWR	2884	2-8-0	1940
—	4144	GWR	5101	2-6-2T	1946
Maindy Hall	4942	GWR	'Hall'	4-6-0	1929
Nunney Castle	5029	GWR	'Castle'	4-6-0	1934
Drysllwyn Castle/ Earl Bathurst	5051	GWR	'Castle'	4-6-0	1936
—	5322	GWR	4300	2-6-0	1917
—	5572	GWR	4575	2-6-2T	1927
Hinderton Hall	5900	GWR	'Hall'	4-6-0	1931
King Edward II	6023	GWR	'King'	4-6-0	1930
King Edward I	6024	GWR	'King'	4-6-0	1930
—	6106	GWR	6100	2-6-2T	1931
—	6697	GWR	5600	0-6-2T	1928
Burton Agnes Hall	6998	GWR	'Hall'	4-6-0	1949
—	7202	GWR	7200	2-8-2T	1934
Cookham Manor	7808	GWR	'Manor'	4-6-0	1938
Duke of Gloucester	71000	BR	8P	4-6-2	1954
Pontyberem	2	Burry Port & Gwendraeth Valley Rly		0-6-0ST	1900
Shannon	5	Wantage Tramway		0-4-0WT	1857

Industrial locomotives

Name	No	Builder	Type	Built
Bonnie Prince Charlie	1	RSH (7544)	0-4-0ST	1949
—	26	Hunslet (5238)	0-6-0DH	1962

Locomotive notes: Locomotives available in 1992 should be: 1466, 3822, 5029, 5572, 6024, 6106, 6998 and 71000. Locomotives under restoration include: 1340, 3650, 3738, 6023, 7202. Construction of the Firefly Trust's reproduction broad gauge locomotive *Firefly* is being undertaken

Stock
Over 40 ex-GWR coaches are preserved along with numerous ex-GWR freight wagons

Owners
5 (on loan from the National Railway Museum)
6024 (the 6024 Preservation Society)
71000 (the Duke of Gloucester Steam Locomotive Trust)

East Anglia Transport Museum

SC

.e East Suffolk Light Railway is
: title given to the 2ft gauge
lway, which winds its way some
0yd or so along the northern
rimeter of the museum site,
tween the stations of Chapel Road
d Woodside. The railway
mmenced operation in 1973 and
ns to re-create a typical
ssenger-carrying light railway of
ars gone by. Many aspects of
lway interest can be found along
length. The track came from
ziate sand-quarry and Canvey
and, as well as from the
uthwold Railway. There is also a
;nalbox from the Lowestoft-Great
rmouth line, and signals from
rious local locations; all of which
lp to set the overall scene

cation: Carlton Colville, three
iles south-west of Lowestoft in
ıffolk

; reference: TM 505903

ɔerating society/organisation:
st Anglia Transport Museum
ciety Ltd, Chapel Road, Carlton
lville, Lowestoft, Suffolk
R33 8BL

:lephone: (0502) 518459

ır park: On site

Industrial locomotives

Name	*No*	*Builder*	*Type*	*Built*
—	1	M/Rail (5902)	4wDM	1932
—	2	M/Rail (5912)	4wDM	1934
—	4	R/Hornsby (177604)	4wDM	1936

Locomotive notes: During the 1992 season, R/Hornsby (177604) is likely to be the sole source of motive-power. The other two locomotives are under course of restoration, as finance and time allows. The return journey takes 10 to 15min.

Stock

Locally designed and built covered coach
Small selection of wagons
Van body ex-Southwold Railway

Access by public transport: Eastern Counties 111 and 171 (Monday-Saturday) and Flying Banana 1, 2 and 171 (Sundays and bank holidays) from Lowestoft. BR, Oulton Broad South (1½ miles)

On site facilities: Refreshments, souvenir and bookshop, toilets, working transport museum, including trams, narrow-gauge railway, trolleybuses, steam-rollers and other commercial and public transport vehicles

Period of public opening: Easter Sunday and Monday, and Sundays from beginning of May to end of September, also other Bank Holidays in this period; open from 11.00. Saturdays from the beginning of June to the end of September, and every weekday during August; open from 14.00

Special notes: Limited facilities for the disabled

Membership details: From the above address

Below:
East Suffolk Light Railway No 4 at Carlton Colville, the site of the East Anglia Transport Museum on 26 August 1991. As well as the railway interest the site is also home to a number of trams and trolleybuses along with a recreated street scene. *John C. Baker*

East Anglian Railway Museum

SC

Location: Chappel & Wakes Colne station, near Colchester CO6 2DS
OS reference: TL 898289
Manager: Michael Stanbury
Operating society/organisation: East Anglian Railway Museum, Chappel & Wakes Colne Station, Station Road, Wakes Colne, Essex CO6 2DS
Telephone: Colchester (0206) 242524
Car park: On site
Access by public transport: Chappel & Wakes Colne BR station. Also Eastern National/Hedingham Omnibus service No 88 Colchester-Halstead. Sundays Eastern National No 188 Colchester-Halstead
On site facilities: Light refreshments, bookshop, museum, souvenir shop, heritage centre and toilets
Public opening: Daily 09.00-17.30
Special events: 19 July — Rolls-Royce Enthusiast's Club, Essex Section, Annual Rally & Concours d'elegance. Annual 'Camra' beer festival, 9-12 September. Santa Specials in December (please see press for details)
Special notes: Special steam days are held first Sunday of month March-October inclusive, plus Banl Holidays, Wednesdays in August. Three restored signalboxes, large goods shed and restoration shed. Victorian country junction station. Schools days and Santa steamings. Disabled visitors welcome — prior advice appreciated. Rail Riders sticker station.
Membership details: Membership Secretary, 50 Ayr Way, Rise Park, Romford, Essex RM1 4UH
Membership journal: *Stour Valle Steam* — 4 times/year

Locomotives

Name	*No*	*Origin*	*Class*	*Type*	*Bu*
A. J. Hill	69621	GER	N7	0-6-2T	192
—	80151	BR	4MT	2-6-4T	195
—	D2279	BR	04	0-6-0DM	196
—	30053	LSWR	M7	0-4-4T	190

Industrial locomotives

Name	*No*	*Builder*	*Type*	*Bu*
Jubilee	—	Bagnall (2542)	0-4-0ST	193
—	1074	Barclay (1047)	0-4-0ST	190
Belvoir	—	Barclay (2350)	0-6-0ST	195
Gunby	68067	Hunslet (2413)	0-6-0ST	194
—	2	M/Vick	0-4-0E	191
—	1438	Peckett (1438)	0-4-0ST	191
—	2039	Peckett (2039)	0-4-0ST	194
Penn Green	54	RSH (7031)	0-6-0ST	194
—	AMW144	Barclay (333)	0-4-0DM	193
—	23	Fowler (4220039)	0-4-0DH	196
—	2029	Simplex (2029)	0-4-0PM	192

Locomotive notes: 69621 will be operational, 30053 will be completed during 1992. 80151 expected to be compelted during 1993

Stock
4 ex-BR Mk 1s; 1 ex-BR sleeping coach; 1 ex-BR Mk 1 full brake; 1 ex-LNER Buffet car; 1 LNER pigeon van; 1 ex-LNER coach; 1 GER 6-wheel full brake; 1 GER 6-wheel family saloon; 1 GER 4-wheel coach; 1 ex-GE bogie coach; 2 MSL 6-wheel coaches; 1 SR PMV; 1 ex-BR CCT; 1 ex-BR 13-ton open wagon; 2 ex-BR 16-ton mineral wagons; 1 Lomac wagon; 1 ex-LMS 12-ton open wagon; 2 Wickham Trolleys; 1 GWR Toad Brakevan; 1 ex-BR brake van

Owners
30053 (the Drummond Locomotive Society)

East Lancashire Railway

A very popular yet newly opened railway by the East Lancs Railway Society in close co-operation with local authorities, the line won the 1987 ARPS award. Visit the line to find out the cause of the line's popularity and success
Location: Bolton Street Station, Bury, Lancashire BL9 0EY
OS reference: SD 803109

Locomotives

Name	*No*	*Origin*	*Class*	*Type*	*Buil*
—	7229	GWR	7200	2-8-2T	193
—	42765	LMS	5P4F	2-6-0	192
Odney Manor	7828	GWR	'Manor'	4-6-0	195
—	45337	LMS	5MT	4-6-0	193
—	46428	LMS	2MT	2-6-0	194
—	73156	BR	5MT	4-6-0	195
—	76079	BR	4MT	2-6-0	195
—	80097	BR	4MT	2-6-4T	195

ıblicity Director: Graham Vevers
perating society/organisation: ıst Lancashire Railway ·eservation Society
elephone: 061 764 7790
ccess by public transport: BR to ·anchester, Bolton, Rochdale and ırnley. Metro-Link from central ·anchester to Bury Interchange. arious bus services also operate to ıry, Ramsbottom or Rawtenstall om the BR stations listed.
n site facilities: Refreshments ormally available when trains are ınning. Buffet car service on most ains. Souvenir shop, transport useum
ngth of line: Approximately 8½ iles
ıblic opening: Steam and diesel-ıuled services operate on ıturdays, Sundays and Bank olidays throughout the year. Santa ·ecials (advanced booking only) in ecember
ecial events: 26 August — Teddy ·ar's Picnic; Santa Specials — eekends in December; Diesel ıthusiasts' Weekend and Friends Thomas the Tank Engine Days — ease apply for details; Irwell ılley Diner, Wine & Dine Trains dvance booking only — please ·ply for details)
ecial Notes: The Society re-·ened the Bury-Summerseat-ımsbottom section in 1987 and the ımsbottom-Irwell-Rawtenstall ction in 1991. Since 1987 over ·0,000 passengers have been rried
embership details: Mrs L. Vevers
embership journal: *The East ıncashire Railway News* — twice arly
arketing name: East Lancs

Name	*No*	*Origin*	*Class*	*Type*	*Built*
Morning Star	92207	BR	9F	2-10-0	1959
Royal Army Ordnance Corps	45112	BR	45	1Co-Co1	1962
—	D335	BR	40	1Co-Co1	1961
—	40145	BR	40	1Co-Co1	1961
Onslaught	D832	BR	42	B-B	1961
Western Prince	D1041	BR	52	C-C	1962
—	D2587	BR	05	0-6-0DM	1959
—	D2767	BR	—	0-4-0DH	1960
—	D2774	BR	—	0-4-0DH	1960
—	D2956	BR	01	0-4-0DM	1956
—	D5054	BR	24	Bo-Bo	1960
—	D7076	BR	35	B-B	1963
—	25901	BR	25	Bo-Bo	1966
—	D7659	BR	25	Bo-Bo	1966
—	D9531	BR	14	0-6-0DH	1965

Industrial locomotives

Name	*No*	*Builder*	*Type*	*Built*
Gothenburg	32	H/Clarke (680)	0-6-0T	1903
Phoenix	70	H/Clarke (1464)	0-6-0T	1921
Sir Robert Peel	8	Hunslet (3789)	0-6-0ST	1953
Shropshire	193	Hunslet (3793)	0-6-0ST	1953
—	1	Barclay (1927)	0-4-0ST	1927
MEA No 1	1	RSH (7683)	0-6-0T	1951
—	DH16	Sentinel (10175)	4wDH	1964
MR Mercury	1	Hibberd (3438)	4wDM	1950
Winfield	—	M/Rail (9009)	4wDM	1948
—	—	Hibbard (3438)	4wDM	1950
—	E2	H/Clark (D1199)	6wDM	1960
—	4002	H/Clarke (D1076)	6wDM	1959

Stock
25 BR Mk 1 coaches; Battery-electric multiple-unit Nos SC79998/9; Diesel multiple-units Nos E51813/51842; Electric multiple-units Nos 65451/65461/77172/77182; 1 L&YR coach; 3 Bogie Guards coaches; 3 Newspaper vans; Cravens 50-ton steam crane RS1013/50 (1930), NER 5-ton hand crane DB915390 (1880) and Smiths 5-ton diesel crane (1939) plus a small number of other goods vehicles

Owners
40145 (the Class 40 Preservation Society)
Battery-electric MU (on loan from the West Yorkshire Transport Museum)

Below:
BR Class 4 2-6-0 No 76079 and GWR 'Manor' class 4-6-0 double-head the 15.00 from Bury to Rawtenstall. Seen at Summerseat on 19 May 1991. *Brian Dobbs*

East Somerset Railway (The Strawberry Line) 

Set up by the artist, David Shepherd, 'the man who loves giants', the railway line is home to *Black Prince* and *The Green Knight* housed in their 'traditional' shed. As one might expect, Cranmore station is well laid out and aesthetically pleasing. A new art gallery is situated at Cranmore station where his paintings and prints can be bought

General Manager: Mr B. Buckfield
Headquarters: East Somerset Railway, (Cranmore Railway Station) Shepton Mallet, Somerset
OS reference: ST 664429
Telephone: Cranmore (074 988) 417
Main station: Cranmore
Car park: Cranmore — free
Refreshment facilities: New restaurant situated in car park offering lunches, snacks, teas, etc. Group catering by arrangement. Picnic areas at Cranmore, Merryfield Lane stations and depot
Souvenir shop: Cranmore
On site facilities: Museum, Victorian style engine shed and workshops, children's play area, wildlife information centre
Depot: Cranmore West
Length of line: 2 miles
Passenger trains: Cranmore West to Mendip Vale. Stations at Cranmore West, Merryfield Lane and Mendip Vale, unlimited train travel
Period of public operation: Depot open daily 27 March-30 October, with trains running each Sunday, Public Holidays; Wednesdays, Thursdays and Saturdays in peak season and on certain other days. Closed January and February (except 1 January). Depot open weekends only November, December, March and April 10.00-16.00. Last admission 30min before closing time. Each day ticket allows unlimited travel on all timetabled trains
Special events: 10 May — Spirit of the 60s (over 500 motorcycles); 13/14 June — David Shepherd, original painting exhbition (Cranmore Village Hall); 1 August — Jazz at the Railway (8pm); 2 August — AEC Vintage Commerical Rally; 31 August —

Locomotives

Name	*No*	*Origin*	*Class*	*Type*	*Bui*
—	6634	GWR	5600	0-6-2T	192
—	32110	LBSCR	E1	0-6-0T	187
—	47493	LMS	3F	0-6-0T	192
The Green Knight	75029	BR	4MT	4-6-0	195
Black Prince	92203	BR	9F	2-10-0	195
—*	390	CGR	7	4-8-0	189
*City of Germiston**	3052	SAR	15F	4-8-2	194

Industrial locomotives

Name	*No*	*Builder*	*Type*	*Buil*
Lord Fisher	1398	Barclay (1398)	0-4-0ST	191
—	705	Barclay (2047)	0-4-0ST	193
Lady Nan	1719	Barclay (1719)	0-4-0ST	192
—	4101	Dubs (4101)	0-4-0CT	190

Stock

9 ex-BR Mk 1 coaches; 25 assorted wagons, mostly LMS and SR; Rhodesian Railways sleeping car 180
Note: *3ft 6in gauge

Owner

6634 (the 6634 Locomotive Co)

Below:
Ex-Rhodesian Railways Class 10 4-8-0 No 930 saw service with a sawmills railway before being repatriated for preservation by David Shepherd. It is seen here at Cranmore on the East Somerset Railway following its arrival from Whipsnade. *Mike Ware*

anmore Village Fayre; 3/4 October Enthusiast's Weekend. Santa's — ›eekends in December
cilities for disabled: Limited, vance notice required

Special Notes: Santa special steam trains on Saturday and Sundays in December
Membership details: Please apply to above address, SAE for brochure

Membership journal: *East Somerset Railway Journal* — quarterly
Marketing name: The Strawberry Line

Embsay Steam Railway SC

›rkshire's 'Friendly Line' is erated by volunteers whose whole n is to reopen the line through to lton Abbey. An atmosphere of the ys of the rural branch line evails
›erating Committee: Stuart Bell
cation: Embsay station, Embsay, ipton, Yorkshire BD23 6QX
; reference: SE 007533
›erating society/organisation: ›phen Walker, Yorkshire Dales ilway Museum Trust
lephone: Skipton (0756) 794727. hr Answerphone (0756) 795189
r park: Embsay
cess by public transport: Pennine s from Skipton
site facilities: Souvenir shop — ecialising in children's gifts, nsport and industrial chaeological titles, plus model lway supplies
tering facilities: Buffet and bar most trains. Buffet on station. ening catering trains will serve ›als on selected dates. Special arters can be arranged. Meals for rties can be arranged on normal rvice trains (subject to advance oking). Please write for further tails
ngth of line: 2½ miles
blic opening: Trains will run, ndays throughout the year, plus turdays in July and August. esdays in July and August. ›dnesdays and Thursdays August ly. Also all Bank Holiday ›ekends. Site open all year until sk. Train times at least hourly .00-16.15
ecial events: 29 March — ›ther's Day; 19/20 April — Easter g Specials; 4 May — Kiddies' Day; '25 May — Friends of Thomas e Tank; 21 June/19 July — Kiddies' Day; 16 August — Teddy Bear's Picnic; 30/31 August — Friends of Thomas The Tank; 20 September — Branch Line Day; 25 October — Halloween Specials; 31 October — Bonfire Night; 22/29 November, 6, 13, 20 December — Santa Trains; 1 January 1993 — Family Day

Locomotives

Name	*No*	*Origin*	*Class*	*Type*	*Built*
—	D2203	BR	04	0-6-0DM	1952
—	NCB 38 (D9513)	BR	14	0-6-0DH	1964

Industrial locomotives

Name	*No*	*Builder*	*Type*	*Built*
Annie	—	Peckett (1159)	0-4-0ST	1908
Gladiator	—	H/Clarke (1450)	0-6-0ST	1922
Slough Estates No 5	—	H/Clarke (1709)	0-6-0ST	1939
Primrose No 2	—	Hunslet (3715)	0-6-0ST	1952
Ann	—	Sentinel (7232)	4wVB	1927
Beatrice	7	Hunslet (2705)	0-6-0ST	1945
Airedale	—	Hunslet (1440)	0-6-0ST	1923
City Link	—	Yorkshire (2474)	0-4-0ST	1949
—	140	H/Clarke (1821)	0-6-0T	1948
Spitfire	S112	Hunslet (2414)	0-6-0ST	1942
Wheldale	—	Hunslet (3168)	0-6-0T	1944
—	69	Hunslet (3785)	0-6-0ST	1953
Monkton No 1	—	Hunslet (3788)	0-6-0ST	1953
—	22	Barclay (2320)	0-4-0ST	1952
Thomas	4	RSH (7661)	0-4-0ST	1950
H. W. Robinson	—	Fowler (4100003)	0-4-0DM	1946
—	MDE15	Baguley/Drewry (2136)	4wDM	1938
—	887	R/Hornsby (394009)	4wDM	1955
—	—	Wickham (7610)	2w-2PMR	1957
—	—	Lister (9993)*	4wPM	1938
—	—	Lister (10225)*	4wPM	1938
—	—	R/Hornsby (175418)*	4wDM	1936
—	—	R/Hornsby*	4wDM	—
—	—	M/Rail (8979)*	4wDM	1946
—	—	M/Rail (5213)*	4wDM	1930
—	—	R/Hornsby	4wDM	1957

*2ft gauge

Stock

11 ex-BR Mk 1 coaches (SK, CK, BCK, 5xTSO, RMB, BSO(T) and SLS)
4 ex-LNER coaches; 2 SR parcels vans; Freight stock and service vehicles, SR and GW brakes

Special notes: Steam rides are on 2½-mile line to new halt and picnic area. Unlimited ride facility. Old Midland Railway buildings, fine collection of industrial locomotives
Membership details: Membership Secretary at above address
Membership journal: *Dalestream, YDR News* — 4 times/year

Foxfield Steam Railway

The railway, built in 1893 to connect a colliery to the national system, closed in 1965, has been re-opened.
Chairman: Ronald H. Whalley
Headquarters: Foxfield Steam Railway, Blythe Bridge, Stoke on Trent
Telephone: (0782) 396210 (weekends), 314532 (weekdays)
Main station: Blythe Bridge (Caverswall Road)
OS reference: SJ 957421
Car park: Blythe Bridge
Access by public transport: BR Blythe Bridge (400yd). PMT bus service to Blythe Bridge
Refreshment facilities: Blythe Bridge
Souvenir shop: Blythe Bridge
Passenger trains: Steam-hauled trains operate from Blythe Bridge (Caverswall Road) to Dilhorne Park and return
Length of line: 2¾ miles
Period of public operation: Steam trains operate Sundays and Bank Holidays only, April-September inclusive between Blythe Bridge and Dilhorne Park.
Special events: Santa Specials, weekends in December (advanced booking essential)

Industrial locomotives

Name	*No*	*Builder*	*Type*	*Bui*
Whiston	—	Hunslet (3694)	0-6-0ST	195
Wimblebury	—	Hunslet (3839)	0-6-0ST	195
Roker	—	RSH (7006)	0-4-0CT	194
Cranford	—	Avonside (1919)	0-6-0ST	192
Lewisham	—	Bagnall (2221)	0-6-0ST	192
Hawarden	—	Bagnall (2623)	0-4-0ST	194
Wolstanton No 3	—	Bagnall (3150)	0-6-0DM	196
Bagnall	—	Bagnall (3207)	0-4-0DH	196
Little Barford	—	Barclay (2069)	0-4-0ST	193
—	—	E/Electric (788)	4wBE	193
Spondon No 2	—	E/Electric (1130)	4wBE	193
Henry Cort	—	Peckett (933)	0-4-0ST	190
Ironbridge No 1	—	Peckett (1803)	0-4-0ST	193
—	11	Peckett (2081)	0-4-0ST	194
C.P.C.	—	Barclay (1964)	0-4-0ST	192
Moss Bay	—	K/Stuart (4167)	0-4-0ST	192
Rom River	—	K/Stuart (4421)	6wDM	192
—	1	Barclay (1984)	0-4-0F	193
Meaford No 4	—	Barclay (486)	0-6-0DH	196
Helen	—	Simplex (2262)	4wDM	192
Coronation	—	N/British (27097)	0-4-0DH	195
—	—	R/Hornsby (395305)	0-4-0DM	195
Gas-oil	—	R/Hornsby (408496)	0-4-0DM	195
Hercules	—	Ruston (242915)	4wDM	194
—	—	Thomas Hill (103C)	0-4-0DH	195

Stock
5 coaches; 4 scenery vans (some converted for other uses); 19 wagons; 1 rail-mounted self-propelled diesel-electric crane

Facilities for disabled: Access to majority of facilities is on the level. For special requirements prior notice is desirable

Membership journal: *Foxfield New* — quarterly

Gloucestershire Warwickshire Railway

Part of an ambitious project to link Cheltenham racecourse with Stratford racecourse, much has been done to recreate the railway and buildings that made up this cross-country route. The railway is home to many owners of private locomotives and rolling stock, so from time to time the items on display may vary
Location: Toddington Station, Toddington
OS reference: SO 050322

Locomotives

Name	*No*	*Origin*	*Class*	*Type*	*Built*
—*	2807	GWR	2800	2-8-0	1905
—	4277	GWR	4200	2-8-0T	1920
Kinlet Hall	4936	GWR	'Hall'	4-6-0	1929
Defiant†	5080	GWR	'Castle'	4-6-0	1939
—§	5619	GWR	5600	6-6-2T	1925
—†	7752	GWR	5700	0-6-0PT	1930
Peninsular and Oriental SNCo	35006	SR	MN	4-6-2	1941
—	76077	BR	4MT	2-6-0	1956
—	D2069	BR	03	0-6-0DM	1959
—	D9537	BR	14	0-6-0DH	1965
—	D9539	BR	14	0-6-0DH	1965
—	D9553	BR	14	0-6-0DH	1965

*Transferred to Birmingham Railway Museum, Tyseley for restoration
†On loan from Birmingham Railway Museum, Tyseley
§On loan from Telford Steam Railway

Operating society/organisation: Gloucestershire Warwickshire Steam Railway PLC, The Station, Toddington, Cheltenham, Glos GL54 5DT
Telephone: Toddington (0242) 621405
Main station: Toddington
Other public stations: Winchcombe
Access by public transport: Public transport is very limited with occasional buses from Cheltenham, Stratford on Avon and Evesham only. Local bus service Castleways will answer timetable queries on (0242) 602949
Car park: On site
On site facilities: Sales, catering, museum, narrow gauge rides, toilets
Length of line: 4 miles
Public opening: During the week the station is unmanned but visitors are welcome. Public services Weekends, Bank Holiday Mondays, between March and October
Special events: Santa Specials in December; Mince Pie Specials and New Year specials
Special notes: The site is being developed as the headquarters of the railway between Cheltenham and Stratford. The GWR owns the railway land between Cheltenham and Honeybourne and operates over four miles from Toddington to Gretton with an intermediate station at Winchcombe
Membership details: From above address
Membership journal: *The Cornishman* — quarterly

Industrial locomotives

Name	*No*	*Builder*	*Type*	*Built*
Huntsman	—	Bagnall (2655)	0-6-0ST	1941
Robert Nelson No 4	—	Hunslet (1800)	0-6-0ST	1936
King George	—	Hunslet (2409)	0-6-0ST	1942
—	19	Fowler (4240016)	0-6-0DH	1964
—	21	Fowler (4210130)	0-4-0DM	1957
—	—	H/Clarke (D615)	0-6-0DM	1938
—	—	Hibberd (2893)	4wPM	1943

Stock
3 ex-GWR coaches; 13 ex-BR coaches; 1 ex-LMS coach; numerous plus wagons

Owners
2807 and 4277 (the Cotswold Steam Preservation Ltd)
35006, 76077 (the P and O Locomotive Society)
D9537, D9539 and D9553 (Cotswold Diesel Preservation Group)

North Gloucestershire Railway

Industrial narrow gauge locomotives (2ft gauge)

Name	*No*	*Builder*	*Type*	*Built*
Isibutu	5	Bagnall (2820)	4-4-0T	1946
George B	—	Hunslet (680)	0-4-0ST	1898
Chaka	—	Hunslet (2075)	0-4-2T	1940
Justine	—	Jung (939)	0-4-0WT	1906
—	—	Henschel (15968)	0-8-0T	1918
—	2	Lister (34523)	4wDM	1949
—	3	M/Rail (4565)	4wPM	1928
Spitfire	—	M/Rail (7053)	4wPM	1937
—	1	R/Hornsby (166010)	4wDM	1932
—	L5	R/Hornsby (181820)	4wDM	1936
—	—	R/Hornsby (354028)	4wDM	1953

Stock
1 coach; 11 wagons

Below:
GWR pannier tank No 7752 arrives at Winchcombe with the 15.00 service from Toddington to Gretton on 31 March 1991. *Tom Heavyside*

Great Central Railway

The original Great Central Railway's extension to London in 1899 was the last main line to be built in this country, most of which was closed in the 1960s. Steam-hauled services are now operating again through attractive rolling Leicestershire countryside crossing the picturesque Swithland reservoir. A project has now commenced to lay double track between Rothley and Loughborough

Headquarters: Great Central Railway, (1976) PLC (Main Line Steam Trust Ltd), Loughborough Central Station, Great Central Road, Loughborough, Leicestershire LE11 1RW
Telephone: Loughborough (0509) 230726
Main stations: Loughborough Central, Leicester North
Other public stations: Quorn & Woodhouse, Rothley
OS reference: SK 543194
Car park: Quorn, Rothley
Access by public transport: Loughborough BR station (¾-mile). Trent, South Notts, and Midland Fox bus services to Loughborough bus station (¾-mile). Some Midland Fox services pass bottom Great Central Road, 300yd
Refreshment facilities: Licensed buffet car and light refreshments on most trains and at all stations. Sunday lunches on mid-day train; evening dining trains on certain Saturday nights, please contact railway for dates and reservations (advance booking only). Private charter trains available on request
Souvenir shop: Loughborough
Museum: Loughborough
Depot: Loughborough
Length of line: 8 miles
Passenger trains: Loughborough-Leicester North
Period of public operation: Weekends throughout the year and Bank Holiday Mondays. Midweek services on certain Tuesdays, Wednesdays and Thursdays in June, July and August
Special events: Thomas Weekends, Steam Galas, Night Steam and Mail runs

Locomotives

Name	*No*	*Origin*	*Class*	*Type*	*Built*
—	68088	NER	Y7	0-4-0T	1923
—	5224	GWR	5205	2-8-0T	1924
Witherslack Hall	6990	GWR	'Hall'	4-6-0	1948
Clun Castle	7029	GWR	'Castle'	4-6-0	1950
Kolhapur	5593	LMS	'Jubilee'	4-6-0	1934
—	47406	LMS	3F	0-6-0T	1926
—	48305	LMS	8F	2-8-0	1943
—	1264	LNER	B1	4-6-0	1947
—	69523	LNER	N2	0-6-2T	1921
Repton	30926	SR	V	4-4-0	1934
Boscastle	34039	SR	WC	4-6-2	1946
Hartland	34101	SR	WC	4-6-2	1950
Canadian Pacific	35005	SR	MN	4-6-2	1941
Brocklebank Line	35025	SR	MN	4-6-2	1948
—	92212	BR	9F	2-10-0	1959
—	D3180	BR	08	0-6-0DE	1955
—	D3101	BR	08	0-6-0DE	1955
—	D4067	BR	10	0-6-0DE	1961
Royal Highland Fusilier	55019	BR	55	Co-Co	1961

3-car DMU, Class 120 M59276, Class 127 M51616 and M51622

Industrial locomotives

Name	*No*	*Builder*	*Type*	*Built*
—	7597	RSH (7597)	0-6-0T	1949
—	68009	Hunslet (3825)	0-6-0ST	1953
Hilda	—	Peckett (1963)	0-4-0ST	1936
Qwag	1	Ruston (371971)	4wDM	1954
Arthur Wright	D4279	Fowler (4210079)	0-4-0DE	1952
—	28	A/Barclay (400)	0-4-0DM	1956

Below:
LMS 'Jubilee' class 4-6-0 No 5593 *Kolhapur* and GWR 0-6-0PT No 7760 leave Loughborough with the 10.45 for Rothley on 28 April 1991. No 7760, the property of the Birmingham Railway Museum was on loan at the time.
W. A. Sharman

Facilities for disabled: Special carriage for wheelchair/disabled persons (advance notice required). Wheelchair access good at Quorn and Rothley, can be arranged at Loughborough with advance notification. Boarding ramps at all stations
Membership & share details: Share enquiries: Company Secretary, Great Central Railway (1976) PLC Membership: Membership Secretary, Main Line Steam Trust PLC. Both c/o above address

Owners
68088 (the Y7 Locomotive Society)
69523 (the Gresley Society)
6990 (the Witherslack Hall Locomotive Society)
61264 (the Thompson B1 Locomotive Society)
92212 (the 92212 Holdings Ltd)
7597 (Railway Vehicle Preservation Society)
55019 (the Deltic Preservation Society)
5593 and 7029 (on loan from the Birmingham Railway Museum)

Hampshire Narrow Gauge Railway Society SC

Operating society/organisation: Hampshire Narrow Gauge Railway Society, c/o 4 Holmdale Road, Gosport, Hants PO12 4PJ
Note: The society held its last open day on 28 December 1991. The site will be abandoned and the stock is to be stored, pending relocation. The stock list alongside is retained for interest. *Railway World* will carry additional details when advised.

Locomotives

Name	*No*	*Builder*	*Type*	*Built*
Wendy	1	Bagnall (2091)	0-4-0ST	1919
AGW1 Pet	2	M/Rail (4724)	4wP	1939
Cloister	3	Hunslet (542)	0-4-0ST	1891
Brambridge Hall	4	M/Rail (5226)	4wP	1936
—	5	R/Hornsby (392117)	4wD	1956
Josephine	6	Hunslet (1842)	0-4-2ST	1936
—	7	Hanomag (8310)	0-8-0T	1918
—	8	O/Koppel (4013)	4wD	1933
Norden	9	O/Koppel (20777)	0-4-0D	1936

Stock
1 bogie coach; Various freight stock; Carriage portion of ex-LSWR 4-2-4T The Bug (standard gauge)

Hollycombe Steam Collection SC

An unusual collection of traction engines, Bioscope, organs, steam gallopers, Mighty Emperor Burrell Steam Engine, sawmill and paddle steamer engine which also includes a 7¼in gauge steam railway which climbs some fair gradients through the woodlands and gardens
Location: Iron Hill, Hollycombe, near Liphook, Hants
OS reference: SU 852295
Operating society/organisation: Hollycombe Steam & Woodland Garden Society, Iron Hill, Liphook, Hants GU30 7LP

Industrial locomotives

Name	*No*	*Builder*	*Type*	*Built*
Excelsior	—	A/Porter (1607)	2-2-0WTG	1880†
Caledonia	70	Barclay (1995)	0-4-0WT	1931*
Jerry M	38	Hunslet (638)	0-4-0ST	1895*
Newcastle	—	H/Leslie (2450)	0-4-0ST	1899
—	16	R/Hornsby	4wDM	1941*

*2ft gauge
†3ft gauge

Telephone: Liphook (0428) 724900 (opening days only); otherwise (04203) 4740
Car park: On site
Access by public transport: Liphook BR station (1½ miles)
On site facilities: Shop and refreshments.
Public opening: Please see press for details
Special events: Please see press for details

Irchester Narrow Gauge Railway Museum SC

The aims of the controlling trust are to acquire and preserve narrow gauge railway locomotives, rolling stock and exhibits associated with Northamptonshire and the east Midlands. To display the collection for the benefit of the public and to restore exhibits to working order so they may be demonstrated in a proper manner
Location: Within Irchester Country Park, 2 miles north of Wellingborough
Operating society/organisation: The Irchester Narrow Gauge Railway Trust, 5 Merchant Lane, Cranfield, Bedford MK43 0DA
On site facilities: Shop, museum, demonstration line, picnic area
Access by public transport: BR Wellingborough (Midland Road) station, buses to Irchester and Little Irchester
Car Parks: Main park car parks
Toilets: Main park complex
Public opening: Every Sunday (summer 10.00-17.30, winter 10.00-16.00), at other times by arrangement. Steam and demonstration weekends are held on last full weekend of the month — March-October
Facilities for disabled: Museum and site on level, staff available if required
Membership details: Membership Secretary, 66 Norton Road, Kingsthorpe, Northampton

Industrial locomotives

Name	*No*	*Builder*	*Type*	*Built*
—	85*	Peckett (1870	0-6-0ST	1934
—	86*	Peckett (1871)	0-6-0ST	1934
Cambrai	—*	Corpet (493)	0-6-0T	1888
—	ND3645*	R/Hornsby (211679)	4wDM	1941
—	—†	R/Hornsby (281290)	0-6-0DM	1949
—	ED10*	R/Hornsby (411322	4wDM	1958
—	—†	M/Rail (1363)	4wPM	1918
—	ND3647†	M/Rail (22144)	4wDM	1962
The Rock	—*	Hunslet (2419)	0-4-0DM	1941

* Metre gauge
† 3ft Gauge

Below:
This metre gauge 0-6-0ST, No 85, is seen in steam on the short demonstration line at Irchester. *R. E. Ruffell*

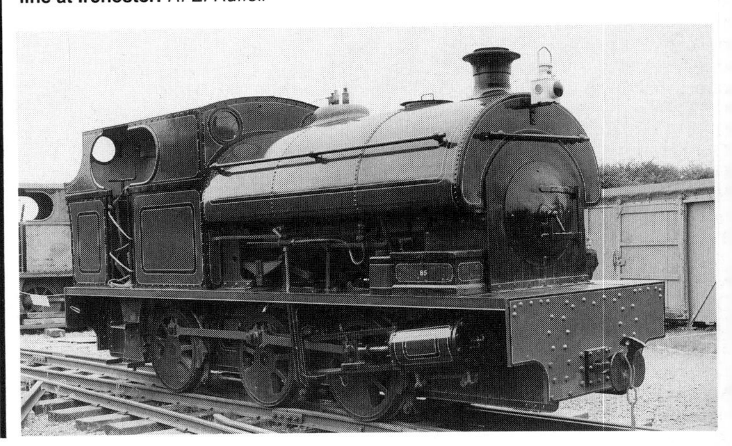

Ironbridge Gorge Museum M

The railway items form only a small part of the displays on two of the museum's main sites, Blists Hill and Coalbrookdale. The Blists Hill site offers an opportunity to see a number of industrial and other activities being operated in meticulously reconstructed period buildings. A working foundry and ironworks are just two of the exciting exhibits. The Ironbridge Gorge was designated a World Heritage Site in 1987
Location: Ironbridge, Shropshire
OS reference: SJ 694033

Industrial locomotives

Name	*No*	*Builder*	*Type*	*Built*
—	—	Sentinel/Coalbrookdale (6185)	0-4-0VBT	1925
—	—	Sentinel/M/Wardle (6155)	0-4-0VBT	1925
—	5	Coalbrookdale	0-4-0ST	1865

All locomotives are at the Museum of Iron, Coalbrookdale

Note: A full-size working replica of Richard Trevithick's 1802 plateway locomotive, built by the Coalbrookdale Co, will be operating outside the Museum of Iron throughout the 1992 season. For further details please telephone the number above, or Telford (0952) 432751,

perating society/organisation: onbridge Gorge Museum Trust, onbridge, Telford, Shropshire F8 7AW
elephone: Telford (0952) 433522
ar park: At the sites
ccess by public transport: Various rivate bus companies, including Midland Red, Williamson's hearings, Elcocks, Boultons.

A frequent 'Park & Ride' bus service operates on weekdays during school holidays, and on weekends from Easter to September. Vintage vehicles are used at weekends
Catering facilities: Licensed Victorian pub, sweet shop and tea rooms at the Blists Hill site, serving drinks and mainly cold snacks. Tea, coffee and light refreshments at the Museum of Iron and Rosehill House, Coalbrookdale
Public opening: Main sites including Museum of Iron and on Blists Hill, daily (except Christmas Eve and Christmas Day) 10.00-17.00, 10.00-18.00 during British Summer Time
Special notes: Tickets for all the sites or just for single sites available

Isle of Wight Steam Railway

eparated from the mainland by the olent, the line's isolation ncouraged the maintenance and tention of Victorian locomotives nd coaching stock which still perate the line today. Its rural harm enhances its attraction for e island's holidaymakers during e summer season
perating manager: Terry Hastings
eadquarters: Isle of Wight Steam ailway, Haven Street station, Ryde, le of Wight PO33 4DS
elephone: Station: Isle of Wight 983) 882204
ain station: Haven Street
S reference: SZ 556898
ther public stations: Wootton and mallbrook Junction
ar park: Haven Street
ccess by public transport: etwork SouthEast 'Island Line' rvice from Ryde or Shanklin to mallbrook Jct

Locomotives

Name	*No*	*Origin*	*Class*	*Type*	*Built*
Freshwater	W8 (32646)	LBSCR	A1X	0-6-0T	1876
—*	11 (32640)	LBSCR	A1X	0-6-0T	1878
Calbourne	W24	LSWR	O2	0-4-4T	1891
—	D2554	BR	05	0-6-0DM	1956
—	D2059	BR	03	0-6-0DM	1959

*depicted as IWCR No 11

Industrial locomotives

Name	*No*	*Builder*	*Type*	*Built*
Invincible	37	H/Leslie (3135)	0-4-0ST	1915
Ajax	38	Barclay (1605)	0-6-0T	1918

Locomotive notes: Ajax is not on public display.

Stock
4 IWR coaches (bodies only); 1 IWR coach; 3 LBSCR coaches; 3 SECR coaches; 1 LCDR coach; 5 LCDR coaches (bodies only); 1 LBSCR coach (body only); 1 crane; 1 ex-BR ballast tamper; 1 Wickham trolley; 30 wagons; 6 parcels vans; 2 ex-LT hoppers; 1 ex-BR Lowmac

Below:
Celebrations took place on the Isle of Wight Steam Railway on 20 July 1991, as it was the date of the opening of the extension to Smallbrook Junction. No 24 *Calbourne* is seen at the head of the special train, civic dignitaries can be seen to the right of the engine. *Theale Photography*

Refreshment facilities: Light refreshments available
Souvenir shop: Haven Street
Museum: Small exhibits museum at Haven Street
Depot: Haven Street
Length of line: 5 miles
Passenger trains: Wootton-Smallbrook Jct
Period of public operation: 26 March to 30 April: Sundays, Thursdays and Bank Holidays, also 21/22 April. May: Sundays, Wednesdays and Bank Holidays, also Tuesdays 5 and 26 May. 2 June to 16 July: Sundays, Tuesdays, Wednesdays and Thursdays. 19 July to 4 September daily EXCEPT Saturdays. 6 to 30 September: Sundays, Tuesdays, Wednesdays and Thursdays. October: Sundays and Thursdays.
Special events: Summer Steam Extravaganza, 22-25 August; Santa Specials, in December until Xmas (please write for details)
Facilities for disabled: Limited facilities but can be catered for singly, or in groups (by prior arrangement), toilets available
Special notes: Summer Steam Show, August Bank Holiday Friday, Saturday, Sunday and Monday. Traction engines, fairground organs, vintage cars etc.
Membership details: Mr J. Price at above address
Membership journal: *Wight Report* — quarterly

Keighley & Worth Valley Railway

The epitome of a volunteer-run railway, a thriving branch line which serves six stations (most of them gas lit) which is host to an extensive and varied collection of locomotives and where everything continues to provide the atmosphere of the days of the steam railway. Immaculate stations, immaculate staff, immaculate trains. Very friendly and very much part of the community
Chairman, Joint Management Committee: David W. Kay
Headquarters: Haworth station, Keighley, West Yorkshire, BD22 8NJ
Telephone: Haworth (0535) 643629 24hr recorded timetable and information service, Haworth (0535) 645214 (other calls)
Main stations: Keighley, Ingrow West, Haworth, Oxenhope
Other public stations: Damems, Oakworth
OS reference: SE 034371
Car parks: Free at Keighley, Ingrow West, Oakworth, Oxenhope. Limited parking at Haworth (pay). Coaches at Ingrow West and Oxenhope only
Access by public transport: British Rail through services from Carlisle, Morecambe, Lancaster, Leeds, Bradford to Keighley station for Worth Valley trains. (Change to platform 4). Also from Preston, Blackburn, Accrington, Burnley, Manchester, Rochdale, Todmorden to Hebden Bridge Station for connection via bus service 500 to Oxenhope. (Operates Saturdays throughout the year, Sundays May to September, Monday to Friday

Locomotives

Name	*No*	*Origin*	*Class*	*Type*	*Built*
—	41241	LMS	2MT	2-6-2T	1949
—	43924	MR	4F	0-6-0	1920
—	45212	LMS	5MT	4-6-0	1935
Bahamas	45596	LMS	Jubilee	4-6-0	1935
—	48431	LMS	8F	2-8-0	1944
—	47279	LMS	3F	0-6-0T	1925
—	1054	LNWR	—	0-6-2T	1888
City of Wells	34092	SR	WC	4-6-2	1949
—	80002	BR	4MT	2-6-4T	1952
—	75078	BR	4MT	4-6-0	1956
—	78022	BR	2MT	2-6-0	1953
—	30072	SR	USA	0-6-0T	1943
—	5775	GWR	5700	0-6-0PT	1929
—	52044	L&Y	2F	0-6-0	1887
—	19*	L&Y	Pug	0-4-0ST	1910
—	51218	L&Y	Pug	0-4-0ST	1901
—	752	L&Y	—	0-6-0ST	1881
—	85	TVR	02	0-6-2T	1899
—	5820	USA TC	S160	2-8-0	1945
—	90733	MoS	WD	2-8-0	1945
—	68077	LNER	J94	0-6-0ST	1947
—	D226	BR	—	0-6-0DE	1956
—	D2511	BR	—	0-6-0DM	1961
—	D3336	BR	08	0-6-0DE	1954
—	D5209	BR	25/1	Bo-Bo	1963
—	D8031	BR	20	Bo-Bo	1960

Industrial locomotives

Name	*No*	*Builder*	*Type*	*Built*
Hamburg	31	H/Clarke (697)	0-6-0T	1903
	67	H/Clarke (1369)	0-6-0T	1919
Nunlow	—	H/Clarke (1704)	0-6-0T	1938
Brussels	118	H/Clarke (1782)	0-6-0ST	1945
Southwick	—	RSH (7069)	0-4-0CT	1942
Fred	—	RSH (7289)	0-6-0ST	1945
—	57	RSH (7668)	0-6-0ST	1950
—	63	RSH (7761)	0-6-0ST	1954
—	2226	Barclay (2226)	0-4-0ST	1946
Tiny	—	Barclay (2258)	0-4-0ST	1949
Merlin	231	H/Clarke (D761)	0-6-0DM	1951
—	1999*	Peckett (1999)	0-4-0	1941
Austins No1	—	Peckett (5003)	0-4-0DM	1961
—	MDHB No 32	Hunslet (2699)	0-6-0DM	1944

*On loan to Southport Railway Museum

Above:
Ex-LNWR 'Coal Tank', No 1054, climbs towards Oakworth with the 13.50 vintage train from Keighley to Oxenhope on 7 April 1991. *Brian Dobbs*

July and August only. Tel: Keighley (0535) 603284 for timings.) A large number of bus services serve Keighley including from Burnley; Burnley & Pendle/Keighley & District Service 25 to Keighley bus station. From Bradford Interchange: services 662/663/664/665/666/667/668/669. From Leeds: service 760. From Huddersfield and Halifax: service 502 via Denholme to Ingrow West. National Coach services Nos 281/2/5/9, 291, 307/8, 318 all serve Keighley from various parts of the country
Refreshment facilities: Buffet restaurant at Oxenhope. Buffet at Keighley station. All normally open when steam trains are operating. Buffet bar car on some trains. Wine and Dine by prior booking only — the 'White Rose Pullman'; Sunday lunch dining car services on the 'Devonian'
Souvenir shops: Haworth, Oxenhope, Keighley, Ingrow carriage museum
Museums: Railway Museum at Oxenhope, Vintage Carriage Trust's carriage and locomotive museum at Ingrow Railway Centre. Open daily May-October, 12.00-16.00. Weekends throughout the year
Depots: Carriage and wagon — Oxenhope; Motive power/loco works — Haworth, 'Bahamas Locomotive Society' workshops at (not yet completed) at Ingrow Railway Centre which is open whenever trains are operating.
Length of line: 4¾ miles
Passenger trains: Steam-hauled services between Oxenhope-Keighley. Some off-peak and local shoppers' services worked by diesel railbus

Frequent bus service between Haworth station and Haworth village top on Sundays (May-September) and bank holidays, 11.00-18.00
Period of public operation: Winter diesel railbus service Saturdays November-February (Keighley-Oxenhope). Winter steam service Sundays November, January and February (Keighley-Oxenhope); December — Santa Specials only from Haworth, Oxenhope and Keighley (pre-booked). Steam/diesel service Saturdays and Sundays March-October. Daily steam service from late June to early September. Easter week and Spring Bank Holiday week
Special events: 2nd weekend before Easter; 'Enthusiast's Weekend', railway horses, Griddle and Restaurant car services, gas and oil lit stations, intensive steam services. Vintage trains in spring and autumn. Carol Service by steam train, last Saturday before Christmas
Facilities for disabled: Toilet on Haworth station forecourt. Wheelchairs accommodated in guard's compartments on trains. Please advise before visit to the Advanced Bookings Officer c/o Haworth station
Special notes: Accompanied children under 5 years of age free. Children 5-15 and Senior Citizens at 50% discount. BR Family Railcard holders 10% discount on full-line tickets. Through bookings from all major BR stations to Haworth and Oxenhope, discount on KWVR portion of ticket
Membership details: Membership Secretary c/o above address
Membership journal: *Push & Pull* — quarterly
Marketing name: *Worth Valley*

Stock
2 ex-BR German-built Waggon und Maschinenbau diesel railbuses; 30 coaches including examples of pre-Grouping types; BR Mk 1 stock including the oldest vehicle in existence, part of the prototype batch; a Pullman car, NER and L&Y observation cars

Owners
19, 752 and 51218 (L&Y Saddletanks)
47279 (South Yorkshire 3F Fund)
75078 and 78022 (the Standard 4 Preservation Society)
Bahamas, Nunlow, Tiny (the Bahamas Locomotive Society)
1054 (the National Trust)

Kent & East Sussex Steam Railway

The epitome of the early Edwardian light railways that were developed on shoestring budgets to open up less populated areas of the countryside. The line is now being extended towards Bodiam Castle and to Robertsbridge providing an interchange with Network SouthEast. The picturesque town of Tenterden remains the headquarters of the railway.
Company Secretary: Raymond Williams
Headquarters: Tenterden Railway Co Ltd, Tenterden Town station, Tenterden, Kent TN30 6HE
Telephone: Tenterden (058 06) 2943 (24 hour talking timetable); Tenterden (05806) 5155 (office)
Main station: Tenterden Town
Other public stations: Rolvenden, Wittersham Road, Northiam
Car parks: Tenterden, Wittersham Road, Northiam
OS reference:
Tenterden TQ 882336,
Rolvenden TQ 865328,
Northiam TQ 834266
Access by public transport: Maidstone & District bus service No 400 from Ashford (Kent) BR station
Refreshment facilities: Tenterden Town. Also on train facilities. Lunch and afternoon teas on Sunday trains
Souvenir shop: Tenterden Town station
Museum: Station Road, Tenterden
Depot: Rolvenden
Length of line: 7 miles
Passenger trains: Tenterden-Northiam.

January, February, March — Sundays only, 11.00-15.00; April —

Locomotives

Name	*No*	*Origin*	*Class*	*Type*	*Built*
	32670	LBSCR	A1X	0-6-0T	1872
Sutton	10 (32650)	LBSCR	A1X	0-6-0T	1876
Knowle	32678	LBSCR	A1X	0-6-0T	1880
—	1556	SECR	P	0-6-0T	1909
Wainwright	21 (30070)	SR	USA	0-6-0T	1943
Maunsell	30065	SR	USA	0-6-0T	1943
—	20	GWR	AEC	diesel railcar	1940
	19	NSB	21c	2-6-0	1919
—	44 (D2023)	BR	03	0-6-0DM	1958
—	45 (D2024)	BR	03	0-6-0DM	1958
—	46 (D2205)	BR	04	0-6-0DM	1958
—	D9504	BR	14	0-6-0DH	1964
—	49 (D9525)	BR	14	0-6-0DH	1965

Industrial locomotives

Name	*No*	*Builder*	*Type*	*Built*
Marcia	12	Peckett (1631)	0-4-0T	1923
Charwelton	14	M/Wardle (1955)	0-6-0ST	1917
Holman F. Stephens	23	Hunslet (3791)	0-6-0ST	1952
William H. Austen	24	Hunslet (3800)	0-6-0ST	1953
Northiam	25	Hunslet (3797)	0-6-0ST	1953
Linda	26	Hunslet (3781)	0-6-0ST	1952
Rolvenden	27	RSH (7086)	0-6-0ST	1943
—	40	BTH	Bo-Bo	1932
—	42	Hunslet (4208)	0-6-0DM	1948
—	—	R/Hornsby (423661)	0-4-0DM	1958

Stock

3 ex-SECR 'Birdcage' coaches; 1 ex-LSWR coach; 5 4-wheel coaches of NLR, GER, SECR and LC&DR origins; 1 LNWR Director's saloon; 1 GER observation car; SECR and LSWR Family saloons; 3 Pullman cars; 8 ex-BR Mk 1 coaches; 1 ex-BR Mk 1 RU 'Diana'; 9 ex-SR Maunsell coaches; 3 steam cranes; large interesting collection of freight vehicles, totalling 51 vehicles

Owners

10 (London Borough of Sutton)
21 and 22 (Kent & East Sussex Loco Trust)
19 (Norwegian Locomotive Trust)

Below:
***Charwelton* and *Sutton* double-head a special on 23 May 1991 bound for Northiam, in connection with the naming of a BR Class 73.** *Brian Morrison*

weekends and daily 17-26, 10.30-16.30; May — weekends and daily 23-31, 10.30-16.30; June — weekends 10.30-16.30; July — weekends 10.30-16.30, daily 10.45-16.00; August — daily 10.30-16.30; September — as June; October — as April; November — weekends 11.00-15.00
Special events: 27/28 June — Friends of Thomas the Tank Engine; 19/20 September — The Good Old Days, a weekend of nostalgia
Facilities for disabled: A special coach for disabled people, 'Petros', is allocated to most trains (telephone for confirmation of availability), reserved parking at Tenterden.
Toilets with disabled access at Tenterden and Northiam, and in coach 'Petros'
Special notes: 'Wealden Pullman' dining car service operates on most Saturday evenings in season. Advance booking is essential for this train. Santa special services operate on each Saturday and Sunday in December. Advanced booking recommended
Membership details: New Members Secretary c/o above address
Membership journal: *The Tenterden Terrier* — 3 times/year

Lakeside & Haverthwaite Railway

Originally this Furness Railway branch line carried passengers and freight from Ulverston to Lakeside but now the only part remaining is the 3½-mile section from Haverthwaite to the terminus at Lakeside where connections are made with the lakeside steamers which ply the 10-mile length of Windermere
General Manager: M. A. Maher
Headquarters: Haverthwaite station, near Ulverston, Cumbria LA12 8AL
Telephone: Newby Bridge (05395) 31594
Main station: Haverthwaite
Other public stations: Intermediate station at Newby Bridge. Terminus at Lakeside
OS reference: SD 349843
Car parks: Haverthwaite, Lakeside
Access by public transport: Lakeside steamers on Windermere call at Lakeside. Ribble bus to Haverthwaite
Refreshment facilities: Haverthwaite
Souvenir shop: Haverthwaite
Depot: All rolling stock at Haverthwaite
Length of line: 3½ miles
Passenger trains: Steam-hauled Haverthwaite-Lakeside
Period of public operation: Easter then daily from early-May to end of October.

Locomotives

Name	*No*	*Origin*	*Class*	*Type*	*Built*
—	2073	LMS	4MT	2-6-4T	1950
—	42085	LMS	4MT	2-6-4T	1951
—	8(D2117)	BR	03	0-6-0DM	1959
—	17(AD601)	LMS	—	0-6-0DE	1945
—	03072	BR	03	0-6-0DM	1959
—	5643	GWR	5600	0-6-2T	1925

Industrial locomotives

Name	*No*	*Builder*	*Type*	*Built*
*Caliban**	1	Peckett (1925)	0-4-0ST	1937
Rachel	9	M/Rail (2098)	4wDM	1924
Repulse	11	Hunslet (3698)	0-6-0ST	1950
Princess	14	Bagnall (2682)	0-6-0ST	1942
Askam Hall	15	Avonside (1772)	0-4-0ST	1935
Alexandra	12	Barclay (929)	0-4-0ST	1902
David	13	Barclay (2333)	0-4-0ST	1953
Cumbria	10	Hunslet (3794)	0-6-0ST	1953
—	7	Fowler (22919)	0-4-0DM	1940
Fluff	16	Hunslet/Fowler	0-4-0DM	1937
—	20	Jones crane	0-4-0DM	1952
—	21	Barclay (1550)	0-6-0F	1917
—	22	Fowler (4220045)	0-4-0DM	1967

*Under restoration at Steamtown, Carnforth

Stock
10 ex-BR Mk 1 coaches; 2-car Class 110 DMU, vehicle Nos 52071, 52077; 1 ex-LNER BG; 1 ex-BR Mk 1 miniature buffet coach, Royal saloon No 5 (built GER, Stratford 1898); Small selection of freight vehicles

Right:
It's 14.23 at Lakeside as L&HR workhorse *Cumbria* arrives with a light train from Haverthwaite on 8 June 1991. *Melvyn Hopwood*

Special events: Santa Specials (advance booking essential) please contact for details
Special notes: Combined railway/lake steamer tickets available, from the station at Haverthwaite and Lakeside steamers piers at Bowness and Ambleside. Lakeside steamers is operated by Windermere Iron Steamboat Co Ltd
Membership journal: *The Iron Horse* — quarterly

Launceston Steam Railway

The railway runs through the beautiful Kensey Valley on a track gauge of 1ft 11½in, following the trackbed of the old North Cornwall line. The locomotives formerly worked on the Dinorwic and Penrhyn railways in North Wales. Launceston station contains a museum of vintage cars and motorcycles and there is also a collection of stationary steam engines which are demonstrated at work. There are catering and gift shop facilities and an exhibition of model railways, together with a very well stocked model shop. At the far end of the line there are pleasant walks and a picnic area. The covered rolling stock ensures an enjoyable visit whatever the weather
Location: Newport Industrial Estate, Launceston, Cornwall
OS reference: SX 328850
Operating Society/organisation: The Spice Settlement Trust Co Ltd, trading as the Launceston Steam Railway, Newport, Launceston
Telephone: (0566) 775665
Stations: Launceston-Hunts Crossing-New Mills. Note: the line now terminates ½-mile from the hamlet of New Mills and refreshments are available at the temporary terminus
Car park: Newport Industrial Estate, Launceston
Length of line: 2 miles, but 2½ miles when New Mills extension opens
Gauge: 1ft 11½in
Access by public transport: BR Gunnislake 13 miles, Plymouth or Bodmin 25 miles
On site facilities: Cafe and restaurant, transport museum, workshop tours, gift and bookshop, and model railway display with model shop, all situated at Launceston
Period of public operation: Easter holiday, then Tuesdays and Sundays until Whitsun. Daily (not Saturdays) Whitsun until end of September. Tuesdays and Sundays in October. Santa Specials every Saturday and Sunday in December, also Christmas Eve and Boxing Day

Above:
Amid historic paraphernalia at the Launceston Steam Railway is Hunslet 0-4-0ST *Covercoat*. It is seen here on 14 April 1991 as it nears the end of an overhaul, but still minus its saddle tank. *Melvyn Hopwood*

Industrial locomotives

Name	*No*	*Builder*	*Type*	*Built*
Lilian	—	Hunslet (317)	0-4-0ST	1883
Velinheli	—	Hunslet (409)	0-4-0ST	1886
Covertcoat	—	Hunslet (679)	0-4-0ST	1898
Sybil	—	Bagnall (1760)	0-4-0ST	1906
Dorothea	—	Hunslet (763)	0-4-0ST	1901
—	—	M/Rail (5646)	4wDM	1933
—	—	M/Rail (9546)	4wDM	1950

Locomotive notes: The three Hunslet locomotives (317/409/679) are expected to be in use during 1991.

Stock
1 electric inspection trolley; 2 bogie carriages and 1 4-wheel carriage

Public opening: Trains run from 10.30-14.30. Departures every 40min and more frequently if required. Unlimited riding on date of issue of ticket
Journey time: Return 35min, no single tickets available
Facilities for disabled: Easy access to all areas except bookshop and motorcycle museum. No toilet facilities for disabled
Special events: Double-headed trains on Wednesdays in July and August (whenever possible)

Lavender Line SC

he neat appearance of the station
nd line at Isfield is largely due to
e care lavished on it by its owner,
avid Milham and his family.
ocation: Isfield Station, Isfield,
ear Uckfield, East Sussex TN22
XB
S reference: TQ 452171
perating society/organisation: The
avender Line Steam Museum
elephone: Isfield (082 575) 515
ar park: On site
ccess by public transport: Train to
ckfield or Lewes, then bus to
field. Buses run every two hours
n site facilities: Refreshments,
censed bar, wine & dine trains
dvanced booking essential),
ouvenir shop, museum
ength of line: 1½ miles

Locomotives

Name	No	Origin	Class	Type	Built
—	15224	BR	12	0-6-0DE	1949

Industrial locomotives

Name	No	Builder	Type	Built
Annie	945	A/Barclay (945)	0-4-0ST	1904
—	68012	Hunslet (3193)	0-6-0ST	1944

Stock
4 ex-BR Mk 1 coaches; 1 ex-GWR 'Toad' brake van

Note: at the time of going to press the future of this line was uncertain

Public opening: Every Sunday and Bank Holiday Monday, March-November, 10.30-17.00
Facilities for disabled: Yes
Special events: Santa specials in December

Special notes: Luxury wine & dine trains every Friday, all year except February, 19.30-20.00, booking essential

Leeds Industrial Museum M

ocation: The Leeds Industrial
Museum, Armley Mills, Canal Road,
eeds LS12 2QF
S reference: SE 275342
perating society/organisation:
eeds City Council, Department of
eisure Services, 19 Wellington
treet, Leeds 1
urator: P. J. Kelly
elephone: (0532) 637861
ar park: Cark park adjacent to the
Museum
ccess by public transport: Nos 5
r 5A from City Square, Leeds
outside the railway station)
ublic opening: April-September:
Tuesdays-Saturdays 10.00-18.00,
undays 14.00-18.00. October-
March: Tuesdays-Saturdays 10.00-
7.00, Sundays 14.00-17.00. Closed
Mondays (except Bank Holidays)
On site facilities: Museum shop,
efreshments (vending machines)
pecial notes: Facilities for the
isabled (toilets, etc), lifts. Museum
an be viewed by visitors in
wheelchairs (most areas are
ccessible)
**Details of locomotive and rolling
tock:** Locomotive collection
ncludes steam, diesel, mines
ocomotives and a narrow gauge
ailway and engines

Below:
Jack **is seen here in all its glory on the 18in gauge line at Leeds Industrial Museum.**

During the year there are a large number of steam-hauled specials that run over British Rail tracks. Here we see former East and West Coast Pacifics posing side by side during Coalville open day on 26 May 1991. Open days at BR depots often have a steam presence and LNER No 4472 ***Flying Scotsman*** and LMS No 46203 ***Princess Margaret Rose*** are seen here. *Robin Stewart-Smith*

46203
66
A

Leicestershire Museum

M

Narrow gauge site railway (1ft 11½in gauge) formerly part of sewage pumping station that now forms museum site. Railway relaid in concrete by MSC scheme during early 1980s to original track layout. New track layout as an extension to original laid with 35lb rail on wooden sleepers. All the railway system is now run by volunteers. Original Simplex locomotive kept on site (non-operational at present). A Planet petrol locomotive and a Ruston diesel are used to demonstrate railway with typical tipper wagons and mine tubs. Line originally used for transferring solid material from screens to tip (about 100yd).
Location: Museum of Technology, Abbey Pumping Station, Corporation Road, off Abbey Lane, Leicester LE4 5PW
Operating group: Leicestershire County Council Museum Department and Museum Volunteer Group
Telephone: (0533) 661330
Car park: Free on site
Access by public transport: BR Leicester (London Road). Leicester City Bus route 29 or 29A direct from station (alight at Beaumont Leys Lane)
Length of line/gauge: About 200yd and 1ft 11½ in gauge. No public riding on line
Period of public opening: Daily, 10.00 to 17.30 Monday to Saturday and 14.00 to 17.30 Sunday
On site facilities: Museum/shop/toilets/car park. Refreshments only on Special Event Days
Facilities for disabled: Access to museum lower floor and grounds. Steps to Engine House and refreshments on event days
Volunteer contact: Mr N. Pell, 211 Broadgate Lane, Anstey, Leics
Museum contact: Mr R. Bracegirdle, Industrial Museum, Snibston Mine, Ashby Road, Coalville, Leicestershire LE6 2LN. Telephone: 0530 510851
Other attractions: Museum holds various other railway items and small exhibition on Leicester & Swannington Railway. Some items only viewable by appointment or on Special Event Days

Industrial locomotive stock list

Narrow gauge:

Name	*No*	*Builder*	*Type*	*Built*
—	—	Motor Rail (52600)	4wPM	1931
Planet	—	(1776)	4wPM	1931
Ruston	—	(223700)	4wPM	1941

All at museum in Leicester

Standard gauge:

Name	*No*	*Builder*	*Type*	*Built*
Mars II	—	RSH (7493)	0-4-0ST	1948
—	2	Barclay (1815)	0-4-0F	1924
—	—	Brush (314)*	0-4-0ST	1906
—	—	Hunslet (3851)	0-6-0ST	1962

*Originally Powiesland & Mason Railway No 6 taken over by GWR in 1924, No 921.
Standard gauge locomotives are at Snibston Mine and not available for viewing.

Stock
Several narrow gauge wagons

Leighton Buzzard Railway

In places, this line bears the air of a Continental roadside tramway, running as it does behind the backs of houses before it passes into the open countryside; there is no denying the quaintness of its engines or the friendliness of the little trains and their staff
General Manager: J. Horsley
Headquarters: Leighton Buzzard Railway, Page's Park station, Billington Road, Leighton Buzzard LU7 8TN
OS reference: Page's Park SP 928242

Locomotives

Name	*No*	*Builder*	*Type*	*Built*
Berlin	—	Freudenstein (73)	0-4-0WT	1901
Alice	—	Hunslet (780)	0-4-0ST	1902
Peter Pan	—	K/Stuart (4256)	0-4-0ST	1922
Chaloner	1	de Winton	0-4-0VBT	1877
Pixie	2	K/Stuart (4260)	0-4-0ST	1922
Rishra	3	Baguley (2007)	0-4-0T	1921
Doll	4	Barclay (1641)	0-6-0T	1919
Elf	5	O&K (12740)	0-6-0WT	1936
Caravan	6	Simplex (7129)	4wDM	1938
Falcon	7	O&K (8986)	4wDM	1939
Gollum	8	Ruston (217999)	4wDM	1942
Madge	9	O&K (7600)	4wDM	1935
Haydn Taylor	10	Simplex (7956)	4wDM	1945
P. C. Allen	11	O&K (5834)	0-4-0WT	1912
Carbon	12	Simplex (6012)	4wPM	1930
Arkle	13	M/Rail (7108)	4wDM	1937
—	14	Hunslet (3646)	4wDM	1946

Telephone: (0525) 373888, 24hr answerphone with service and event details
Main station: Pages Park (A4146, Leighton Buzzard)
Other public stations: Halts at Vandyke Road and Stonehenge Works
Car park: Pages Park
Access by public transport: Leighton Buzzard BR station then by bus to town centre
Refreshment facilities: Pages Park
Souvenir shop: Pages Park
Depots: Pages Park and Stonehenge Works Museum project display at Stonehenge Works open
Length of line: 3 miles, 2ft gauge
Journey time: Single 25min, return 60min
Passenger trains: Pages Park-Stonehenge Works
Period of public operation: Sundays 5 April-4 October; Good Friday; Easter Saturday; Bank Holiday Mondays 20 April, 4/25 May, 31 August; Wednesdays 5 August-2 September; Thursdays 6 August-3 September
Special events: 21 June-25th Birthday Steam Gala; 2 August-13 September — Leighton Buzzard Steam Festival on operational days; 12/13 September — Festival Steam-Up '92
Facilities for disabled: Access to shop, buffet, platform. Toilet facilities are specially available June-September. Wheelchairs can be conveyed on trains. Those persons who can be transferred from chair to train are conveyed by first available train
Membership details: Membership secretary c/o above address
Membership journal: *Chaloner* — quarterly
Marketing name: England's Friendly Little Line

Name	*No*	*Class*	*Type*	*Built*
Tom Bombadil	15	Hibberd (2514)	4wDM	1941
Thorin Oakenshield	16	Lister (11221)	4wDM	1939
Damredub	17	Simplex (7036)	4wDM	1936
Feanor	18	M/Rail (11003)	4wDM	1956
—	19	M/Rail (11298)	4wDM	1965
—	20	M/Rail (60s317)	4wDM	1966
Festoon	21	Simplex (4570)	4wPM	1929
Fingolfin	22	under construction	—	—
—	23	Ruston (164346)	4wDM	1932
Ad-a-Cab	25	Simplex (7214)	4wDM	1938
Yimkin	26	Ruston (203026)	4wDM	1942
Poppy	27	Ruston (408430)	4wDM	1957
RAF Stanbridge	28	Ruston (200516)	4wDM	1949
Creepy	29	Hunslet (6008)	4wDM	1963
—	30	M/Rail (8695)	4wDM	1941
—	31	Lister (4228)	4wDM	1931
—	32	Ruston (172892)	4wDM	1934
—	33	Hibberd (3582)	4wDM	1954
—	34	Hunslet (2536)	4wDM	1941
—	35	Hunslet (6619)	0-4-0DM	1966
T. W. Lewis	39	Ruston (375316)	4wDM	1954
—	43	Simplex (10409)	4wDM	1954
Kestrel	44	Simplex (7933)	4wDM	1941

Dismantled for spares: M/Rail 4805, 5613, 5612, 5603; Ruston 218016 converted to brake vans: M/Rail 5608, 5875

Locomotive notes: 20 of these locomotives operated during 1991 and steam locomotives 1, 3, 4, 5 11, *Alice* and *Peter Pan* are potentially operational during 1992.

Stock
10 coaches and a number of miscellaneous vehicles

Liverpool Museum M

A fine selection of vehicles in a traditional 'stuffed and mounted' display. *Lion* may be absent at certain times during the year, depending on developments. Visitors are advised to enquire by telephone as to her availability
Location: William Brown Street, Liverpool
Curator: Dr K. J. Jump (Land Transport and Industrial Collections)
Operating society/organisation: National Museums and Galleries on Merseyside, William Brown Street, Liverpool L3 8EN
Telephone: 051-207 0001
Car parks: Public car parks nearby
Access by public transport: Adjacent Lime Street stations (BR and Merseyrail). Numerous bus routes
On site facilities: Cafe, shop
Public opening: Please contact for details
Special notes: Transport gallery within large general museum. Facilities for disabled visitors
Journal: *Focus*, covering entire activities of National Museums & Galleries on Merseyside; every four months

locomotives

Name	*No*	*Origin*	*Class*	*Type*	*Built*
*Lion**	57	L&MR	—	0-4-2	1838

**Lion* is the oldest working locomotive in the world

Industrial locomotives

Name	*No*	*Builder*	*Type*	*Built*
—	1	Avonside (1465)	0-6-0ST	1904

Stock
LOR electric coach of 1893
L&MR replica coach built Derby 1929

London Transport Museum

M

The museum was opened in the converted Flower Market in March 1980. The displays cover nearly two centuries of public transport in London
Location: Covent Garden, London WC2E 7BB
OS reference: TQ 303809
Operating society/organisation: London Regional Transport
Telephone: 071-379 6344
Access by public transport: Underground to Covent Garden, Leicester Square or Charing Cross. Buses to Strand or Aldwych
On site facilities: Museum shop, lecture theatre, photo and research libraries (by appointment)
Public opening: Daily 10.00-18.00 (last admissions 17.15). Closed 24/25/26 December. Reduced admission prices for children, students, senior citizens, UB40 holders and pre-booked parties. Free admission for registered disabled
Facilities for disabled: Disabled toilets available, wheelchair access to most of the displays. Also taped guide for visually handicapped visitors. Free admission for registered disabled visitors and person accompanying them. Please advise in advance if a party of disabled visitors would like to visit
Special notes: Visitors can operate the controls of a tram, a bus, an Underground train, signals and points. In addition to the vehicles and rolling stock there are models, signs, posters, paintings, audio-visual displays and a 1906 Otis lift car. At certain times there will be films and temporary exhibitions. In addition to the vehicles on display there is a growing reserve collection
Membership details: There is a friends of the London Transport Museum, please contact above address for details

Locomotives

Name	No	Origin	Class	Type	Built
—	23	Met Rly	A	4-4-0T	1866
John Hampden	5	Met Rly		Bo-Bo	1922

Industrial locomotives

Origin	Builder	Type	Built
Wotton Tramway	A/Porter (807)	0-4-0TG	1872

Electric stock
4248 District Rly Q23 stock driving motor coach 1923
11182 LPTB 1938 stock driving motor coach
400 Met Rly bogie stock coach 1899
30 City & South London Rly 'Padded Cell' coach 1890
Great Northern Piccadilly & Brompton Railway 'Gate stock' car 1906
13 City & South London Railway locomotive of 1890, on loan from Science Museum for 'Tube Centenary' exhibition

Stock
1 Met Rly milk van; 3 electric trams; 2 horse buses; 5 motor buses; 1 trolleybus

Mid-Hants Railway

The Mid-Hants line was often used by the Bournemouth expresses on diversions during steam days and was therefore built to main line standards. This has enabled the line's new owners to operate large and powerful locomotives over the line which now has a direct connection with BR
Managing Director: Ian Dean
Headquarters: Mid-Hants Railway PLC, Alresford station, Alresford, Hants SO24 9JG
Telephone: Alresford (0962) 733810/734200
Main station: Alresford
Other public stations: Ropley, Medstead & Four Marks, Alton

Locomotives

Name	No	Origin	Class	Type	Built
—	30499	LSWR	S15	4-6-0	1920
—	506	LSWR	S15	4-6-0	1920
—	31625	SR	U	2-6-0	1929
—	31806	SR	U	2-6-0	1926
—	31874	SR	N	2-6-0	1925
Bodmin	34016	SR	WC	4-6-2	1945
Tangmere	34067	SR	BB	4-6-2	1947
Swanage	34105	SR	WC	4-6-2	1950
British India Line	35018	SR	MN	4-6-2	1945
—	73096	BR	5MT	4-6-0	1956
—	76017	BR	4MT	2-6-0	195[illegible]
Sturdee	601	MoS	WD	2-10-0	194[illegible]
Franklin D. Roosevelt	701	USATC	S160	2-8-0	194[illegible]
—	D3358	BR	08	0-6-0DE	195[illegible]
—	D5217	BR	25	Bo-Bo	196[illegible]
—	D5353	BR	27	Bo-Bo	196[illegible]

Industrial locomotives

Name	No	Builder	Type	Built
—	4	Fowler (22889)	0-4-0DM	193[illegible]

Right:
The Mid-Hants Railway decided to fool visitors to the line on Easter Monday, 1 April 1991, by disguising No 34105 *Swanage* as No 34067 *Tangmere*. No 34067 is seen at Medstead & Four Marks with the 11.15 Alresford-Alton as 'S160' class 2-8-0 No 701 *Franklin D. Roosevelt* rolls in with the 11.30 ex-Alton. The real 34067 is undergoing a protracted rebuild at Ropley.
John Bird

Stock
2 steam cranes; 1 Plasser & Theurer AL250 lining machine; 36 ex-BR Mk 1 coaches; 7 ex-BR Mk 2 coach; 4 ex-SR coaches; 3 ex-LSWR coaches; Numerous goods vehicles

Owners
30499 and 506 (the Urie Locomotive Society)
34105 (the 34105 Light Pacific Group)
76017 (the Standard 4 Locomotive Group)

OS reference: Alresford SU 588325, Ropley SU 629324
Car park: Alresford, BR car park Alton
Access by public transport:
BR train services — just over 1hr from London. Through ticketing arrangements available from Waterloo and all BR stations. Alternatively, travel to Winchester station and take the bus to Alresford.
Bus services — are operated by Alder Valley; telephone Guildford 575226 or Aldershot 23322 for details.
Refreshment facilities: Buffet service on most trains; 'West Country' buffet at Alresford; tea/coffee available at Alton when information office open
Catering facilities: The 'Watercress Belle' operates on alternate Saturdays April-October. Early booking is essential, please telephone to confirm seat availability
Souvenir shops: Alresford and Alton. Collector's corner at Ropley
Depot: Ropley
Length of line: 10 miles
Passenger trains: Alton-Alresford. Sundays 5 January-1 November; Saturdays and Bank Holidays 4 April-31 October; Tuesdays, Wednesdays and Thursdays 26 May-23 July; Daily 25 July-6 September. Santa Specials 28/29 November, 5/6, 12/13, 19-24 December (bookings commence end of August)
Journey time: Round trip 1hr 40min max
Special events: 23 March — Coach Operator's Day; 28 March — Over the Alps II (sponsored walk); 4/5 April — Spring Enthusiast's Weekend; 19 April — the 'Rambling Rose' (first public operation of luncheon and cream teas train); 24 May — Austin Day; 7 June — Paddington's Day Out; 14 June — Father's Day; 27/28 June — Special Event (provisional); 4/5 July — American Weekend; 19 July — Morris Day; 23 August — Barnado's Day; 6 September — Bus Bonanza; 13 September — Commercial Vehicle & Road Transport Club road run to Watercress Line; 27 September — Local Locomotion Day; 3/4 October — Scouts & Guides Weekend; 18 October — 1950s Agricultural Show
Facilities for disabled: Toilets at Ropley, special facilities for disabled passengers on selected trains
Membership details: Membership Secretary, c/o above address

Middleton Railway

SC

This is a preserved section of one of the world's oldest railways, authorised by Act of Parliament in 1758, and also the first to be re-opened by volunteers
Headquarters: Middleton Railway Trust Ltd, Moor Road, Leeds LS10 2JQ

Locomotives

Name	No	Origin	Class	Type	Built
—	1310	NER	Y7	0-4-0T	1891
—	54	LNER	Y1	0-4-0VB	1933
—	385	DSB	HsII	0-4-0WT	1893
—	7401	LMS	—	0-6-0DM	1932

Industrial locomotives

Name	No	Builder	Type	Built
John Blenkinsop	—	Peckett (2003)	0-4-0ST	1941
Henry de Lacy II	—	H/Clarke (1309)	0-4-0ST	1917
Mirvale	—	H/Clarke (1882)	0-4-0ST	1955

Telephone: (0532) 710320 (Ansaphone) or (0532) 711089 after 6pm
Main station: Moor Road, Hunslet
OS reference: SE 302309
Car parks: Tunstall Road/Moor Road (free)
Access by public transport: Any bus from Corn Exchange to Tunstall Road, walk down the troad, across Waterway and the MR is on the right, walking time 5min
Souvenir shop: Moor Road
Museum: Depot now open 10.00 to 18.00 during season (10.00 to 16.00 during winter). There is no charge for admission to site
Length of line: 1¼ miles
Passenger trains: Sunday trains all steam operated. Saturday services may be diesel hauled. Special trains operate on request, contact J. Wickinson, Tel: (0532)719785
Period of public operation: Every Saturday, Sunday and Bank Holiday Monday from 4 April to 27 September. Normal Sunday steam timetable; 13.00 then ½-hourly until 16.30. Normal Saturday diesel timetable; 13.30 then every 45min until 16.30. Wednesdays 13.30 then every 45min until 16.30
Special events: 18-21 April — Easter train service; 2-4 May — May Day holiday trains; 13 May — Schoolday trains; 23-25 May — Spring Bank Holiday trains; 18 July — 60 Years of the Diesel; 27/28 June

Name	No	Builder	Type	Built
Brookes No 1	—	Hunslet (2387)	0-6-0ST	1941
Windle	—	Borrows (53)	0-4-0WT	1909
Matthew Murray	—	Bagnall (2702)	0-4-0ST	1943
Harry	—	A/Barclay (1823)	0-4-0ST	1926
Arthur	—	M/Wardle (1601)	0-6-0ST	1901
—*	—	Brush (91)	0-4-0DE	1958
—	No 6	H/Leslie (3860)	0-4-0ST	1935
Carroll	—	H/Clarke (D631)	0-4-0DM	1946
—	—	Hunslet (1786)	4wD	1935
Mary	—	H/Clarke (D577)	0-4-0DM	1932
—	—	Fowler (3900002)	0-4-0DM	1945
—	—	Fowler (4200038)	0-4-0DH	1966
—	—	Thomas Hill (138C)	0-4-0DH	1963
Rowntrees No 3†	—	R/Hornsby (441934)	4wDM	1960

*On loan from BSC Orb Works, Newport
†On loan from North Yorkshire Moors Railway

Stock
2 CCTs converted for passenger use Nos 1867 and 2048; CCT as stores van No 2073; Norwegian brake coach; Various goods vehicles; 5-ton Booth rail crane; 1 3-ton Smith steam crane; 1 3-ton Isles steam crane; 7.5 ton steam crane

Owners
1310, 385 (the Steam Power Trust)
Harry (owned by Crossley Bros, Shipley)

— 'Friends of Thomas' Weekend; 2 August — Cops 'n Robbers Day; 29-31 August; Bank Holiday Trains; 26/27 September — Children's Weekend; 5/6, 12/13, 19/20 December — Santa trains (special timetable in operation on special days, schooldays are pre-booking only)

Facilities for disabled: Access very good
Special notes: It was the first standard gauge railway to be opened by volunteers, in June 1960. The railway terminates in a large car park and a nature trail has been provided by the local council

Midland Railway Centre

This centre is being established as not only an operating railway, but also as a 57-acre museum site and a 35-acre country park which will make the centre unique. A wide variety of exhibits are being collected
Location: Midland Railway Centre, Butterley station, near Ripley, Derbyshire DE5 3TL
OS reference: SK 403520
General Manager: John Hett
Operating society/organisation: Midland Railway Trust Ltd
Telephone: Ripley (0773) 747674/570140
Fax: (0773) 570271
Car park: Butterley station on B6179 1-mile north of Ripley

Locomotives

Name	No	Origin	Class	Type	Built
Princess Margaret Rose	46203	LMS	8P	4-6-2	1936
—	44027	LMS	4F	0-6-0	1924
—	44932*	LMS	5MT	4-6-0	1945
—	45491	LMS	5MT	4-6-0	1943
—	47564	LMS	3F	0-6-0T	1928
—	47327	LMS	3F	0-6-0T	1926
—	47357	LMS	3F	0-6-0T	1926
—	47445	LMS	3F	0-6-0T	1927
—	9395	LNWR	7F	0-8-0	1921
—	158A	MR	—	2-4-0	1866
—	53809	S&DJR	7F	2-8-0	1925
—	73129	BR	5MT	4-6-0	1956
—	80080	BR	4MT	2-6-4T	1954
—	80098	BR	4MT	2-6-4T	1955
—	92214	BR	9F	2-10-0	1959
—	92219	BR	9F	2-10-0	1959
—	D2138	BR	03	0-6-0DM	1960
—	12077	BR	11	0-6-0DE	1950
—	20227	BR	20	Bo-Bo	1967
Experiment	24061	BR	24	Bo-Bo	1960
—	D7671	BR	25	Bo-Bo	1967

site facilities: Newly opened useum, award winning country rk, souvenir shop
freshment facilities: Restaurants Butterley and Butterley Park, bar most trains and extensive Wine Dine service, the 'Midlander' etails from above address)
ngth of line: 3½ miles
blic opening: Every Sunday and nk Holiday Weekend throughout e year. Every Saturday April-ctober and December. Daily -26 April, 23-31 May, throughout ugust, 1-6 September; 24 October; November; Tuesdays, Wednesdays d Thursdays 30 June-30 July; idays 24, 31 July
urney time: Approximately 1hr
ecial events: Every Sunday from March-27 September will be a la day, please contact for details specific events
cilities for disabled: Toilets, ecial coach, access to shop and feteria, special weekend
embership details: J. Hancock, at ove address
embership journal: *The Wyvern* quarterly
arketing names: 'More than just a ilway'; Golden Valley Light ilway (narrow gauge); Butterley rk Miniature Railway (miniature ne)

Name	*No*	*Origin*	*Class*	*Type*	*Built*
Aureol	40012	BR	40	1Co-Co1	1959
Great Gable	D4	BR	44	1Co-Co1	1959
—	45133	BR	45/1	1Co-Co1	1961
Tulyar	55015	BR	55	Co-Co	1961

*Shares time between here and Steamtown, Carnforth

Locomotive notes: In service 44932, 46203, 47357, 53809, 80080, 48151, 12077, D4, 45133, 55015 and D7671. Under restoration 44027, 47327, 80098, 40012, D2138. Awaiting repairs or stored 47445, 73129. Boiler and frames only 47564. Static display 158A, 9395.

Industrial locomotives

Name	*No*	*Builder*	*Type*	*Built*
Gladys	—	Markham (109)	0-4-0ST	1894
Stanton	24	Barclay (1875)	0-4-0CT	1925
Victory	—	Peckett (1547)	0-4-0ST	1917
Lytham No 1	—	Peckett (2111)	0-4-0ST	1949
—	4	N/Wilson (454)	0-4-0ST	1894
—		Sentinel (9370)	4wVBT	1947
Andy	—	Fowler (16038)	0-4-0DM	1923
—	RS9	M/Rail (2024)	0-4-0DM	1921
—	RS12	M/Rail (460)	0-4-0DM	1912
—	—	M/Rail (1930)	0-4-0PM	1919
Boots	2	Barclay (2008)	0-4-0F	1935
Boots	—	R/Hornsby (384139)	0-4-0DE	1955
*Handyman**	—	H/Clarke (573)	0-4-0ST	1900
Albert Fields	—	H/Clarke (D1114)	0-6-0DM	1958
—†	—	Deutz (10249)	4wDM	1932
Campbell Brick Works†	—	M/Rail (60S364)	4wDM	1968
—†	—	M/Rail (5906)	4wDM	1932
—†	—	M/Rail (11246)	4wDM	1963
Hucknall Colliery§	1	Ruston (480080)	4wDM	1963
Hucknall Colliery§	3	Ruston	4wDM	1963
Oddson†	—	Marshall	4wVBT	1970
—†	—	Hunslet (7178)	4wDH	1971
*Princess Elizabeth***	6201	H/Clarke (D611)	4-6-2DM	1938
*Princess Margaret Rose***	6203	H/Clarke (D612)	4-6-2DM	1938

*3ft gauge
†2ft gauge
§2ft 6in gauge
**21in gauge

Locomotive notes: In service Sentinel 9370, D2959, Deutz 10249, *Albert Fields*, *Oddson* M/Rails 5906/60S364. Under restoration *Andy* RS12.

elow:
ammersmith station at the Midland ailway Centre on 31 August 1991. inty' No 47357 is seen at the head of train of vintage stock.
obin Stewart-Smith

Awaiting repairs or stored Stanton, RS9, Ruston 480080, Hunslet 7178. Static display *Gladys*, 4, Boots No 2, *Handyman*, Hucknall 1.
Victory and M/Rail (1930) on loan to Derby Industrial Museum

Stock
Numerous carriages, wagons and cranes including MR Royal saloon, MR six-wheeled coach, BR horsebox, LMS travelling Post Office, MR brake van, L&YR saloon — all on display in new museum. LD&ECR six-wheel coach should be restored and on display for 1992

Owners
158A, 9395, 44027 (on loan from the National Railway Museum)
53809 (the 13809 Preservation Group)
47357, 47327, 47445, 47564, 73129 (Derby City Council)
80080, 80098 (the 80080 Holdings Ltd)
55015 (the Deltic Preservation Society)
D4 (the Peak Locomotive Preservation Co Ltd)
D7671 (Derby Industrial Museum)

Moseley Railway Museum SC

The collection concentrates on diesel and petrol power with some battery units and one steam outline locomotive. There are also hand, rope and chain operated vehicles on site. Emphasis is placed on operational locomotives and stock which, by prior appointment, can be observed and photographed performing the tasks for which they were originally designed. There are a number of unique running exhibits including the Kent petrol and Greenbat electric locomotives, and single cylinder Simplex and Ruston diesel units. Passenger train rides are always available on official open days
Location: Grounds of Margaret Danyers College, Northdowns Road, Cheadle, Cheshire SK8 5HA
OS reference: SJ 864871
Operating society: The Moseley Industrial Narrow Gauge Tramway Museum Society (MTM), address as above
Telephone: School hours 061-485 4372, any other time 061-485 4448, Colin Saxton (curator)
Car park: Extensive, free, adjacent to the museum buildings
Station: One boarding area adjacent to the museum. Other request stops
Length of line and gauge: Approximately ½-mile, 2ft gauge. Static lines in short lengths at other gauges
Access by public transport: Nearest BR station Cheadle Hulme (10min walk). Bus from Manchester 157, bus from Stockport S13, ask for Cheadle Adult Education Centre/Margaret Danyers College

Industrial locomotives

Name	*No*	*Builder*	*Type*	*Built*
—	—	G/Batley (2345)	4wBE	1951
—	—	G/Batley (2960)	4wBE	1959
—	—	G/Batley (420172)	4wBE	1969
—	—	H/Hunslet (6299)	4wDM	1964
—	—	Hunslet (4758)	4wDM	1954
—	—	Kent	4wPM	c192[illegible]
Ald Hague	—	Hiberd (3465)	4wPM	1954
—	—	Lister (3834)	4wPM	1931
—	—	Lister (8022)	4wDM	1936
—	—	Lister (52031)	4wDM	1960
—	—	L/Blackstone (52885)	4wDM	1962
—	—	M/Rail (4565)	4wPM	1928
—	—	M/Rail (7512)	4wDM	1938
—	—	M/Rail (7552)	4wDM	1948
—	—	M/Rail (8663)	4wDM	1941
—	—	M/Rail (8669)	4wDM	1941
—	—	M/Rail (8878)	4wDM	1944
The Lady D	—	M/Rail (8934)	4wDM	1944
Nick the Greek	—	M/Rail (8937)	4wDM	1944
—	—	M/Rail (9104)	4wPM	1942
—	—	M/Rail (11142)	4wDM	1960
Knothole Worker	—	M/Rail (22045)	4wDM	1959
Moseley	—	R/Hornsby (177639)	4wDM	1936
—	—	R/Hornsby (198278)	4wDM	1940
—	—	R/Hornsby (223667)	4wDM	1943
—	—	R/Hornsby (229647)	4wDM	1944
Neath Abbey	—	R/Hornsby (476106)	4wDM	1964
—	—	R/Hornsby (192846)	4wDM	1939
—	—	Wichham (4091)	2w-2PMR	1946
—	—	Wickham (4092)	2w-2PMR	1946
—	—	Wickham (4131)	2w-2PMR	1947

Stock
Nearly 100 items of rolling stock, gauges from 10 1/4 in to 2ft; 3 Wickham Target Trolleys

On site facilities: Free access and parking, a small selection of hot and cold drinks and chocolate, access to all site

Period of public operation: Throughout the year. Second Sunday of every month plus any other time by appointment

:ain services: Return journey ɔund trip) approximately 20min
ıcilities for the disabled: The ıuseum operates policy as ockport Education Authority. ⁄ery effort is made to accommodate disabled persons who will find a visit easier during school hours when the main school premises are open
Special notes: Museum buildings and displays are now open
Membership details: Colin Saxton, Member of Staff in charge. School address or 60 Pingate Lane, Cheadle Hulme, Cheshire SK8 7LT or John Rowlands, Chairman, College address

Museum of Army Transport M

ɔerating a substantial network of ilways in wartime the Army is ll responsible for railways feeding oD depots in this country. Not ıly does the Museum hold tensive archives and display some scinating maps, drawings and ıotographs, it contains some very teresting stock from the former ilitary railways
ıcation: Museum of Army ansport, Flemingate, Beverley, ɔrth Humberside HU17 0NG
S reference: TA 041392
ɔerated by: The Museum of Army ansport Ltd (Charitable Status ɔmpany)
:lephone: Hull (0482) 860445
ır park: Yes, 1¼ acres
:cess by public transport: Rail: min walk from Beverley station. ıs: served by East Yorks Motor rvice
ı site facilities: Museum — The ɔyal Corps of Transport Collection road, rail, sea, air and movement ntrol artefacts. Licensed cafeteria. ıop in building. Lavatories, cluding special for handicapped. rge car and bus park
ıcilities for disabled: The ıuseum is on one floor. This allows ɔwing of all vehicles. Access is ailable by ramp into the Armoured Train. Access is not possible into the Beverley aircraft, the railway locos and the signalbox frame
Public opening: 10.00-17.00 every day except 24-26 December
Special notes: Please bear in mind that while what is reported here deals with railways, other parts of this extensive museum cover movement by road, sea and air
Honorary Railway (and Port) Consultant: Major J. A. Robins (Retd)

Locomotives

Name	*No*	*Builder*	*Type*	*Built*
Gazelle	—	Dodman	0-4-2WT	1893
Woolmer	—	Avonside (1572)	0-6-0ST	1910
Waggoner	92	Hunslet (3792)	0-6-0ST	1953
Rorke's Drift	—	Drewry (2047)	0-4-0DM	1934
—	110	R/Hornsby (411319)	4wDM	1958
—	1035	Wickham Rail Car	4w	1958
—	3282*	Wickham Target Trolley	4w	1943
—	WD2182†	M/Rail (461)	4wDM	1917
—	—†	M/Rail (3849)	4wDM	1927
—	LOD 758228†	M/Rail (8667)	4wDM	1941
—	LOD 758208†	M/Rail (8855)	4wDM	1943

*2ft 6in gauge
†2ft gauge

Rolling stock
Collection of various rolling stock items including Lord Kitchener's coach (c1885), a World War 1 Armoured Train gun truck and a World War 2 ramp wagon

Owners
Gazelle (the National Railway Museum)

A 2ft gauge system based on the ADLR of World War 1, some 200yd long, and worked by World War 2 Simplex rail tractors operated by volunteers, on Saturday and Sunday afternoons and at other times as advertised locally during the summer. Intending travellers should check the line is operating.

Museum of Science & Industry M

ıcation: Liverpool Road Station, ıstlefield, Manchester (off ːansgate near Granada)
S reference: SJ 831987
ɔerating society/organisation: ıuseum of Science & Industry, verpool Road Station, Liverpool ɔad, Castlefield, Manchester M3 P
:lephone: 061 832 2244

Locomotives

Name	*No*	*Origin*	*Class*	*Type*	*Built*
Magpie	44806	LMS	5MT	4-6-0	1944
Pender	3*	IoMR	—	2-4-0T	1873
Novelty	Powered replica of 1829 locomotive using some original parts				
—	3157†	PR	—	4-4-0	1911
—	2352§	SAR	GL	4-8-2+2-8-4	1929
Ariadne	1505 (27001)	BR	EM2 (77)	Co-Co	1954
Hector	26048	BR	EM1 (76)	Bo-Bo cab only	—

Car parks: On site, plus parking in the area (museum car park £1)
Access by public transport: Manchester Victoria, Piccadilly and Oxford Road BR stations. GM bus 33
On site facilities: Oldest passenger railway station, weekend train rides, former railway warehouses containing exhibitions about science, industry, aviation, space, water supply and sewage disposal and electricity. New exhibitions include Xperiment!, the hands-on science centre and the 'out of this world' space gallery. Also a licensed buffet and shop
Public opening: Daily except 23, 24 and 25 December, including Saturdays and Sundays, 10.00-17.00. Entrance in Lower Byrom Street. Admission charged
Special events: Castlefield Carnival held during the August Bank Holiday weekend
Special notes: Some wheelchair access, toilets for the disabled, lecture and conference facilities

Industrial locomotives

Name	No	Builder	Type	Bui
Agecroft No 3	—	RSH (7681)	0-4-0ST	195
—	—	Barclay (1964)	0-4-0ST	192
—	—	E/Electric (1378)	4wBE	194
—	—	H/Leslie (3682)	Bo-Bo	192
—	—	Fowler	0-6-0	—

*Ex-Isle of Man Railways, 3ft gauge, sectioned (B/Peacock 1255)
†Ex-Pakistan Railways, 5ft 6in gauge (V/Foundry 3064)
§Ex-South African Railways, 3ft 6in gauge (B/Peacock 6693)

Rolling stock
BR Restaurant Car (RU(A), BRCW Co Ltd, 1959; 31217 BR passenger bogie brake van, LMS (Wolverton), 1944; BR, Metro-Cam, LDY30515, 1960; BR Mk 2 SO E5241, 1966

c1908 L&YR 3rd class carriage re-built 1923 as Medical Examination Ca LMS No 10825
B955209 20-ton goods brake van, BR (Ashford), 1962
B782903 4-wheeled covered goods van, BR (Wolverton), 1961
B783709 4-wheeled covered goods van, BR (Wolverton), 1962
3-plank loose coupled goods wagon, MSLR (Dukinfield)?, c1890

Owners
Novelty on loan from the Science Museum, London
L&YR coach, Dinting Railway Centre
Magpie on loan from Mr K. Aldcroft
MSLR Wagon on loan form G. Muslin
Industrial locomotives (except Fowler) on loan from National Power/Power Gen

National Railway Museum M

Location: National Railway Museum, Leeman Road, York YO2 4XJ
OS reference: SE 594519
Operating society/organisation: Part of the National Museum of Science and Industry
Telephone: York 621261 (STD Code 0904)
Car park: Limited parking for cars and pre-booked coaches at the Museum. York City's Leeman Road car park for cars and coaches visiting the NRM adjoins the main entrance
Access by public transport: The Museum is within a few minutes' walking distance of the railway and bus stations in York. The York City and District Bus Service operates to the door
On site facilities: Museum shop, restaurant and toilets. Reference Library (free by appointment)
Public opening: Daily, weekdays 10.00-18.00. Sundays 11.00-18.00. Closed on New Years' Day, Christmas Eve, Christmas Day and Boxing Day
Facilities for disabled: Most areas of the museum are accessible by the disabled
Special notes: The Museum has been open since 1975 and has welcomed over 15 million visitors.

A completely new exhibition, the Great Railway Show, on the theme of Travelling by Train, was opened in 1990 and the Museum's former public display hall was closed for re-roofing. The new exhibition won the prestigious Museum of the Year Award in 1991.

From Easter 1992 the re-roofed Great Hall will open once more to the public in addition to the award-winning exhibition in the South Hall. Thus the Museum's public display space will be doubled and more of the National Railway Collection will be shown in York than ever before.

The details of the Great Hall displays are still evolving as *Railways Restored* goes to print but will be on the theme of the technology of railways. Once again there will be magnificent display of railway locomotive development round the turntable. Signalling, permanent way, the modern railv and the Channel Tunnel will all have a place too.

The South Hall will continue t illustrate the concept of travel by train — for passengers and freigh Short but representative trains wi be drawn up at platforms and several footplates and some carriages will be open to the visitors. A temporary display building will house a rotating exhibition of famous locomotives under the general title of 'Record Breakers and Workhorses'. Magician's Road, an interactive educational exhibition, will provi booked school parties — and oth visitors out of school hours — wi 'hands-on' experience of various aspects of railway operation.

The Museum's extensive Reference Library (including the Photographic and Drawings collections) continues to be free t all booked enquirers every weekd from 10.30-17.00.

The Tables which follow indic the whereabouts (display, on loa in store) of the items in the National Railway Collection. It must be emphasised that the appearance of any particular item on public display cannot be guaranteed. If it is vital to discover the exact whereabouts of a specific item enquirers should contact the Museum in York before making a visit.

The National Railway Museum is open for evening hire for private viewings and celebrations; menus and details are available on request.

Details of membership of the Museum's support group, including free entry and a quarterly newsletter are available from: The Secretary, Friends of the National Railway Museum, c/o the above address.

Important Note: a number of stock movements are taking place as *Railway Restored* goes to press. The Tables that follow must only be taken as a guide and not as a wholly accurate picture of the whereabouts of all the items in the National Railway Collection.

TABLE 1

Exhibits in the Great Hall
Locomotives

Name	*No*	*Origin*	*Builder*	*Class*	*Type*	*Built*
Agenoria	—	Shutt End Colliery	Foster/Raistrick	—	0-4-0	1929
Columbine	1868	LNWR	Crewe	—	2-2-2	1845
Coppernob	3	FR	Bury, Curtis & Kennedy	—	0-4-0	1846
Aerolite	66	NER	Gateshead	X1(LNER)	2-2-4T	1869
—	1	GNR	Doncaster	—	4-2-2	1870
—	1275	NER	Dübs & Co	—	0-6-0	1874
Livingston Thompson	—	FR	Boston Lodge	—	0-4-4-0T	1885
—	1008	LYR	Horwich	—	2-4-2T	1889
Hardwicke	790	LNWR	Crewe	—	2-4-0	1892
—	563	LSWR	Nine Elms	T3	4-4-0	1893
—	1	NER	BTH	—	Bo-Bo electric	1902
—	251	GNR	Doncaster	C1	4-4-2	1902
—	1000	MR	Derby	4	4-4-0	1902
—	87	GER	Stratford	J69	0-6-0T	1904
—	1217	GER	Stratford	J17	0-6-0	1905
—	K1	TGR	B/Peacock	—	0-4-0 + 0-4-0	1909
—	1	NSR	Stoke	—	Bo battery/elec	1917
Butler Henderson	506	GCR	Gorton	'Director'	4-4-0	1920
—	8143	SR	—	4-SUB	EMU	1925
—	2700	LMS	Horwich	5P4F	2-6-0	1926
Rocket (sectioned)	—	Replica	R. Stephenson	—	0-2-2	1935
—	KF7	Chinese Govt Rlys	Vulcan	KF	4-8-4	1935
Duchess of Hamilton	46229	LMS	Crewe	'Coronation'	4-6-2	1938
Mallard	4468	LNER	Doncaster	A4	4-6-2	1938
Ellerman Lines	35029	BR(SR)	Sectioned	—	4-6-2	1949
—	26020	BR	Gorton/Metrvick	76	Bo-Bo Electric	1951
—	—	Imperial Paper Mills	Barclay	—	0-4-0P	1956
—	—	Tees-Side Bridge & Engineering Co	Sentinel	—	4wTG	1957
—	D8000	BR	E/Electric	20	Bo-Bo	1957
—	D200	BR	E/Electric	40	1Co-Co1	1958
Evening Star	92220	BR	Swindon	9F	2-10-0	1960
—	41001	BR	Crewe	Prototype HST	Bo-Bo	1972

Departmental Stock
899 GWR Hand Crane No 537
906 NER Dynamomter Car No 902502
907 NER Steam Breakdown Crane No CME 13

Exhibits in the South Hall
Locomotives

Name	*No*	*Origin*	*Builder*	*Class*	*Type*	*Built*
Boxhill	82	LB&SCR	Brighton	A1	0-6-0T	1880
Gladstone	214	LB&SCR	—	—	0-4-2	1882
—	1621	NER	Gateshead	M	4-4-0	1893
—	245	LSWR	Nine Elms	M7	0-4-4T	1897
—	673	MR	Derby	—	4-2-2	1899
—	1247	GNR	S/Stewart (4492)	152	0-6-0ST	1899

Name	No	Origin	Builder	Class	Type	Built
—	737	SECR	Ashford	D	4-4-0	1901
—	2818	GWR	Swindon	2800	2-8-0	1905
Cheltenham	925	SR	Eastleigh	V	4-4-0	1934
—	5000	LMS	Crewe	5MT	4-6-0	1935
Green Arrow	4771	LNER	Doncaster	V2	2-6-2	1936
Rocket (replica)	—	—	Loco Enterprises	—	0-2-2	1979
Iron Duke (broad gauge replica)	—	GWR	RESCO	—	4-2-2	1985

Rolling Stock

Carriages

1842 L&BR Queen Adelaides' Saloon
1869 LNWR Queen Victoria's Saloon
1885 MR 6-wheel composite brake No 901
1885 WCJS 8-wheel TPO No 186
1887 GNR 6-wheel brake No 948
1898 ECJS 3rd class No 12
1899 Privately owned Duke of Sutherland's Saloon 57A
1900 LNWR (ex-WCJS) Dining Car LMS 76
1902 LNWR King Edward's Saloon No 800
1902 LNWR Queen Alexandra's Saloon No 801
1903 LSWR Tricomposite brake No 3598
1908 ECJS Royal Saloon No 395
1908 ECJS Passenger Brake van LNER 109
1913 Pullman Car Co 1st class parlour car *Topaz*
1914 MR Dining car No 3463
1936 CIWL Night Ferry sleeping car No 3792
1937 LNER Buffet Car No 9135
1941 LMS Royal Saloon 799
1985 GWR broad gauge carriage replica

Exhibits in Record Breakers & Workhorses

Locomotives

Name	No	Origin	Builder	Class	Type	Built
City of Truro	3440	GWR	Swindon	City	4-4-0	1903
—	03090	BR	—	03	0-6-0DM	1960
—	84001	BR	N/British	84	Bo-Bo	1960
The King' Own Yorkshire Light Infantry	55002	BR	E/Electric	55	Co-Co	1961
Western Fusilier	D1023	BR	Swindon	52	Co-Co	1963

TABLE 2

In store at the National Railway Museum, York

Locomotives

Name	No	Origin	Builder	Class	Type	Built
Wren	—	LYR	B/Peacock	—	0-4-0ST	1887
Henry Oakley	990	GNR	Doncaster	C2	4-4-2	1898
—	75S	W&CR	Siemens (6)	—	Bo electric·	1898
—	102	GCR	Gorton	O4	2-8-0	1911
—	—	WD	Simplex (60cm gauge)	—	0-4-0	1918
—	—	Berry Wiggins & Co	Simplex	—	0-4-0	1931
—	—	Yorks Water Auth	R/Hornsby (2ft gauge)	—	0-4-0	1937
Winston Churchill	34051	SR	Brighton	BB	4-6-2	1946
Mine loco (3ft gauge)	—	NCB	H/Clarke (3ft gauge)	—	0-6-0 DM	1950
—	08064	BR	Darlington	08	0-6-0 DE	1953
—	3	CEGB	RSH (7746)	—	0-6-0 DM	1954
—	D2860	BR	YEC	02	0-4-0 DH	1960

Powered Units

1931 GPO Post Office Railway Car No 809
1972 BR APT-E prototype experimental Advanced Passenger Train
1977 Leyland Motors LEV-1 experimental railbus

Departmental Stock

1891 NER Snow plough No DE 900566
1899 GWR Hand crane No 537
1904 MR Officers' saloon No 2234
1931 LNER Petrol-driven platelayers' trolley No 960209
1932 LMS Ballast plough brake van No 197266
1938 LMS Mobile test unit No 1, No 45053
1949 BR(LMS) Dynamometer car No 3, No 45049
1957 BR Track recording trolley No DX 50002
1974 BR Matisa tamping machine No 74/007
Uncertain LNWR Tender/water carrier

Passenger Stock

1834 B&WR 1st & 2nd composite
1834 B&WR 2nd class
1834 B&WR 3rd class
1851 ECR 1st class No 1
1895 Cambrian luggage composite No 238
1896 Glasgow Subway Car No 7
1897 Lynton & Barnstaple Rly brake composite No 6992
1925 LMS 3rd class vestibule No 7828
1925 LMS 3rd class vestibule No 7863
1927 LMS 3rd class vestibule No 8207
1936 LNER 3rd class open No 13251

36	LNER 3rd class open No 13254
50	BR(LMS) Corridor 3rd class brake No 27093
55	BR Lavatory composite No E43046
56	BR 2nd class open No E4286
60	BR Griddle car No Sc1100
60	Pullman Car Co 1st class Kitchen car No 311 *Eagle*
60	Pullman Car Co 1st class Parlour car No 326 *Emerald*
62	BR Prototype Mk II 1st class corridor No 13252
	Freight & non-passenger carrying stock
28	Two replica chaldron wagons
38	GJR replica TPO
50	South Hetton Colliery chaldron wagon No 1155
39	Shell-Mex oil tank wagon No 512
94	LSWR Brake van No 99
95	LSWR Open carriage truck No 5830
02	NER 20-ton wooden hopper wagon
900	CR Bogie trolley wagon No 300041
	GCR Single bolster wagon No 110
	GCR Double bolster wagon No 111
12	LB&SCR Open wagon No 27884
12	LSWR Gunpowder van No KDS61209
12	NER Sand wagon No DE14974
12	GNR 8-ton van No E432764
14	GWR Shunters' truck No W94988
17	Shell tank wagon No 3171 (precise identity not known)
17	MR 8-ton open wagon (precise identity not known)
17	GCR Van (precise identity not known)
17	NER Van (precise identity not known)
24	LMS Van
24	LNER Fitted tube wagon No 181358
26	GWR Fitted open wagon No 108246
28	ICI Nitric acid tank wagon No 14

c1933	LMS Gunpowder van No 288824
1935	SR Bogie goods brake van No 56297
1935	GWR Motor car van No 126438
1936	LNER 20-ton goods brake van No 187774
1936	LMS Tube wagon No 499254
1937	GWR Siphon bogie milk van No 2775
1938	LMS Single bolster wagon No 722702
1940	WD Warflat No 161042
1944	LMS Lowmac No M700728
1944	GWR 13-ton open wagon No DW143698
1945	GWR Loriat P No 42367
1946	SNCF 16-ton mineral wagon No ADB192437
1946	LMS Bogie trolley wagon No 300041
1946	LNER 20-ton hopper wagon No E270919
1948	BR(SR) 12-ton shock absorbing wagon No 14036
1949	BR 40-ton Gain-A No DB996724
1949	BR Bogie bolster D No B941000
1950	BR 22-ton iron ore hopper wagon No B436275
1951	ICI Liquid chlorine tank wagon No 47484
1951	BR(SR) Show cattle wagon No S3733S
1951	BR 8-ton cattle wagon No B893343
1952	BR 30-ton bogie bolster wagon No B943139
1954	National Benzole oil tank wagon No 2022
1955	BR 16-ton mineral wagon No B234830
1955	BR 16-ton mineral wagon No B227009
1957	BR Horse box No S96369
1959	BR Fish van No B87905
1959	BR Conflat No B737725
1960	BR 25-ton Weltrol WP No ADB 900916
1961	BR Presflo cement wagon No B873368
1962	BR Speedfreight container No BA 4324B
1970	Phillips Petroleum 100-ton GLW tank wagon No PP85209
?	Yorkshire Water Authority two tip wagons (2ft gauge)

'able 3

ıms on Loan from the NRM

ıcomotives

ʻiginal type/No/Name	*Location*	*Builder*	*Built*
ıtton Colliery 0-4-0	Beamish	G. Stephenson	1822
)R 0-4-0 *Locomotion*	Darlington	R. Stephenson & Co	1825
ːMR 0-2-2 *Rocket*	Science Mus	R. Stephenson & Co	1829
ːMR 0-4-0 *Sans Pareil*	Science Mus	T. Hackworth	1829
ːMR 0-2-2 *Novelty*	Museum of Science & Technology (Manchester)	Braithwaite & Ericsson	1829
VR 2-2-2 *North Star*	Swindon GWR Mus	R. Stephenson	1837
)R 0-6-0 No 24 *Derwent*	Darlington Nth Rd Mus	A. Kitching	1845
antage Tramway 0-4-0WT No 5 *Shannon*	Didcot Rly Ctr	G. England	1857
JWR 0-4-0ST *Pet*	Tywyn NG Museum	Crewe	1865
R 2-4-0 No 158A	Midland Rly Ctr	Derby	1866
ɔuth Devon Rly 0-4-0WT *Tiny*	South Devon Rly	Sara	1868
SWR 2-4-0WT No 0298	South Devon Rly	B/Peacock	1874
ɔbburn Works 0-4-0ST No 2 *Bauxite*	Science Mus	B/Hawthorn	1874
ER 2-4-0 No 910	Darlington Nth Rd Mus	Gateshead	1875
ER 2-4-0 No 1463	Darlington Nth Rd Mus	Gateshead	1885
ːSL Bo electric No 1	Science Mus	B/Peacock	1890
ːMR 0-4-2WT *Gazelle*	Mus of Army Transport, Beverley	Dodman	1893
ER 2-4-0 No 490	Bressingham	Stratford	1894
WR 0-6-0 No 2516	Swindon GWR Mus	Swindon	1897
VR 0-6-2T No 28	Caerphilly Rly Soc	TVR	1897
SWR 4-4-0 No 120	Swanage Rly	Nine Elms	1899
WR 4-6-0 No 4003 *Lode Star*	Swindon GWR Mus	Swindon	1907
T&SR 4-4-2T No 80 *Thundersley*	Bressingham	R. Stephenson	1909

Original type/No/Name	*Location*	*Builder*	*Bui*
Nord (France) 4-6-0 No 3.628	Nene Valley Rly	Henschel	191
NER 0-8-0 No 901	North York Moors Rly	Darlington	191
LNWR 0-8-0 No 485	Midland Rly Ctr	Crewe	192
GWR 4-6-0 No 4073 *Caerphilly Castle*	Science Mus	Swindon	192
LMS 0-6-0 No 4027	Midland Rly Ctr	Derby	192
SR 4-6-0 No 777 *Sir Lamiel*	Humberside Loco Preservation Group, Hull	N/British	192
SR 4-6-0 No 850 *Lord Nelson*	Steamtown	Eastleigh	192
LMS 2-6-4T No 2500	Bressingham	Derby	193
SR 0-6-0 No C1	Bluebell Rly	Eastleigh	194
GWR 0-6-0PT No 9400	Swindon GWR Mus	Swindon	194
BR 4-6-2 No 70013 *Oliver Cromwell*	Bressingham	Crewe	195
English Electric Co-Co DE *Deltic*	Science Mus	E/Electric	195
BR A1A-A1A No 5500	Steamtown	Brush Traction	195

Powered Units
NER electric parcels van No 3267, Tyne & Wear Mus
LPTB driving motor car No 3327, Science Mus
GWR diesel railcar No 4, Swindon GWR Mus
LMS electric motor brake 2nd No 28361, Southport Transport Mus
LMS electric driving trailer composite No 29896, Southport Transport Mus
BR APT-P pre-production Advanced Passenger Train, Crewe Heritage Ctr

Departmental Stock
LNWR Match truck No 284235, Steamtown
LNWR Steam breakdown crane No 2987, Steamtown

Passenger Stock
SDR 1st & 2nd composite No 31, Darlington Nth Rd MusΠ
SDR 3rd No 179, Timothy Hackworth Mus, Shildon
ECJS Royal saloon No 396, Bressingham
1910 GCR Open 3rd class No 666, Great Central Railway
1925 GWR 3rd class dining car No 9653, Severn Valley Rly
1925 GWR 3rd class dining car No 9654, Severn Valley Rly
1928 Nord (France) 2nd class corridor No 7122, Nene Valley Rly
1930 GWR composite dining car No 9605, Science Mus (Wroughton)
1930 L&MR replica 1st class *Experience*, Liverpool Mus
1930 L&MR replica 2nd class, Liverpool Mus
1937 SR buffet car No S125295, Nene Valley Rly
1937 LMS corridor 3rd class brake No 5987, Steamtown
1941 LMS Royal saloon No 798, Glasgow Museum of Transport
1947 SR 3rd class open No 1456, Bluebell Rly

Freight & non-passenger carrying stock
1907 NER bogie van No 041273, Humberside Loco Preservation Group
1917 GWR Hydra-D No 42193, Didcot Railway Ctr
1922 LB&SCR cattle truck No 7116, Isle of Wight Steam Rly
1939 SR postal sorting van No 4920, Nene Valley Rly
1947 GWR Motorcar van No 65814, Bristol Industrial Mus
1949 BR(LMS) Postal sorting van No M30272M Birmingham Rly Mus

National Tramway Museum

A journey back in time — an experience of living transport history with vintage horse-drawn, steam and electric trams running through a recreated townscape of authentic buildings, stone setts, iron railings and historic street furniture. The heart of the Museum is its collection of about 50 vintage trams and you can enjoy the thrill of travelling on the scenic mile-long track

Locomotives

Name	*No*	*Builder*	*Type*	*Buil*
—	—	B/Peacock (2464)	0-4-0VB tram loco	188
—	—	E/Electric (717)	4wE	192
Rupert	—	R/Hornsby (223741)	4wDM	194
GMJ	—	R/Hornsby (326058)	4wDM	195
—	—	R/Hornsby (373363)	4wDM	1954

Also some 50 trams (including examples from Czechoslovakia, Portugal, USA and South Africa), about a third of which have been restored to working order

Location: Crich, near Matlock, Derbyshire DE4 5DP
OS reference: SK 345549
Manager: David Lardge
Operating society/organisation: Tramway Museum Society
Telephone: 0773 852565
Car park: Site, coach parking also available
Access by public transport: Nearest stations: Cromford (BR) or Alfreton & Mansfield Parkway (BR) then by bus; or Whatstandwell (BR) and steep uphill walk
On site facilities: Souvenir shop, bookshop and picnic areas. 1-mile electric tramway. Tramway period street, depots, displays, exhibitions and video theatre. Large new exhibition hall now open
Refreshment facilities: Hot and cold snacks and meals
Public opening: Saturdays, Sundays and bank holidays, 4 April to 1 November, plus Mondays to Thursdays mid-April to end September. Also open Fridays, 29 May and 3 July through to 4 September. Additional openings: daily during autumn half-term weeks. Open: 10.00am to 5.30pm (6.30pm Saturdays/Sundays/ Bank Holidays)
Facilities for disabled: Access available for most of site, but most trams excluded. Advanced notice required
Special Notes: Crich houses the largest collection of preserved trams in Europe and has a 1-mile working tramway on which restored electric trams are regularly operated. Special events are arranged at weekends and bank holidays throughout the season. Part of tram line occupies route of narrow gauge mineral railway built by George Stephenson
Membership details: From above address
Membership journal: *The Journal* — quarterly

Nene Valley Railway

This unique railway's collection includes locomotives and coaches from 10 countries and two continents. It is a regular location for TV and film makers — from films like *Octopussy* with Roger Moore as 007 to TV — *Hannay*, *Christobel* — to commercials for cars, beer and soft drinks. The railway and the pleasant Cambridgeshire countryside have doubled for as diverse locations as Russia and Spain
General Manager: Mr M. A Warrington
Headquarters: Nene Valley Railway, Wansford station, Stibbington, Peterborough, Cambs PE8 6LR
Telephone: Stamford (0780) 782854; talking timetable (0780) 782921
Main station: Wansford
Other public stations: Orton Mere, Ferry Meadows, Peterborough NVR ½-mile from city centre
OS reference: TL 903979
Car park: Wansford, Orton Mere, Ferry Meadows, Peterborough NVR
Access by public transport: Buses from Peterborough to Orton Mere and Ferry Meadows
Refreshment facilities: Wansford, (restaurant bar coach on platform 4). Orton Mere. Light snacks available. Bar coach on most trains
Souvenir shops: Wansford, Orton Mere, Ferry Meadows
Museum: Wansford

Locomotives

Name	No	Origin	Class	Type	Built
—	80.014	DB	80	0-6-0T	1927
—	996	DSB	E	4-6-2	1950
—	7173	DB	52	2-10-0	1943
—	656	DSB	F	0-6-0T	1949
Danish Seaways	740	DSB	S	2-6-4T	1928
—	101	SJ	B	4-6-0	1944
—	1178	SJ	S	2-6-2T	1914
—	3.628	Nord	3500	4-6-0	1911
Mayflower	1306	LNER	B1	4-6-0	1948
92 Squadron	34081	SR	BB	4-6-2	1948
—	5231	LMS	5MT	4-6-0	1936
City of Peterborough	73050	BR	5MT	4-6-0	1954
—	D2122	BR	03	0-6-0DM	1959
—	D9516	BR	14	0-6-0DH	1964
—	D9523	BR	14	0-6-0DH	1964
—	14029 (D9529)	BR	14	0-6-0DH	1965
Atlantic Conveyor	D306	BR	40	1Co-Co1	1960
—	64.305-6	DB	64	2-6-2T	1936

Industrial locomotives

Name	No	Builder	Type	Built
—	804	Alco (77778)	Bo-Bo	1949
—	—	Avonside (1945)	0-6-0ST	1926
Toby	—	Cockerill (1626)	0-4-0VBT	1890
Muriel	—	E/Electric (1123)	0-4-0DH	1966
Derek Crouch	—	H/Clarke (1539)	0-6-0ST	1924
Thomas	—	H/Clarke (1800)	0-6-0T	1947
Jacks Green	—	Hunslet (1953)	0-6-0ST	1939
—	68081	HUnslet (2855)	0-6-0ST	1943
—	740	O&K (2343)	0-6-0T	1907†
—	—	R/Hornsby (294268)	4wDM	1951
Doncaster	—	YEC (2654)	0-4-0DE	1957
—	11	Rebuilt Hill	4wD	1963

†2ft gauge

Stock
14 BR Mk 1 coaches; Wagons Lits sleeping car, Italian-built; Wagons Lits sleeping car, Belgian-built; 6 coaches from Denmark; 1 coach from France; 4 coaches from Belgium; Leyland Vehicles Experimental coach; 3 steam rail cranes; SR Travelling Post Office; Various items of freight stock

Depot: Wansford
Length of line: 7½ miles
Passenger trains: Yarwell Mill-Wansford-Orton Mere-Peterborough NVR
Period of public operation: Weekends April-end-October; Sundays March and November, Wednesdays, Spring Bank Holiday to end August; schools specials mid-June and Bank Holidays, mid-week June, July and August
Special events: Enthusiasts events; Thomas events and vintage weekend. Santa Specials in December (phone for details)

Owners
34081 (the Battle of Britain Locomotive Preservation Society)
73050 (Peterborough City Council)
3.628 (Science Museum)
996 and 804 (Museum of World Railways)
Other locomotives privately owned

Facilities for disabled: Ramp access to all stations and shops. Toilets adjacent to Wansford station souvenir shop. Disabled persons and helpers are eligible for concessionary fares. Passengers can be assisted on and off trains
Membership details: Bill Foreman and Wendy Reed, 87 Flamborough Close, Woodstow, Peterborough PE2 9LP
Membership journal: *Nene Steam* — 3 times/year
Marketing names: Britain's International Steam Railway

North Downs Steam Railway SC

The North Downs Steam Railway is a rapidly developing society, establishing a museum and working railway, on a greenfield site at Stone Lodge, Dartford
General Manager: Eric Usher
Location: Stone Lodge Centre, Dartford, Kent
Operating society: North Downs Steam Railway, Stone Lodge Centre, Catton Lane, Stone, Nr Dartford, Kent
Telephone: Dartford (0322) 228260
Main station: Cotton Lane — free car parking available
Other station: London Road — (new station to open during 1992)
Directions: By car — leave M25 Junction 1a (Dartford Tunnel). Follow Stone Lodge/Historic Dartford signs up Cotton Lane (2min).
By train — Network SouthEast to Dartford. Then Kentish Bus to Stone Lodge Farm entrance (routes 480 and 481), 5min walk
Length of line: ½-mile
Public opening: Every Sunday and bank holiday. Saturdays April-September inclusive.
Special events: Please ring for details
Facilities for disabled: Special compartment in train for wheelchairs and special toilet facilities
Membership and service details: North Downs Steam Railway, 29 Southbourne, Washford Farm, Ashford, Kent TN23 2UB
Tel: Ashford (0233) 646170
Membership journal: *Downsline* — quarterly

Industrial locomotives

Name	*No*	*Builder*	*Type*	*Built*
Scottie	1	R/Hornsby (412427)	4wDM	1957
Burt	2	M/Rail (9019)	4wDM	1951
North Downs	3	RSH (7846)	0-6-0T	1955
—	4	Fowler (4220008)	0-4-0DH	1959
Princess Margaret	6	Barclay (376)	0-4-0DM	1948
Telemon	7	Drewry/Vulcan (D295)	0-4-0DM	1955
Octane	8	YEC (2686)	0-4-0DE	1960
Topham	10	Bagnal (2193)	0-6-0ST	1922
Paxman	—	R/Hornsby (412718)	0-4-0DE	1958

Stock
2 ex-LT T stock DMB cars, 2758 and 2749; 1 ex-LCDR 4-wheel carriage (body only); 1 ex SECR carriage (body only); 2 ex-BP oil tanks; 1 ex-Blue Circle open cement wagon; 1 ex-LT brake van chassis; 1 ex-SR Bogie van; 1 ex-SR PMV' 1 ex-LT brake van; 1 Grafton 5-ton diesel-hydraulic crane; 1 ex-Esso oil tank

Below:
On 23 December 1990 *Topham* awaits the first Santa Special train of the day, seen in the background. This was its last day in service prior to withdrawal for a major overhaul. *A. I. Cottenham*

North Norfolk Railway

art of the former Midland & Great 'orthern Joint Railway, other lements of the LNER have crept in the guise of the Great Eastern 15', the 'B12' now being restored nd a variety of Gresley coaches. he newly opened extension to Holt as opened up extensive views of 1e Norfolk coast and the steep radients belie the county's putation for flatness

enaral Manager: Mr D. P. Madden
eadquarters: North Norfolk ailway, Sheringham station, heringham, Norfolk, NR26 8RA
elephone: Sheringham (0263) 22045. Talking timetable: (0263) 25449
ain station: Sheringham
ther public stations: Weybourne, elling Heath Park, Holt
S reference: Sheringham TG 56430, Weybourne TG 118419
ar parks: Sheringham (old goods ard), Weybourne, Holt
ccess by public transport: ieringham BR station (200 yards)
efreshment facilities: Sheringham, 'eybourne
ouvenir shops: Sheringham, 'eybourne
useum: Sheringham
epot: Weybourne
ength of line: 5¼ miles
assenger trains: Steeply graded, ieringham-Weybourne-Holt
eriod of public operation: Please ntact for details

Locomotives

Name	No	Origin	Class	Type	Built
—	564	GER	J15	0-6-0	1912
—	61572	LNER	B12	4-6-0	1928
—	12131	BR	11	0-6-0DE	1952
—	27066	BR	27	Bo-Bo	1962

Industrial locomotives

Name	No	Builder	Type	Built
Ring Haw	—	Hunslet (1982)	0-6-0ST	1940
—	3809	Hunslet (3809)	0-6-0ST	1954
Harlaxton	—	Barclay (2107)	0-6-0T	1941
Birchenwood	4	Bagnall (2680)	0-6-0ST	1944
—	12	RSH (7845)	0-6-0T	1955
—	10	E/Electric (C8431)	0-4-0DH	1963
Wissington	—	H/Clarke (1700)	0-6-0ST	1938
—	—	Bagnall (2370)	0-6-0F	1929
Edmundsons	—	Barclay (2168)	0-4-0ST	1940

Stock
2 Wagon und Maschinenbau ex-BR diesel railbuses; 10 ex-BR coaches; 2 ex-SR 'Brighton Belle' Pullman cars; 7 ex-LNER coaches; Small number of wagons

Owners
564 and 61572 (the Midland & Great Northern Railway Society)

Special events: Santa Specials in December
Facilities for disabled: Specially adapted Pullman Car available, advanced booking essential
Membership details: Midland & Great Northern Joint Railway Society, Clive Morris, c/o above address
Membership journal: *Joint Line* — quarterly
Marketing names: The Poppy Line

Below:
Holt station on the North Norfolk Railway with one of the German-built 4-wheel railbuses providing accommodation for the days passengers. The line provides a vital link from Holt and Weybourne for shoppers to the line's main station at Sheringham, 19 May 1991. *Nigel Hunt*

North Woolwich Old Station Museum — M

No expense has been spared in the very imaginative restoration of this attractive Victorian terminus building overlooking the Thames. Railway artefacts, documents, drawings, etc are well displayed in glass cases or on the walls, the stock being stabled in the platform area. Convenient for the new City airport and connections for the Docklands Railway
Location: North Woolwich Old Station Museum, Pier Road, North Woolwich, London E16 2JJ
OS reference: TQ 433798
Organisation: Passmore Edwards Museum Governors
Telephone: 071-474 7244

Locomotives

Name	*No*	*Origin*	*Class*	*Type*	*Built*
—	229	GER	209	0-4-0ST	1876

Industrial locomotives

Name	*No*	*Builder*	*Type*	*Built*
—	—	Hibberd (3294)	4wDM	1948
—	—	Peckett (2000)	0-6-0ST	1942
—	—	RSH (7667)	0-6-0ST	1950

Stock
1 ex-LNER coach; 2 compartment sections of LTSR coach; NLR Luggage Van

Car park: Only in adjoining streets
Public transport: BR North London Link. Buses: 101, 69 and 276
Facilities: Museum shop
Public opening: Saturday to Wednesday, 10.00-17.00. Sunday and Bank Holidays, 14.00-17.00. Closed Thursday and Friday

North Yorkshire Moors Railway

This 18-mile line runs through the picturesque North York Moors National Park and is host to an extensive collection of main line locomotives
General Manager: F. R. Pearce
Headquarters: Pickering station, Pickering, North Yorkshire
Telephone: Pickering (0751) 72508 or 73535
Operating Manager: J. P. Russell
Main station: Pickering
Other public stations: Grosmont, Goathland, Newtondale Halt, Levisham
OS reference: Pickering NZ 797842, Levisham NZ 818909, Goathland NZ 836013, Grosmont NZ 828053
Car parks: Grosmont, Goathland, Levisham, Pickering
Access by public transport: BR service to Grosmont from Whitby and Middlesbrough. Bus services Malton-Pickering, York or Scarborough-Pickering and Whitby-Goathland and Pickering
Refreshment facilities: Available on most trains and at Grosmont, Goathland and Pickering
Souvenir shops: Pickering, Goathland, Grosmont

Locomotives

Name	*No*	*Origin*	*Class*	*Type*	*Bui*
Eric Treacy	45428	LMS	5MT	4-6-0	193
George Stephenson†	44767	LMS	5MT	4-6-0	194
—	2238	NER	T2	0-8-0	191
—	2392**	NER	P3	0-6-0	192
Bittern†	19	LNER	A4	4-6-2	193
Blue Peter†	60532	LNER	A2	4-6-2	194
—	2005	LNER	K1	2-6-0	194
—	63460	NER	T3	0-8-0	191
—	69023	LNER	J72	0-6-0T	195
—	3814	GWR	2884	2-8-0	194
—	6619	GWR	5600	0-6-2T	192
—	841	SR	S15	4-6-0	193
Repton§	30926	SR	V	4-4-0	193
—	75014	BR	4MT	4-6-0	195
—	80135	BR	4MT	2-6-4T	195
—†	92134	BR	9F	2-10-0	195
Dame Vera Lynn	3672	MoS	WD	2-10-0	194
—	D2207	BR	04	0-6-0DM	195
—	D5032	BR	4	Bo-Bo	195
—	D7029	BR	35	B-B	196
—	25191	BR	25	Bo-Bo	196
—	D7628	BR	25	Bo-Bo	196
Alycidon†	55009	BR	55	Co-Co	196

The line is aiming to import two American-built Class S160 2-8-0 locomotives during late 1992
†Not on site
§On loan to Great Central Railway
**Expected to be loaned to Llangollen Railway, May-August 1992

Industrial locomotives

Name	*No*	*Builder*	*Type*	*Bui*
—	29 Kitson (4263) 0-6-2T 1904			
—	5	RStephenson (3377)	0-6-2T	190
Stanton	No 44	Yorkshire (2622)	0-4-0DE	195
No 21	—	Fowler (4210094)	0-4-0DH	195

Above:
'Battle of Britain' class 4-6-2 No 34072 *257 Squadron* was a visitor to the North Yorkshire Moors Railway during 1991, being seen here on 26 May leaving Goathland with the 15.55 Grosmont-Pickering service. *John S. Whitley*

luseum: Situated at locomotive epot, Grosmont
epot: Grosmont
ength of line: 18 miles
assenger trains: Steam-hauled ervices Grosmont and Pickering. 'he 'North Yorkshireman' runs egularly. A GWR saloon is also vailable for special occasions (eg edding parties, conferences etc)
eriod of public operation: Daily aster to early November, Santa pecials and other Xmas services in ecember
acilities for disabled: The NYMR relcomes visitors who may be uffering from a disability and pecial attention will gladly be rovided if advanced notice is given
pecial notes: Operates through Iorth York Moors National Park.

Name	*No*	*Builder*	*Type*	*Built*
Antwerp	—	Hunslet (3180)	0-6-0ST	1944
Redcar	12139	E/Electric (1553)	0-6-0DE	1948
—	16	Drewry	0-4-0DM	1941
—	2	R/Hornsby (421419)	4wDM	—
—	3*	R/Hornsby (441934)	4wDM	1960
—	1	Vanguard (129V)	0-4-0DM	1963
—	2	Vanguard (131V)	0-4-0DM	1963

*On loan to Middleton Railway

Stock
33 × BR Mk 1, 4 × Pullman, 2 × BR XP64, 1 × BR Mk 2, 3 × GUV, 7 × Gresley, 6 × Thompson, 1 × GW Saloon, 1 × SR Bulleid, 3 × LMS, 1 × GCR Barnum, 1 × GNR Brake, 3 × NER, 2 × H&BR, 2 × diesel cranes, 2 × 45ton steam cranes, over 40 wagons.

Owners
841 (Essex Locomotive Society)
2005, 2238, 2392, 69023 (the North Eastern Locomotive Preservation Group)
19 and 60532 (on loan to the North Eastern Locomotive Preservation Group)
63460 (on loan from the National Railway Museum)
75014 (75014 Locomotive Operators Group)
92134 (the Standard Nine Loco Group)
Antwerp (the National Coal Board)
D821, D1015, D7029, D8568 (Diesel Traction Group)
55009 (the Deltic Preservation Society)
21, 44 (British Steel Corporation)
29 (Lambton 29 Syndicate)
5, 926, 3814, 6619 and 80135 (private)

Northampton & Lamport Railway

Headquarters: Pitsford & Brampton Station
Location: About 5 miles north of Northampton, Pitsford road off A50 or A508
Operations Manager: Mr B. Faulkner
Operating society/organisation: Northampton Steam Railway Preservation Society
Telephone: (0604) 22709
Car parks: On site
Access by public transport: None
On site facilities: NSR sales shop
Length of line: ¾-mile at present
Public opening: Construction work underway, and open for viewing on Sundays 10.30-17.00.
Special events: Open days planned for 26 April, 21 June, 20 September
Membership details: Mr J. Douglas, 222 Spinney Hill Road, Northampton NN3 1DP
Membership journal: *Premier Line* — 4 times a year
Marketing name: Harboro Line

Locomotives

Name	*No*	*Origin*	*Class*	*Type*	*Built*
—	3862	GWR	2884	2-8-0	1942
Castel Dinas Bran	25035	BR	25	Bo-Bo	1963
—	27024	BR	25	Bo-Bo	1962
—	27056	BR	27	Bo-Bo	1962
The Royal Artilleryman	45118	BR	45	1Co-Co1	1962

Industrial locomotives

Name	*No*	*Builder*	*Type*	*Built*
Colwyn	45	Kitson (5470)	0-6-0ST	1933
Yvonne	2945	Cockerill (2945)	0-4-0VBT	1920
—	2104	Peckett (2104)	0-4-0ST	1948
Bunty	—	Fowler (4210018)	0-4-0DM	1950
—	1	R/Hornsby (275886)	4wDM	1949
Sir Gyles Isham	764	R/Hornsby (319286)	0-4-0DM	1953

Stock

Coaches: 1 ex-SR double-decker motor coach; 1 Pullman car; 1 BR Mk 1 FK; 1 BR Mk 1 TSO; Mk 1 BSO; 1 Mk 1 CK; 2 BR Mk 1 SK; 1 Mk 2 BSO (micro buffet); 1 SR CCT van; 2 BR Suburban coaches (1 CL, 1 BS); 1 BR Mk 2 SO; 1 BR Mk 1 BSK; 2 GWR coaches; 1 GWR Siphon; 2 LMS coaches; 1 BR full brake; 1 BR GUV
Wagons — A number of various wagon types

Owners

3862 (the LNWR Preservation Society)
Colwyn (the *Colwyn* Preservation Society)

Right:
One of the last surviving carriages from a unique double-deck electric multiple-unit survives at the Northampton Steam Railway. It is seen here in company with several other coaches and a BR Class 27 diesel.
Will D. Downing

Northamptonshire Ironstone Railway Trust SC

Location: Hunsbury Hill Industrial Museum. Hunsbury Hill Country Park, Hunsbury Hill Road, Camp Hill, Northampton
OS reference: SP 735584
Operating organisation: Northamptonshire Ironstone Railway Trust Ltd, c/o Mr B. Denny, 5 Forest Road, Far Cotton, Northants NN4 9NZ
Telephone: Northampton (0604) 767216

Industrial locomotives

Name	*No*	*Builder*	*Type*	*Built*
Vigilant	—	Hunslet (287)	0-4-0ST	1882
Brill	14	M/Wardle (1795)	0-4-0ST	1912
—	87	Peckett (2029)	0-6-0ST	1942*
Belvedere	—	Sentinel (9365)	0-4-0TG	1946
Musketeer	—	Sentinel (9369)	0-4-0TG	1946
Hylton	—	Planet (3967)	0-4-0DH	1961
Spitfire	39	R/Hornsby (242868)	4wDM	1946
—	16	Hunslet (2087)	0-4-0DM	1940
—	—	R/Hornsby (386875)	0-4-0DM	1955
—	—	M/Rail (9711)	0-4-0DM	1946†

ccess by public transport: erminus of Northampton ransport bus routes, 24, 26 to amp Hill from Northampton reyfriars bus station. Operated by nited Counties Bus Co on Sundays
n site facilities: Light refreshments, hop, toilets in car park. Brake van des given on standard gauge ailway. Children's playground and icnic areas within the park oundary
ength of line: 2¼ miles
ublic opening: Easter Sunday to nd of September and Bank olidays

Name	No	Builder	Type	Built
—	—	M/Rail	0-4-0DM	1954†
—	—	Lister (14006)	0-4-0PM	1950†

*Metre gauge
†2ft gauge

Times of opening: Museum: 11.00-17.00. Railway: First train 14.00, last train 17.10
Facilities for the disabled: Site relatively flat. Members willing to assist.
Special notes: Museum to the Ironstone Industry of Northamptonshire, the museum houses photographs, documents and other items connected with the Ironstone Industry of Northamptonshire. The railway has been relaid on part of the trackbed of the former 3ft 8½in gauge line of now defunct Hunsbury Ironstone Co
Membership details: Mrs J. Clayton, 9 High Street, Hallaton, Leicestershire

Paignton & Dartmouth Steam Railway

line that succeeds in imparting ie feeling of running from A to B, nking, as it does, the Dartmouth erry at Kingswear to Paignton and R. A trip in the observation car is vell worth the supplement for the iews of the sea, the climb through ie tunnel, and the descent through ie wooded hillside to Brunel's erminus at Kingswear on the banks f the River Dart
irector & General Manager: B. S. Cogar
leadquarters: Paignton Queen's ark station, Paignton, Devon
elephone: Paignton (0803) 555872
lain station: Paignton Queen's ark
ther public stations: Goodrington, hurston, Kingswear (for artmouth)
S reference: SX 889606
ar parks: Paignton municipal car ark, Goodrington, Dartmouth (ferry Kingswear)
ccess by public transport: djacent to both BR station and evon General bus station
efreshment facilities: Kingswear

Locomotives

Name	No	Origin	Class	Type	Built
—	4555	GWR	4500	2-6-2T	1924
—	4588	GWR	4575	2-6-2T	1927
Dumbleton Hall	4920	GWR	Hall	4-6-0	1929
Goliath	5239	GWR	5205	2-8-0T	1924
Lydham Manor	7827	GWR	7800	4-6-0	1950
Volunteer	D3014	BR	08	0-6-0DE	1954
Mercury	D7535	BR	25	Bo-Bo	1965

Stock
16 ex-BR Mk 1 coaches; 1 Pullman observation coach; 2 DMU trailer vehicles, Class 116 Nos 59003/59004; 1 auto-coach

Owners
4920 (the South Devon Railway Trust)

Depot: Churston
Length of line: 7 miles
Passenger trains: Paignton-Kingswear, views of Torbay and Dart estuary, 495yd tunnel
Period of public operation: Easter to October
Facilities for disabled: Limited
Special events: Santa Specials — please see press for details
Membership details: Torbay & Dartmouth Railway Society, Mrs P. Mackey, Renewals Officer, 68 Osney Crescent, Paignton TQ4 5EZ
Membership journal: *Torbay Express* — quarterly

ight:
icturesque Dartmouth is seen over ie top of Kingswear station sidings as o 6435 prepares a rake of wagons for demonstration goods train on unday 16 June 1991 during the aignton & Dartmouth Railway's gala eekend. The weather looks somewhat amp! *Mark S. Wilkins*

Peak Rail PLC SC

Locations: Buxton Midland Station Site, Buxton, Derbyshire; BR station, Matlock, Derbyshire; Darley Dale Station, Darley Dale, Derbyshire
OS reference: Buxton SK 296603, Matlock SK 060738
Operating society/organisation: Peak Rail PLC, Matlock Station, Matlock, Derbyshire
Car parks: On sites
Access by public transport: BR DMU service between Manchester Piccadilly and Buxton daily. Monday to Saturday between Derby and Matlock
Length of line: 2 miles between Matlock and Darley Dale (scheduled to open 1992)
On site facilities: Shop and buffet at Matlock
Public opening: Shop and buffet at Matlock open daily. Buxton site currently closed to public
Facilities for disabled: Advance notice not necessary but contact telephone is (0298) 79898
Special events: Please contact for details
Special notes: Peak Rail (Operations) Ltd, has outline permission to relay the 20-mile line from Buxton to Matlock from all relevant local authorities. At the time of writing track laying on the first 2 miles from Matlock to Darley Dale is almost complete and is scheduled to open in 1992

Locomotives

Name	No	Origin	Class	Type	Built
—	48624	LMS	8F	2-8-0	1943
Penyghent	D8*	BR	44	1Co-Co1	1959
3rd Carabinier	D99*	BR	45	1Co-Co1	1961
Sherwood Forester	D100*	BR	45	1Co-Co1	1961
—	D3429†	BR	08	0-6-0DE	1958
—	D5705*	BR	28	Bo-Bo	1958
—	D7615†	BR	25	Bo-Bo	1963

*At Matlock
†At Darley Dale

Industrial locomotives

Name	No	Builder	Type	Built
Vulcan	—	V/Foundry (3272)	0-4-0ST	1918
The Duke	2746	Bagnall (2746)	0-6-0ST	1944
*William**	—	Sentinel (9599)	0-4-0T	1956
—	E1	H/Clarke (D1199)	0-6-0DM	1960
—	1684	Hunslet (1684)	0-4-0T	1931
*Warrington**	150	RSH (7136)	0-6-0ST	1944
Meteor	7604	RSH (7604)	0-6-0T	1956
Moorbarrow	47	RSH (7849)	0-6-0T	1955
*Janine**	—	YEC	0-6-0DE	1963
—*	—	Simplex	0-4-0D	—
Robert	2068	Avonside (2068)	0-6-0ST	1933
*Cynthia**	—	R/Hornsby	0-4-0DM	—

*At Darley Dale

Owners
D8 (the North Notts Loco Group)
Vulcan (the Vulcan Loco Trust)

Plym Valley Railway M

A scheme dedicated to the restoration of services over the former GWR Marsh Mills-Plym Bridge line, a distance of 1½ miles
Location: 5 miles from centre of Plymouth, Devon, north of A38. From Marsh Mills roundabout, take B3416 to Plympton, follow signs
OS reference: SX 517564
General Manager: Malcolm Stead
Operating society/organisation: Plym Valley Railway Co Ltd, Marsh Mills Station, Coypool Road, Marsh Mills, Plymouth, Devon PL7 4NL

Locomotives

Name	No	Origin	Class	Type	Built
Wadebridge	34007	SR	WC	4-6-2	1945
—	75079	BR	4MT	4-6-0	1956
—	D3002	BR	08	0-6-0DE	1953

Industrial locomotives

Name	No	Builder	Type	Built
—	3	H/Leslie (3597)	0-4-0ST	1926
—	—	T/Hill (125V)	4wDH	1963

Access by public transport: Buses from Plymouth, Nos 20, 20A, 21, 22A, 51. Stop close to site
On site facilities: Shop and refreshments at Marsh Mills, Coypool (Sundays only)
Public opening: Site open most days from 10.00
Special events: Please see press for details
Special notes: Visitors are advised that, at the moment, the railway and

its locomotives are still under restoration. Prospective visitors are advised to take the advice of their guides. Steam and diesel operating on various weekends

Membership details: Marsh Mills Station, Coypool Road, Marsh Mills, Plymouth PL7 4NL

Membership journal: *Plym Valley News* — quarterly
Marketing name: The Woodland Line

Ravenglass & Eskdale Railway

Originally built to serve iron ore mines in Eskdale, this delightful line makes an ideal 'tourist' line running as it does through wooded valleys and along rugged hillsides
General Manager: Douglas Ferreira
Headquarters: Ravenglass & Eskdale Railway, Ravenglass station, Cumbria
Telephone: 0229 717171
Main station: Ravenglass
Other public stations: Muncaster Mill, Irton Road, The Green, Eskdale (Dalegarth)
OS reference: SD 086964
Car parks: All stations
Access by public transport: BR services to Ravenglass
Refreshment facilities: Ravenglass, Dalegarth. Bar meals at 'Ratty Arms'
Souvenir shops: Ravenglass, Dalegarth
Museum: Ravenglass
Length of line: 7 miles, 15in gauge
Passenger trains: Steam or diesel-hauled narrow gauge trains Ravenglass-Dalegarth

Locomotives

Name	*No*	*Builder*	*Type*	*Built*
River Irt	—	Heywood	0-8-2	1894
River Esk	—	Davey Paxman (21104)	2-8-2	1923
River Mite	—	Clarkson (4669)	2-8-2	1966
Northern Rock	—	R&ER	2-6-2	1976
Bonny Dundee	—	K/Stuart (720)*	0-4-2WT	1901
Shelagh of Eskdale	—	R&ER/Severn-Lamb	4-6-4DH	1969
Quarryman	—	Muir-Hill (2)	0-4-0P/Paraffin	1928
Perkins	—	Muir Hill (NG39A)	0-4-4DM	1929
Silver Jubilee	—	R&ER	DMU	1977
Lady Wakefield	—	R&ER	Bo-Bo	1980
Synolda	—	Bassett-Lowke	4-4-2	1912
—	—	Greenbat (2782)	0-4-0B	1957
Cyril	—	Lister	0-4-0DM	1987

*Rebuilt to 15in gauge 1981

Period of public operation: Daily from late March-late October. Limited winter service November-March
Special events: Family Day 23 May
Facilities for disabled: Special coaches for wheel-chair passengers. Advance notice preferred. Wheelchair access to toilets and museum at Ravenglass; toilets, shop and cafe at Eskdale (Dalegarth)
Special notes: At Ravenglass the R&ER has two camping coaches and the company also operates the 'Ratty Arms' public house formed by conversion of the former BR station buildings. During the high summer, mid-July through August, five steam locomotives are normally in use Monday-Thursday
Membership details: A. N. Grayston, 'Brunel', 10 Harriot Hill, Cockermouth, Cumbria CA13 0BL
Membership journal: *The R&ER Magazine* — quarterly
Marketing names: 'Ratty' or 'T' laal Ratty'

Romney, Hythe & Dymchurch Railway

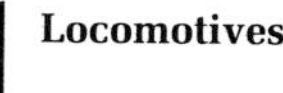

This line was built in 1926/27 as a one-third size miniature main line, and is by far the longest and most fully-equipped 15in gauge railway in the world. It carries not only daytrippers and holidaymakers but also children to and from the local school at New Romney.
Headquarters: Romney, Hythe & Dymchurch Railway, New Romney station, Kent TN28 8PL
Telephone: New Romney (0679) 62353/63256

Locomotives

Name	*No*	*Builder*	*Type*	*Built*
Green Goddess	1	Davey Paxman	4-6-2	1925
Northern Chief	2	Davey Paxman	4-6-2	1925
Southern Maid	3	Davey Paxman	4-6-2	1926
The Bug	4	Krauss (8378)	0-4-0TT	1926
Hercules	5	Davey Paxman	4-8-2	1926
Samson	6	Davey Paxman	4-8-2	1926
Typhoon	7	Davey Paxman	4-6-2	1926
Hurricane	8	Davey Paxman	4-6-2	1926
Winston Churchill	9	YEC (2294)	4-6-2	1931
Doctor Syn	10	YEC (2295)	4-6-2	1931
Black Prince	11	Krupp (1664)	4-6-2	1937
John Southland	12	TMA Birmingham	Bo-Bo	1983
—	14	TMA Birmingham	Bo-Bo	1989
—	PW1	M/Rail (7059)	4wDM	1938

OS reference: TR 074249
Main station: Hythe
Other public stations: Dymchurch, Jefferstone Lane, New Romney, Romney Sands, Dungeness
Car parks: Hythe, Dymchurch, New Romney, Dungeness
Access by public transport: Sandling Junction BR station (1½ miles), Folkestone Central BR station — 4 miles: bus connection from Folkestone bus station to Hythe
Refreshment facilities: New Romney, Dungeness. Also an observation coach on certain trains
Souvenir shops: Hythe, New Romney
Museum: New Romney
Depot: New Romney
Length of line: 13½ miles, 15in gauge

Name	*No*	*Builder*	*Type*	*Built*
—	PW2	RH&DR	4wPM	1965
Redgauntlet	PW3	RH&DR	4wPM	1975

Stock
42 saloon bogie coaches; 12 open bogie coaches; 3 semi-open coaches; 5 luggage/brake saloons; 1 Parlour car; 1 mess coach; 40 assorted wagons

Passenger trains: Train frequency depends on the time of year: maximum frequency is 45 minutes
Period of public operation: Daily from Easter until end of September, and at weekends in March and October
Special events: 17 May — Steam & Diesel Gala Day; 21 June — New Romney Bus Rally; 13 September — Romney on Parade
Special notes: Senior citizen concession Fridays, Saturdays, Sunday, (return journey for single fare). The 'Romney Toy and Model Museum' at New Romney. Parties can be catered for at New Romney
Membership details: RH&DR Association, 26 Norman Close, Battle, East Sussex TN33 0BD
Membership journal: *The Marshlander* — quarterly

Ruislip Lido Railway SC

The 12in gauge line is operated by enthusiast volunteers as an attraction within Ruislip Lido, a country park which is maintained by the London Borough of Hillingdon
Location: Ruislip Lido, Reservoir Road, Ruislip, Middlesex
Operating society/organisation: Ruislip Lido Railway Society Ltd, Membership Secretary, Mrs S. E. Simmons, 9 Wiltshire Lane, Eastcote, Pinner, Middx HA5 2LH
Telephone: 081-866 9654
Car park: Available at Lido
Access by public transport: Ruislip Underground station (Metropolitan and Piccadilly lines) then by bus H13 (Monday-Saturday), 114 (Sundays) or E2 (Summer Sundays). Lido is off the A4180 road

Locomotives

Name	*No*	*Builder*	*Type*	*Built*
Robert	3	Severn-Lamb	B-2 PH	1973
Lady of the Lakes	5	Ravenglass & Eskdale Railway	B-B DM	1985
Graham Alexander	7	Severn-Lamb	B-B DM	1990

Locomotive notes: All locomotives are available for service and a steam locomotive is under construction

Stock
10 open coaches; 5 closed coaches; miscellaneous service stock

Refreshment facilities: Available at Lido site
Length of line: 1-mile single journey, 2 miles return with a planned extension of about 1 mile which will terminate beside main entrance to car park
Public opening: The line is open Sundays throughout the year, Monday, Wednesday, Friday and Saturday in April, May, September and October. Every day in June, July and August, also daily during all school holidays.

24-hour recorded train information service 0895 622595
Journey time: Single 12min, return 22min
Facilities for disabled: Limited number of wheelchair passengers can be accepted for travel
Membership details: c/o above address
Memership jornal: *Woody Bay News* — quarterly

Rutland Railway Museum SC

This museum is dedicated to portraying the railway in industry, particularly iron ore mining, and has a wide range of industrial locomotives and rolling stock. Indeed, its collection of freight rolling stock is probably the most comprehensive in the country and regular demonstrations are a feature of the 'steam days'.
Location: Cottesmore Iron Ore Mines Siding, Ashwell Road, Cottesmore, near Oakham, Leicestershire — museum situated

nid-way between villages of ;ottesmore and Ashwell, pproximately 4 miles north of)akham (locally signposted)
)S reference: SK 886137
)perating society/organisation: ;utland Railway Museum, ;ottesmore Iron Ore Mines Siding, shwell Road, Cottesmore, Nr)akham, Leicestershire LE15 7BX
'elephone: Information, Stamford)780) 63092/62384; Site, Oakham)572) 813203
;ar park: Free car park on site
ccess by public transport: Nearest R station, Oakham. Blands bus ervice, Leicester-Oakham- ;ottesmore. Bartons buses, Iottingham-Melton Mowbray-)akham-Ashwell, ;orby/Peterborough-Oakham- shwell (services 117 and 125).
)n site facilities: Free train rides, emonstration freight trains, efreshments, toilets, museum, hop, picnic sites, demonstration ne with lineside walk and viewing reas, static displays of over 30 team and diesel locomotives; over 0 wagons, vans and coaches)elieved to be the largest collection f preserved freight stock in the UK)
ength of line: ¾-mile
assenger trains: Regular shuttle ervice operates on open days using rake vans (approximately every 5min)
ublic Opening: Open weekends or y arrangement, some weekdays)lease telephone prior to visit).)pen 11.00-17.00
pecial events: Please contact for etails
acilities for disabled: Site elatively flat. Members willing to ssist.
pecial notes: The museum houses n extensive collection of industrial ocomotives and rolling stock 'pifying past activity in local onstone quarries, nationwide nines and factories. A emonstration line approximately -mile long has been relaid on the rmer MR Cottesmore mineral ranch (originally built to tap local onstone quarries), on which estored locomotives and stock are ın. Among the latter is the only ırviving Wisbech & Upwell ramway coach and the last

Locomotives

Name	No	Origin	Class	Type	Built
NCB No 7	(D9518)	BR	14	0-6-0DH	1964
NCB No 3	(D9521)	BR	14	0-6-0DH	1964
BSC45	(D9520)	BR	14	0-6-0DH	1964
—	D9555	BR	14	0-6-0DH	1965

Industrial locomotives

Name	No	Builder	Type	Built
Albion	—	Barclay (776)	0-4-0ST	1896
Uppingham	—	Peckett (1257)	0-4-0ST	1912
Rhos	39	H/Clarke (1308)	0-6-0ST	1918
BSC No 2	—	Barclay (1931)	0-4-0ST	1927
Dora	—	Avonside (1973)	0-4-0ST	1927
Elizabeth	—	Peckett (1759)	0-4-0ST	1928
Singapore	Yard No 440	H/Leslie (3865)	0-4-0ST	1936
Swordfish	—	Barclay (2138)	0-6-0ST	1941
Drake	—	Barclay (2086)	0-4-0ST	1940
Sir Thomas Royden	—	Barclay (2088)	0-4-0ST	1940
Carlton No 3	—	Barclay (352)	0-4-0DM	1941
*Salmon**	8410/39	Barclay (2139)	0-6-0ST	1942
Coal Products No 6	—	Hunslet (2868) (Rebuilt Hunslet 3883 1963)	0-6-0ST	1943
—	8	Peckett (2110)	0-4-0ST	1950
—	3	N/British (27656)	0-4-0DH	1957
—	—	R/Hornsby (306092)	4wDM	1950
—	—	R/Hornsby (305302)	4wDM	1951
Phoenix	—	Hibberd (3887)	4wDM	1958
Stanton No 50	—	YEC (2670)	0-6-0DE	1958
Janus	No 28	YEC (2791)	0-6-0DE	1962
Colsterworth	1382	YEC (2872)	0-6-0DE	1962
—	65	Hunslet (3889)	0-6-0ST	1964
—	20-90-01	Barclay (499)	0-4-0DH	1965
—	20-90-02	R/Hornsby (504565)	0-4-0DH	1965
Betty	8411/04	R/Royce (10201)	0-4-0DH	1965
—	—	E/Electric (D1231)	0-6-0DH	1967
—	No 1	Hunslet (6688)	0-4-0DH	1968

*Currently on loan to British Steel Scunthorpe as 'Appleby Frodingham Steel Co' No 15

'ight:
***almon* is seen at the head of a rake of rake vans during Rutland Railway useum's gala on 23 August 1991.**
obin Stewart-Smith

locomotive built for BR service at Swindon Works
Membership details: Membership Secretary, c/o above address

Locomotive notes: In service *Singapore, Dora, Salmon*, BSC45, NCB 3, D9555, *Colsterworth, Betty, Janus*, E/Electric D1231 and 1.

Stock
4 coaches; 5 brake vans; 12 covered goods vans; 57 wagons (includes rakes of wagons as used in local ironstone and industrial railways); 2 rail cranes

Science Museum M

Built on land acquired with the profits from the Great Exhibition of 1851, the Science Museum was one of the first to include industrial archaeology. Here you will find the originals featured in the history books, such as Robert Stephenson's *Rocket*.
Location: South Kensington
OS reference: TQ 268793
Operating society/organisation: Science Museum, Exhibition Road, South Kensington, London SW7
Telephone: 071-938 8000
Access by public transport: South Kensington Underground station
Catering facilities: Cafe on 3rd floor, tea, coffee, sandwiches etc
On site facilities: Book shop
Public opening: Weekdays 10.00-18.00, Sundays 11.00-18.00. Closed 1 January, Good Friday, May Day Monday, 24-26 December
Special events: All organised by the National Railway Museum, York, which is part of the Science Museum. Telephone (0904) 621261 for details

Locomotives

Name	No	Origin	Class	Type	Built
Caerphilly Castle	4073	GWR	'Castle'	4-6-0	1923
Deltic	—	E/Electric	—	Co-Co	1955
Rocket	—	L&MR	—	0-2-2	1829
Rocket	—	(Replica)	—	0-2-2	1935
Sans Pareil	—	L&MR	—	0-4-0	1829
	13	C&SLR	—	4wE	1890
Puffing Billy	—	Wylam Colliery	—	0-4-0	1813

Industrial locomotives

Name	No	Builder	Type	Built
Bauxite	2	B/Hawthorn (305)	0-4-0ST	187[illegible]
Agenoria	—	Shutt End Colliery	0-4-0	182[illegible]

Stock
LPTB Underground coach, 3327 (built 1927)

Locomotive notes: All restored to static display condition

Owners
*On loan from London Transport Museum, Covent Garden
†On loan to the National Railway Museum, York

Facilities for disabled: Toilets on ground floor, ramp and lifts to all floors (except basement). Parties should contact before arrival if extra assistance is required
Special notes: Static exhibits only

Seaton & District Electric Tramway

A passenger-carrying 2ft 9in gauge electric tramway, operating on the trackbed of the former LSWR Seaton branch
Location: Seaton, Devon
OS reference: SY 252904
Operating society/organisation: Seaton & District Electric Tramway Co, Riverside Depot, Harbour Road, Seaton, Devon EX12 2NQ
Telephone: Seaton (0297) 21702/20375
Access by public transport: Located near to centre of Seaton

Locomotives

Name	No	Builder	Type	Built
—	—	R/Hornsby (435398)	4wDM	195[illegible]

On site facilities: Shops Seaton and Colyton, tea bar at Colyton, adventure playground
Length of line: 3 miles, 2ft 9in gauge
Period of public operation: Daily Good Friday-end September, weekdays in October, also limited winter service
Special notes: Services operated by open top deck bogie tramcars and enclosed single-deck winter car
Disclaimer: The company reserves the right to cancel the tram service without giving prior notice, although this would apply in extreme circumstances only

Severn Valley Railway

'he railway hosts more main line ngines than any other preserved ine in the country, enjoying the ackup of a large volunteer and rofessional workforce and xtensive engineering workshops nd equipment. Railway travel like t used to be

ieneral Manager: Michael J. Draper

)perating Superintendent: ohn F. Hill

Ieadquarters: Severn Valley ailway Co Ltd, Railway Station, ewdley, Worcs DY12 1BG

'elephone: Bewdley (0299) 403816; 4hr timetable — Bewdley (0299) 01001

Aain stations: Bridgnorth, Bewdley, idderminster Town

)ther public stations: Arley, Iighley, Hampton Loade, Jorthwood Halt

)S reference: Bridgnorth SO '15926, Bewdley SO 793753

ar parks: At all stations

ccess by public transport: Aidland Red bus service X92 to idderminster and Bewdley and

Locomotives

Name	No	Origin	Class	Type	Built
The Great Marquess	3442	LNER	K4	2-6-0	1938
Gordon	AD600	LMR	WD	2-10-0	1943
—	43106	LMS	4MT	2-6-0	1951
—	46443	LMS	2MT	2-6-0	1950
—	46521	LMS	2MT	2-6-0	1953
RAF Biggin Hill	45110	LMS	5MT	4-6-0	1935
Leander	5690	LMS	'Jubilee'	4-6-0	1936
Galatea	5699	LMS	'Jubilee'	4-6-0	1936
—	47383	LMS	3F	0-6-0T	1926
—	8233	LMS	8F	2-8-0	1940
—	2968	LMS	5P4F	2-6-0	1933
—	813	GWR	—	0-6-0ST	1901
—	2857	GWR	2800	2-8-0	1918
—	5164	GWR	5101	2-6-2T	1930
—	4150	GWR	5101	2-6-2T	1947
—	5764	GWR	5700	0-6-0PT	1929
—	7714	GWR	5700	0-6-0PT	1930
Raveningham Hall	6960	GWR	'Hall'	4-6-0	1944
—†	4566	GWR	4500	2-6-2T	1924
Bradley Manor	7802	GWR	'Manor'	4-6-0	1939
*Erlestoke Manor**	7812	GWR	'Manor'	4-6-0	1939
Hinton Manor	7819	GWR	'Manor'	4-6-0	1939
Hagley Hall	4930	GWR	'Hall'	4-6-0	1929
—	1501	GWR	1500	0-6-0PT	1949
—	9303	GWR	4300	2-6-0	1932
Taw Valley	34027	SR	WC	4-6-2	1946
—	80079	BR	4MT	2-6-4T	1954
—	78019	BR	2MT	2-6-0	1954
—	75069	BR	4MT	4-6-0	1955
Western Ranger	D1013	BR	52	C-C	1962
Western Courier	D1062	BR	52	C-C	1963
—	D3022	BR	08	0-6-0DE	1952
—	D3586	BR	08	0-6-0DE	1953
—	12099	BR	11	0-6-0DE	1952
—	D7633	BR	25	Bo-Bo	1965
—	D5410	BR	27	Bo-Bo	1962

*Undergoing overhaul at Swindon Heritage Centre
†On loan to Llangollen until October 1992

Right:
tanier Mogul No 2968 at Haye Bridge n 20 April 1991 whilst heading the 3.45 Kidderminster-Bridgnorth during he Severn Valley Railway's spring gala veekend. *John S. Whiteley*

890 to Bridgnorth. BR Sprinter service to Kidderminster (BR) with immediate connections to SVR station. Through tickets available from a wide range of BR stations
Refreshment facilities: Bridgnorth, Hampton Loade, Bewdley, Arley, Highley, Kidderminster Town and on most trains. Fully licensed bars at Bridgnorth and Kidderminster Town
Souvenir shops: Bridgnorth, Bewdley, Kidderminster Town
Depots: Bridgnorth (locomotives), Bewdley (stock)
Model railways: At Bewdley, Kidderminster and Hamtpon Loade
Length of line: 16¼ miles
Passenger trains: Steam-hauled trains running frequently from Kidderminster Town to Bewdley and Bridgnorth. Diesel-hauled service on limited occasions
Period of public operation: Weekends March-October and Santa Steam specials in late November and December. Daily service mid-May to early October and all public Bank Holidays. Open for limited viewing at other times
Special events: Steam Enthusiasts' weekends in April and September; Diesel Gala weekends in May and October; Santa Specials end November and December; Mince Pie Specials in December/early January 1992
Facilities for disabled: Facilities available, special vehicle available to carry wheelchairs
Special notes: A number of special enthusiasts' weekends and special events are held when extra trains are operated. In addition supplementary trains with diesel haulage may be run on special occasions. 'Severn Valley Limited' Restaurant Car service operates on Sundays and dining car service on selected Saturday evenings. Advanced booking recommended

Industrial locomotives

Name	No	Builder	Type	Built
—	4	Peckett (1738)	0-4-0ST	1928
Warwickshire	—	M/Wardle (2047)	0-6-0ST	1926
The Lady Armaghdale	—	Hunslet (686)	0-6-0T	1898
—	—	Ruston (319290)	0-4-0DM	1953
Alan	—	R/Hornsby (414304)	0-4-0DM	1957
William	—	R/Hornsby (408297)	0-4-0DM	1957

Stock
27 ex-GWR coaches; 13 ex-LMS coaches; 24 ex-BR Mk 1 coaches; 8 ex-LNER coaches; Numerous examples of ex-GWR, LMS and other freight vehicles and two 30-ton steam cranes

Owners
3442 (family of the late Earl of Lindsay)
AD600 (The Royal Corps of Transport Museum Trustees)
43106 (the Ivatt 4 Fund)
46443 (SVR 46443 Fund)
47383 (the Manchester Rail Travel Society)
8233 (the Stanier 8F Locomotive Society)
2968 (the Stanier Mogul Fund)
813 (the GWR 813 Fund)
2857 (the 2857 Fund)
5164 (The 51XX Fund)
4150 (the 4150 Locomotive Fund)
5764, 7714 (the Pannier Tank Fund)
4566 (the 4566 Fund)
7802, 7812 (the Erlestoke Manor Fund)
7819 (the Hinton Manor Fund)
1501 (the 15XX Trust)
9303 (the Great Western (SVR) Association)
80079 (the Passenger Tank Fund)
75069 (the 75069 Fund)
6960, 34027, 46521, 78019, D1013 (private)
D1062 (the Western Locomotive Association)
D3022 (the Class 08 Society)
D5410 (Sandwell Metropolitan Council)
D7633 (the SVR P/W Fund)

Membership details: Mrs Pauline Stribblehill c/o above address
Membership journal: *Severn Valley Railway News* — quarterly
Share details: Mr M. J. Draper, c/o above address

Sittingbourne & Kemsley Light Railway

The Sittingbourne & Kemsley Light Railway is part of the 2ft 6in gauge railway built to convey paper and other materials between mills at Sittingbourne and Kemsley and the Dock at Ridham on the banks of the Swale. The first section of the line opened in 1906 and two of the engines then in use remain on the line today.

Locomotives

Name	No	Builder	Type	Built
Alpha	—	Bagnal (2472)	0-6-2T	1932
Triumph	—	Bagnall (2511)	0-6-2T	1934
Superb	—	Bagnall (2624)	0-6-2T	1940
Unique	—	Bagnall (2216)	2-4-0F	1924
Premier	—	K/Stuart (886)	0-4-2ST	1905
Leader	—	K/Stuart (926)	0-4-2ST	1905
Melior	—	K/Stuart (4219)	0-4-2ST	1924
Edward Lloyd	—	R/Hornsby (435403)	4wDM	1961
Victor	—	Hunslet (4182)	4wDM	1953

Industrial standard gauge locomotives

Name	No	Builder	Type	Built
—	4	H/Leslie (3718)	0-4-0ST	1928

The railway is now leased from U.K. Paper Group and is operated as a tourist attraction. Passenger trains are normally steam-hauled and are formed of a varied selection of open and covered coaches. For the first half mile of the journey the train twists and turns through Milton Regis on a concrete viaduct which was one of the first reinforced concrete structures to be built
General Manager: Malcolm Burton
Headquarters: Sittingbourne & Kemsley Light Railway Ltd, The Wall, Milton Regis, Sittingbourne, Kent
Telephone: Sittingbourne (0795) 424899 (talking timetable) or (0634) 852672 (other enquiries)
Main station: Sittingbourne
Car park: Sittingbourne
Party bookings and enquiries: General Manager, 85 Balmoral Road, Gillingham, Kent ME7 4QG
Access by public transport: Sittingbourne BR station, A2 and M2 roads
OS reference: Sittingbourne 905643, Kemsley Down 920662

Name	*No*	*Builder*	*Type*	*Built*
Bear	—	Peckett (614)	0-4-0ST	1896
—	1	Barclay (1876)	0-4-0F	1925

Locomotive notes: In service: *Triumph, Melior, Premier.* Under repair: *Leader, Superb.* On static display *Alpha, Unique* and standard gauge exhibits

Stock
10 bogie coaches (4 ex-Chattenden & Upnor Railway); 2 open coaches; various wagons

Refreshment facilities: Kemsley Down
Souvenir shop: Sittingbourne
Depot: Kemsley Down (access by rail only)
Length of line: 2 miles, 2ft 6in gauge
Passenger trains: Ex-industrial line Sittingbourne-Kemsley Down
Journey time: 15min each way
Period of public operation: Good Friday, Easter Monday and bank holidays; Saturdays 18 April; 2, 23 May, and during August; Sundays 19 April-mid October; Wednesdays 27 May and 5-26 August. Santa specials, contact for details
Special events: 20 April — Easter Bunny Day; 21 June — Friendly Engines Day; 12 July — Teddy Bear Day; 1 August — Enthusiast's Day; 20 September — Wild West Day; 11 October — Special Open Day
Special notes: There is no public access to Kemsley Down other than by the railway on operating dates. When the line is closed all stock is stored in security compounds, on the mill premises. Family ticket available, special rates for parties and senior citizens
Membership details: Mrs Stickler, Lite Hjem, Woodlands Estate, Blean, Canterbury, Kent CT2 9JN
Marketing name: Sittingbourne Steam Railway

South Devon Railway – 'The Primrose Line'

A typical West Country branch line meandering up the Dart Valley to Buckfastleigh which is home to the railway's workshops, a butterfly and otter farm and several other attractions
General Manager: R. Elliot
Headquarters: South Devon Railway, Buckfastleigh station, Buckfastleigh, Devon
Telephone: Buckfastleigh (0364) 42338
Main station: Buckfastleigh
Other public stations: Staverton
OS reference: Buckfastleigh SX 747663, Staverton SX 785638
Car park: Buckfastleigh
Access by public transport: Bus, X 38/9 Exeter-Plymouth; 188 Newton Abbot-Buckfastleigh
Refreshment facilities: Buckfastleigh
Souvenir shop: Buckfastleigh
Museum: Buckfastleigh
Depot: Buckfastleigh
Length of line: 7 miles

Locomotives

Name	*No*	*Origin*	*Class*	*Type*	*Built*
—	0298	LSWR	0298	2-4-0WT	1874
Bulliver	1420§	GWR	1400	0-4-2T	1933
Ashburton	1450§	GWR	1400	0-4-2T	1935
—	1369	GWR	1366	0-6-0PT	1934
Dartington	1638	GWR	1600	0-6-0PT	1951
—	3803*	GWR	2884	2-8-0	1939
—	6435	GWR	6400	0-6-0PT	1937
—	D2192§	BR	03	0-6-0DM	1961
Tiny†	—	SDR	—	0-4-0VBT	1868

*Undergoing restoration at the Birmingham Railway Museum, Tyseley
†Broad gauge (7ft 0 1/4 in)
§Property of DVLR plc, stored at Buckfastleigh

Industrial locomotives

Name	*No*	*Builder*	*Type*	*Built*
Ashley	1	Peckett (2031)	0-4-0ST	1942
Lady Angela	1690	Peckett (1690)	0-4-0ST	1926
—	—	Bagnall (2766)	0-6-0ST	1944
Barbara	—	Hunslet (2890)	0-6-0ST	1943
Glendower	—	Hunslet (3810)	0-6-0ST	1954
—	—	Fowler (421014)	0-4-0DM	1958
Errol Lonsdale	68082	Hunslet (3796)	0-6-0ST	1953

Stock
DMU vehicles, Class 127 Nos 51592 and 51604; 6 ex-BR Mk 1 coaches; 7 ex-GWR coaches; 2 ex-GWR auto trailers
Certain items are the property of DVLR plc and are on loan to the SDR

Above:
No 69023 was built by British Railways in 1951, but was based on a North Eastern Railway design of 1898. During the summer of 1991 the locomotive was loaned to the South Devon Railway and is seen here on 6 July leaving Staverton Bridge bound for Little Hempston Riverside

Passenger trains: Buckfastleigh-Littlehempston Riverside alongside the River Dart
Period of public operation: Telephone above for details
Facilities for disabled: Good
Membership details: South Devon Railway Association, Mrs J. Perring, 12 Spencer Road, Newton Abbot, Devon TQ12 1BQ
Membership journal: *Bulliver* — quarterly
Marketing name: The Primrose Line

Owners
0298 (30587) (on loan from the National Railway Museum)
Tiny, 7ft 0 1/4 in gauge, part of the National Collection
3803 (the South Devon Railway Trust)
Glendower, *Barbara* and Bagnall 2766 (the Glendower Group)
1690 (the South Devon Railway Association)

South Tynedale Railway

A narrow gauge line passing through the attractive scenery of the South Tyne valley, in the North Pennine area of outstanding natural beauty
Location: Approximately ¼-mile north of Alston town centre, on A686 Hexham road
OS reference: NY 717467
Operating society: South Tynedale Railway Preservation Society, The Railway Station, Alston, Cumbria CA9 3JB
Telephone: Alston (0434) 381696
Car park: Alston station
Access by public transport: Wright Bros buses, Haltwhistle-Alston and Newcastle-Alston-Keswick.

Locomotives

Name	No	Builder	Type	Built
Phoenix	1	Hibberd (2325)	4wDM	1941
Sao Domingos	3	O/K (11784)	0-6-0WT	1928
Naworth	4	H/Clarke (DM819)	0-6-0DM	1952
Thomas Edmondson	6	Henschel (16047)	0-4-0T	1918
—	9	Hunslet (4109)	0-4-0DM	1952
Naklo	10	Chrzanow (3459)	0-6-0WTT	1957
—	11	Hunslet (6646)	0-4-0DM	1967
—	12	Hunslet (4110)	0-4-0DM	1953
Chaka's Kraal No 6	—	Hunslet (2075)	0-4-2T	1940
Helen Kathryn	—	Henschel (28035)	0-4-0T	1948
Tiny Tim	—	Hunslet (6619)	0-4-0DM	1966

Locomotive notes: In addition to several of the above, the visiting Hunslet steam locomotive *Chaka's Kraal No 6* is expected to be in service during the 1991 season

Stock
7 bogie coaches; 1 brake van; 1 bogie box van; 1 bogie open wagon; 5 4-wheel open wagons; 1 4-wheel box van; 1 4-wheel flat wagon; 1 fuel tank wagon; 2 bogie well wagons; 6 bogie hopper wagons

Enquiries: Tel: Alston (0434) 381200. Also summer Sunday buses from Stanhope in connection with 'Heritage Line' trains. Details: (091) 386 4411 ext 2410. Bus links from Langwathby in connection with Settle-Carlisle line trains on certain dates (details: (0228) 812812
On site facilities: Book and souvenir shop, tourist information centre, refreshments, picnic area, toilets (including disabled persons)
Catering facilities: Tea room at Alston, serving selection of snacks and home baking
Length of line: 1½ miles, 2ft gauge
Public opening: Passenger train service from Alston to Gilderdale: April — Easter week; May — Saturdays, Sundays, May Day Holiday, Spring Bank Holiday Week; June and September — Tuesdays, Wednesdays, Thursdays, Saturdays, Sundays; July and August — daily; October — Sundays. Departures from 11.15 until 16.00 or 17.00. Steam haulage scheduled at weekends from Spring Bank Holiday until end of September, also Easter and May Day weekends
Journey time: c40min (round trip)
Special events: Children's Day — 27 May; Steam Enthusiasts' Weekend — 25/26 July; Santa Specials — 6, 12/13, 20 December. Mince Pie Specials — 27/28 December
Special notes: The line has been constructed on the trackbed of the former BR Haltwhistle-Alston branch. Extension of the line from Gilderdale towards Slaggyford, a further 3 miles, is in progress
Membership details: Membership Secretary c/o above address
Membership journal: *Tyndalesman* — bi-monthly
Marketing name: England's Highest Narrow Gauge Railway

Owners
3, 4 and 12 (the Durham Narrow Gauge Group)
Tiny Tim (the Ayle Colliery Co)
Chaka's Kraal No 6 (the North Gloucestershire Narrow Gauge Co)
Helen Kathryn (privately-owned)

South Yorkshire Railway SC

Location: Barrow Road Railway Sidings, Barrow Road, Meadowhall, Wincobank, Sheffield S9 1LA
OS Reference: SK389922
General Manager: John Wade
Secretary: Andrew Hayle
Operating Society: South Yorkshire Railway
Telephone: 0742 424405 or 0742 451214
Car Park: Car parking facilities available, more facilities being developed nearby
Access by public transport: From Sheffield: By bus, No 93 Firth Park, alight at the top of Barrow Road, and follow the signposts.
From Rotherham, Doncaster and Sheffield No X77 bus alighting on Barrow Road.
By rail: Meadowhall, 100yd
Refreshment facilities: Light refreshments available
Other on site facilities: Small shop
Length of line: 3½ miles in total, although only ¾-mile is currently occupied
Period of public operation: Not operating a service as yet
Journey time: See above
Membership details: 11 Linnet Mount, Thorpe Hesley, Rotherham S61 2TR
Membership journal: *41Z* — quarterly

Locomotives

Name	*No*	*Origin*	*Class*	*Type*	*Built*
—	D2953	BR	01	0-4-0DM	1956
—	D2854	BR	02	0-4-0DH	1960
—	D2027	BR	03	0-6-0DM	1958
—	03066	BR	03	0-6-0DM	1959
—	D2070	BR	03	0-6-0DM	1959
—	03094	BR	03	0-6-0DM	1960
—	D2124	BR	03	0-6-0DM	1959
—	D2199	BR	03	0-6-0DM	1961
—	D2229	BR	04	0-6-0DM	1955
—	D2284	BR	04	0-6-0DM	1960
—	D2334	BR	04	0-6-0DM	1961
Dorothy	D2337	BR	04	0-6-0DM	1961
—	D2420	BR	06	0-4-0DM	1958
—	07001	BR	07	0-6-0DE	1962
Gwyneth	D3019	BR	08	0-6-0DE	1953
—	D3476	BR	10	0-6-0DE	1957
Christine	D4092	BR	10	0-6-0DE	1962
—	12074	BR	11	0-6-0DE	1950
—	12088	BR	11	0-6-0DE	1951
Andania	40013	BR	40	1Co-Co1	1959

Industrial locomotives

Name	*No*	*Builder*	*Type*	*Built*
—	2	Hunslet (3183)	0-6-0ST	1944
Sunbrite	8	Hunslet (3192) (68006)	0-6-0ST	1944
—	7	H/Clarke (1689)	0-4-0ST	1937
Cathyrn	—	H/Clarke (1884)	0-4-0ST	1955
George	—	Sentinel (9596)	4wVBT	1955
Ken	67	Sentinel (10180)	0-6-0DH	1964
Bigga	—	Fowler (4200019)	0-4-0DH	1947
Rotherham	2	YEC (2480)	0-4-0DE	1950
—	—	Hibbard (3817)	0-4-0DM	1956
—	44	Hunslet (6684)	0-6-0DH	1968
—	48	Hunslet (7279)	0-6-0DH	1972
—	47	T/Hill (249V)	0-6-0DH	1974
Speedy	—	Barclay (361)	0-4-0DM	1942
Hotwheels	—	Barclay (422)	0-6-0DM	1958

Nº 120

Great Southern Railways is the joint marketing name for the Bluebell, Isle of Wight, Kent & East Sussex, Swanage and Watercress Lines. A special 'passport' is available from the participating lines that gives you the opportunity to save money on the cost of the fares, as well as the chance to win a holiday.

During this year each line will hold an Ian Allan 50th Anniversary event at which the opportunity will arise to participate in a free draw and purchase books and magazines.

All events will be advertised in *Railway World,* the enthusiasts' magazine for railway news.

Owned by the National Railway Museum this former LSWR Class T9 4-4-0 No 120 is currently on loan to the Swanage Railway. No 120 is seen at the head of a Harmans Cross-bound train during 1991. *Andrew P. M. Wright*

South Yorkshire Railway

Name	No	Builder	Type	Built
Toffo	2	R/Hornsby (432479)	4wDM	1959
BP21	—	H/Clarke (D707)	0-6-0DM	1950
Enterprise	—	H/Clarke (D810)	0-6-0DM	1953
—	406	NBL (277427)	0-4-0DH	1955

Rolling stock
2 diesel-electric cranes; 5 Mk 1 coaches; 6 Mk 1 General Utility Vehicles; 1 Mk 1 bogie van; 1 Covered Carriage Truck; 2 LNER brake vans; Several other wagons

Southall Railway Centre SC

During the autumn of 1988 the GWRPG moved all their stock into the former BR diesel depot adjacent to their old site. At the time of writing the area was being upgraded to allow the general public into the site, this involves fencing the centre off from the adjacent BR tracks. Please see press for details of open days etc
Location: The former BR diesel depot, approximately 10min from BR station. Access is only possible via the footbridge at the London end of the station, during opening times only
Operating society/organisation: GWR Preservation Group
Telephone: 081-574 1529 R. A. Gorringe (evening and weekend only)
Facilities for disabled: Access to the site is not possible, involving two flights of steps, those wishing to visit are advised to make contact before their visit and alternative arrangements will be made

Locomotives

Name	No	Origin	Class	Type	Built
—	2885	GWR	2884	2-8-0	1938
—	4110	GWR	5101	2-6-2T	1936
—	9682	GWR	5700	0-6-0PT	1949
—	68078*	LNER	J94	0-6-0ST	1946

*Not on site

Industrial locomotives

Name	No	Builder	Type	Built
—	—	AEC Southall	4wDM	1938
—	2100	Peckett (2100)	0-4-0ST	1949
Birkenhead	7386	RSH (7386)	0-4-0ST	1948
Francis Baily of Thatcham	AD251	R/Hornsby (390772)	0-4-0DM	1957

Stock
1 BR 'Gane' wagon; 1 BR 'Rectank' wagon; 1 BR Generator van; 1 BR Goods van; 1 GWR 'Mink' van; 1 GWR brake van; 2 BP oil tank wagons; 1 GWR bogie bolster wagon; 1 LMS parcels van; 1 LMS stores van; 1 Staff coach, former LMS BCK; 1 Wagons Lits coach

Owners
2100 (The City of Portsmouth Museum)

Southport Railway Centre SC

Exhibits include ex-Liverpool Riverside signalbox and the restored turntable facilities using the

Right:
Back home on Lancashire & Yorkshire Railway metals for the first time in years is L&YR No 19. The locomotive is on a 12 month loan from the K&WVR. It is seen alongside the locomotive shed at Steamport Railway Museum.

ırntable from York (Queen St). A working ex-Midland Railway water olumn from London St Pancras is a ominant feature of the site. teamport has been a servicing oint for the annual Southport-Ianchester steam specials since 985

ocation: Five minutes from BR ation, via London Street. Behind ar park

S reference: SD 341170

ecretary: H. J. M Royden

perating society/organisation: outhport Railway Centre, Steamport, Southport Ltd), Derby oad, Southport PR9 0TY

elephone: Southport (0704) 30693

ar park: Derby Road

ccess by public transport: BR ation, Merseyrail from Liverpool

n site facilities: Souvenir shop. afe open Sundays and Bank olidays at weekends. Steam auled rides in passenger coaches MS brake vans June-mid eptember, plus special events. uffet car in operation on special vents. Santa Steam trains in ecember

ength of line: 600yd

ublic opening: October-April 3.00-17.00; Weekdays June-mid eptember 13.00-16.30 (July-August 0.30-16.30)

acilities for disabled: Access to all arts of museum. Limited access to ilets. No advanced notice required or disabled visitors — groups lways welcome. Enquiries always elcomed

Locomotives

Name	No	Origin	Class	Type	Built
Cecil Raikes	5	Mersey Railway	—	0-6-4T	1886
—	19†	L&Y	Pug	0-4-0ST	1910
—	5193	GWR	5101	2-6-2T	1934
—	D2148	BR	03	0-6-0DM	1960
—	D2953	BR	05	0-6-0DM	1959
—	24081	BR	24	Bo-Bo	1958

†On loan from L&Y Saddletanks Fund (K&WVR)

Industrial locomotives

Name	No	Builder	Type	Built
—	5	Peckett (2153)	0-6-0ST	1954
North Western Gas Board		Peckett (1999)	0-4-0ST	1941
Fitzwilliam	—	Hunslet (1954)	0-6-0ST	1939
—	—	Hunslet (3155)	0-6-0ST	1943
Glasshoughton	4	Hunslet (3855)	0-6-0ST	1954
Persil	—	Fowler (4160001)	0-4-0DM	1952
*Efficient**	—	Barclay (1598)	0-4-0ST	1918
Agecroft No 2	—	RSH (7485)	0-4-0ST	1948
St Monans	—	Sentinel (9373)	4wVBT	1947
Hornet	—	Peckett (1935)	0-4-0ST	1937
Whitehead	—	Peckett (1163)	0-4-0ST	1908
—	—	Greenwood & Batley	0-4-0BE (2000)	1958
Sefton	—	T/Hill (123V)	4wDM	1963
Stanlow No 4	4	T/Hill (160V)	0-4-0DM	1966
—	—	N/British (27653)	0-4-0DH	1956
—	D2870	YEC (2677)	0-4-0DM	1960

Stock

Small selection of rolling stock including Class 502 EMU, M28361M and M29896M on loan from NRM, and buffet car Sc1839, TSO 4886 and BSK 35128

1 Smith-Rodley diesel crane

Owner

Cecil Raikes (Liverpool Museum)

*Stock (Liverpool Locomotive Preservation Group)

Membership journal: *27C*

Newsletter — quarterly

Steamtown, Carnforth

SC

ormerly BR Carnforth motive ower depot. Carnforth is a centre or 'Steam on BR' steam-hauled ailtours over BR main lines.

ocation: Steamtown Railway entre, Warton Road, Carnforth, ancashire LA5 9HX

S reference: SD 496708

perating society/organisation: teamtown Railway Museum Ltd

elephone: Carnforth (0524) 732100

ar park: Free car park on site

ccess by public transport: BR ervices to Carnforth station. Bus

Locomotives

Name	No	Origin	Class	Type	Built
Flying Scotsman†	4472	LNER	A3	4-6-2	1923
Sir Nigel Gresley†	4498	LNER	A4	4-6-2	1937
Lord Nelson	850	SR	LN	4-6-0	1926
Sovereign†	44871	LMS	5MT	4-6-0	1945
—	44932§	LMS	5MT	4-6-0	1945
—	48151	LMS	8F	2-8-0	1942
—	5407	LMS	5MT	4-6-0	1937
—	6441	LMS	2MT	2-6-0	1950
—	1300	L&Y	27	0-6-0	1896
—	D2381	BR	03	0-6-0DM	1960
—	03120	BR	03	0-6-0DM	1959
—	08220	BR	08	0-6-0DE	1956
—	D5500	BR	31	A1A-A1A	1957
La France	231K22	SNCF	231K	4-6-2	1914
—	01.2104-6	DB	01	4-6-2	1940

†Visiting locomotives used on BR for main line running
§Shares time between here and Midland Railway Centre

services to Carnforth by Ribble and Lancaster City Transport
Catering facilities: Buffet car for meals and snacks, several picnic areas
On site facilities: Model railway, signalbox, collectors' corner, shop, cafe, 15in gauge railway
Length of line: Standard gauge ¾-mile, 15in gauge 1-mile
Public opening: Daily Easter-October. Summer 09.00-17.00, winter 10.00-16.00, closed 24-26 December. Locomotives in steam on Bank Holidays, Sundays from Easter-October, and daily during July-August
Facilities for disabled: Limited, toilets available, standard gauge trains can accommodate wheelchairs
Special notes: Scheduled steam hauled excursions during summer season, operate from Carnforth with through connections from main centres

Industrial locomotives

Name	*No*	*Builder*	*Type*	*Buil*
Sirapite	6158*	A/Porter (6158)	0-4-0TG	190
Pitsford	—	Avonside (1917)	0-6-0ST	192
John Howe	5	Barclay (1147)	0-4-0ST	190
J. N. Derbyshire	—	Barclay (1969)	0-4-0ST	192
Coronation	3	Barclay (2134)	0-4-0ST	194
Cooke & Nuttal	1	Barclay (2230)	0-4-0ST	194
British Gypsum	4	Barclay (2343	0-4-0ST	195
Glenfield	1*	Barclay (880)	0-4-0CT	190
May	—	Peckett (1370)	0-4-0ST	191
Trimpell	—*	Bagnall (3019)	0-6-0F	195
Cranford No 2	—	Bagnall (2668)	0-6-0ST	194
Great Central	39	RSH(6947)	0-6-0T	193
Barrow Steel No 7	FR 18	S/Stewart (1435)	0-6-0ST	186
Barrow Steel No 17	FR 25	S/Stewart (1585)	0-4-0ST	186
Lindsay	—	Wigan Coal & Iron Co	0-6-0ST	188
Joyce	—*	Sentinel (7109)	4wVBTG	195
Gasbag	—	Sentinel (8024)	4wVBTG	192
Esso	—	General Electric (30483)	Bo-Bo	194
Lord Trenchard	—	Barclay (401)	0-4-0DM	195
Tom Rolt	7049	Hunslet (2697)	0-6-0DM	194

*Expected to transfer to private site in Shropshire

Stock

4 pre-Grouping vehicles; 1 GWR saloon; 5 LNER coaches; 2 LMS coaches; 6 BR coaches; Small selection of freight vehicles; 3 steam cranes; 1 diesel crane

Owners

1300 (the Fairclough Corporation)
850 and D5500 (on loan from the National Railway Museum)

Stephenson Rly Museum & North Tyneside Steam Rly SC

A display in buildings which began life as the Tyne-Wear Metro Test Centre now features locomotives and exhibitions which illustrate railway development from waggonways to the present day
Location: Middle Engine Lane, North Tyneside
OS reference: NZ 396576
Operating society/organisation: Tyne & Wear Museums operates Stephenson Railway Museum and North Tyneside Steam Railway Association operates North Tyneside Steam Railway for North Tyneside Council, address c/o Stephenson Railway Museum,

Locomotives

Name	*No*	*Origin*	*Class*	*Type*	*Buil*
—	03078	BR	03	0-6-0DM	195
—	12098	BR	11	0-6-0DE	195
*Bittern**	4464	LNER	A4	4-6-2	193

*Externally restored as 2509 *Silver Link* of 1935

Industrial locomotives

Name	*No*	*Builder*	*Type*	*Built*
Billy	—	Killingworth or RS & Co (1)	0-4-0	1816-2
—	A5	Kitson (2509)	0-6-0PT	1883
—	E4	Siemens	Bo-BoWE	1909
Thomas Burt MP 1837-1902	401	Bagnall (2994)	0-6-0ST	1950
—	10	Consett (10)	0-6-0DM	1958

Right:
Regular passenger service on the North Tyneside Steam Railway commenced on 14 July 1991. No 401, a Bagnall 0-6-0ST of 1950, leaves Percy Main with a train conveying school children to Museum station. *Ian S. Carr*

Middle Engine Lane, West Chirton, North Shields NE29 8DX
Car park: On site
Length of line: North Tyneside Steam Railway, 1¾ miles, Stephenson Railway Museum to Percy Main
Access by public transport: Tyne & Wear Metro to Percy Main when North Tyneside Steam Railway is in operation. Bus routes 300/307 (operated by Go-Ahead Northern Co) from Newcastle (Eldon Square or Worswick Street) to North Shields, Tynemouth, Whitley Bay, stops at Museum

Stock
1 NER electric parcels van; 1 LNER Gresley BFK; 3 BR non-gangwayed coaches

Owners
12098 (private)
Bittern (on loan from NELPG)
NER van (National Railway Museum)

Public opening: Please contact for details
Special notes: Stephenson Railway Museum and North Tyneside Steam Railway share facilities in buildings Managed by Tyne & Wear Museums at Middle Engine Lane. North Tyneside Steam Railway Association operates and maintains exhibits from the Museum Collection
Facilities for disabled: Access for wheelchairs to Museum building at Middle Engine Lane

Swanage Railway — The Purbeck Line

Overlooked by the historic ruins of Corfe Castle, this railway is slowly extending towards Wareham and a connection to the BR network
Location: Swanage station
Operations Manager: Derek Montague
Operating society/organisation: Swanage Railway Co Ltd, Station House, Railway Station, Swanage, Dorset
Telephone: Swanage 425800. Purbeck Line 24hr Talking Timetable — Swanage 424276
Main station: Swanage
Other public stations: Herston Halt, Harman's Cross
OS reference: SZ 026789
Car park: Swanage
Access by public transport: Wilts & Dorset buses from Bournemouth, Poole and Wareham stop outside station

Locomotives

Name	*No*	*Origin*	*Class*	*Type*	*Built*
—	6695	GWR	5600	0-6-2T	1928
—	30053	LSWR	M7	0-4-4T	1905
—	120	LSWR	T9	4-4-0	1899
257 Squadron	34072	SR	BB	4-6-2	1948
Holland America Line	35022	SR	MN	4-6-2	1948
Port Line	35027	SR	MN	4-6-2	1948
—	45160	LMS/WD	8F	2-8-0	1941
—	80078	BR	4MT	2-6-4T	1954
—	80104	BR	4MT	2-6-4T	1955
—	1708	MR	IF	0-6-0T	1880
—	30075	JZ	USA	0-6-0T	1950s
—	—	7069	LMS	0-6-0DM	1936
—	D3591	BR	08	0-6-0DE	1958
—	D7594 (25244)	BR	25	Bo-Bo	1964

Locomotive notes: 30053 is due to re-enter service in 1992/3 following restoration at East Anglian Railway Museum. 34072 will be away

Right:
Preserved diesels as well as steam locomotives require overhaul. Here we see ex-LMS No 7069 having its diesel engine removed to facilitate overhaul on 11 May 1991. A number of railways now have 'off site' restoration facilities, this Swanage-based locomotive is being overhauled at a private site at Hamworthy *R. Lingley*

On site facilities: Souvenir shop, buffet car on certain trains, hot and cold snacks. Shop open every weekend throughout the year, and on all operating days
Length of line: 3 miles, Swanage-Herston Halt-Harman's Cross
Public opening: Weekends throughout the year. Daily from June to September (inclusive). Thursdays in April, May and October. DEMU early and late trains from July to September
Special events: Please contact for details
Facilities for disabled: Access to station, shop and toilets and special coach on train
Membership details: Nrs N. Noble, Secretary, Southern Steam Trust, c/o above address
Membership journal: *Swanage Railway News* — quarterly
Marketing name: The Purbeck Line

periodically on short-term loans. 35027 is on loan to the Bluebell Railway. 45160 and 7069 undergoing restoration at Hamworthy. 80104 is at Avon Valley Railway undergoing restoration

Industrial locomotives

Name	*No*	*Builder*	*Type*	*Built*
Cunarder	47160	Hunslet (1690)	0-6-0T	1931
May	2	Fowler (4210132)	0-4-0DM	1957
Beryl	—	Planet (2054)	4wPM	1937
—	2150	Peckett (2150)	0-6-0T	1954
—	—	Hunslet (1684)	0-4-0T	1931

Stock
Hastings line DEMU (3 coaches); 3 ex-LSWR coach bodies; 4 ex-SR vans; 9 ex-SR coaches; 18 ex-BR Mk 1 coaches; 1 ex-LNWR CCT; 1 ex-LMS coach; 18 various types of wagons; 1 ex-BR Sleeping coach; 1 ex-SR 15ton diesel-electric crane; 1 Wickham trolley (WD9024); 1 ex-London Transport Plasser & Theurer ballast tamper; 1 ex-BR Corridor 2nd, converted to disabled persons coach

Owners
120 (the National Railway Museum)
6695 (the Great Western Railway Preservation Group)
35022 (the Southern Steam Trust)
Cunarder (owned by 1708 Locomotive Preservation Trust Ltd)
34072, 35027 and 80104 (the Port Line Project)
30053 (the Drummond Locomotive Society)

Swindon & Cricklade Railway SC

This is the only preserved section of the former Midland & South Western Junction Railway, the society having had to relay track and associated works
Location: Tadpole Lane, Blunsdon (approximately mid way between Blunsdon St Andrew and Purton)
Chairman: J. Larkin
Operating society/organisation: Swindon & Cricklade Railway, Blunsdon Station, Blunsdon, Swindon, Wiltshire SN2 4DZ
Telephone: Swindon (0793) 771615 (weekends only)
Station: Blunsdon
OS reference: SU 110897
Length of line: 1-mile
Car park: Tadpole Lane, Blunsdon
Refreshment facilities: Blunsdon station amenities building
Souvenir shop: Blunsdon station amenities building. Various sales stands on Open Days around station area. Museum in converted coach
Depot: Blunsdon
Public opening: Saturdays and Sundays throughout the year.

Locomotives

Name	*No*	*Origin*	*Class*	*Type*	*Built*
Foremarke Hall	7903	GWR	'Hall'	4-6-0	1949
—	5637	GWR	56xx	0-6-2T	1924
—	1506 (08114)	BR	08	0-6-0DE	1955
—	D5222	BR	25	Bo-Bo	1965

Industrial locomotives

Name	*No*	*Builder*	*Type*	*Built*
—	—	Fowler (4210137)	0-4-0DM	1958
Woodbine	—	Fowler (21442)	0-4-0DM	1936
Richard Trevithick	—	Barclay (2354)	0-4-0ST	1955
Merlin/Myrddin	1371	Peckett (1967)	0-4-0ST	1939

Stock
5 BR Mk 1 coaches; 1 BR DMU vehicle; 2 GWR coaches; Selection of goods rolling stock; Wickham railcar

Owners
7903 (the Foremarke Hall Locomotive Group)
5637 (the 5637 Locomotive Group)

Passenger trains: Passenger trains operate 1 January; 19/20 April; 24/25 May; 27/28 June; 5/6 September; 31 October; 1 November. Details from Public Relations Manager c/o above address
Special events: 24/25 May — Friends of Thomas Weekend; 5/6, 12/13, 19/20 December — Santa Specials
Facilities for disabled: Access to shop and refreshments
Membership details: Membership Secretary c/o above address
Membership journal: Quarterly
Marketing names: Tiddlydyke

Swindon GWR Museum

M

he Great Western Railway
useum began life as a lodging
ouse for railway workers, and was
en a Wesleyan Methodist Chapel
r 90 years before being acquired
/ Swindon Borough Council and
onverted into a museum.
longside the museum, in the heart
' the railway village, visitors can
impse the living conditions of the
ilworkers at the turn of the
entury, in the carefully restored
orkman's house
eeper: T. Bryan
ocation: Faringdon Road,
windon, Wiltshire
S reference: SU 145846
perating society/organisation:
orough of Thamesdown, GWR
useum, Faringdon Road,
windon, Wiltshire
elephone: Swindon (0793) 493189

Locomotives

Name	No	Origin	Class	Type	Built
—	2516	GWR	2301	0-6-0	1897
Lode Star	4003	GWR	'Star'	4-6-0	1907
—	9400	GWR	9400	0-6-0PT	1947
*North Star**	—	GWR	—	2-2-2	1837
—	4	GWR	Diesel railcar	Bo-Bo	1934
—	—	A38W	Petrol railcar	2w-2PMR	c1960

*Broad gauge (7ft 0¼in) replica

Owners
All locomotives are part of the National Railway Museum Collection

Please note that No 4003 Lode Star *has been transferred to the National Railway Museum, replaced by No 6000* King George V

Car park: Swindon BR station and street parking
Access by public transport: Swindon BR (10 minutes)
On site facilities: A selection of souvenirs is available
Public opening: Weekdays 10.00-17.00, Sundays 14.00-17.00. Closed Good Friday, Christmas Day, Boxing Day
Special Notes: The Museum also houses a considerable number of photographs depicting scenes of the GWR along with nameplates, models, posters, tickets, etc. 1992: Return to Swindon Exhibition continues this year
Membership details: The Friends of Swindon Railway Museum, c/o The GWR Museum
Membership journal: *North Star* — quarterly

Tanfield Railway

he oldest railway in the world,
aving opened in 1725, the site
aintains its basic appearance of an
idustrial railway but contains an
nusual assortment of stock as well
s the Tyneside Locomotive
ollection
ocation: Off the A6076 Sunniside
Stanley road
S reference: NZ 207573
perating Superintendent: P.
'eightman
perating society/organisation: The
anfield Railway, Marley Hill
ngine Shed, Sunniside, Gateshead,
yne & Wear. Postal address: 33
tocksfield Avenue, Newcastle-
pon-Tyne NE5 2DX
elephone: Newcastle (091)
742002
ar park: Marley Hill Engine Shed
ccess by public transport:
ımmer — X30 weekdays and X75
undays, stop outside main
ntrance. *Winter* — X30 weekdays,
utside main entrance, 706, 708,
22 Sundays to Sunniside only,
ear Sunniside station

Industrial locomotives

Name	No	Builder	Type	Built
—	9	AEG (1565)	4w-4wE	1913
Gamma	—	Bagnall (2779)	0-6-0ST	1945
Horden	—	Barclay (1015)	0-6-0ST	1904
—	6	Barclay (1193)	0-4-2ST	1910
—	17	Barclay (1338)	0-6-0T	1913
—	32	Barclay (1659)	0-4-0ST	1920
—	3	E. Borrows (37)	0-4-0WT	1898
Wellington	—	B/Hawthorn (266)	0-4-0ST	1873
Enterprise	—	R&W Hawthorn (2009)	0-4-0ST	1884
Cyclops	—	H/Leslie (2711)	0-4-0ST	1907
—	2	H/Leslie (2859)	0-4-0ST	1911
Stagshaw	—	H/Leslie (3513)	0-6-0ST	1923
—	3	H/Leslie (3575)	0-6-0ST	1923
—	13	H/Leslie (3732)	0-4-0ST	1928
—	3	H/Leslie (3746)	0-6-0F	1929
Irwell	—	H/Clarke (1672)	0-4-0ST	1937
—	38	H/Clarke (1823)	0-6-0T	1949
—	4	Sentinel (9559)	0-4-0T	1953
—	169	RSH (6980)	0-4-0DM	1940
Hendon	—	RSH (7007)	0-4-0CT	1940
—	62	RSH (7035)	0-6-0ST	1940
—	3	RSH (7078)	4w-4wE	1940
—	49	RSH (7098)	0-6-0ST	1943
Progress	—	RSH (7298)	0-6-0ST	1946
Cochrane	—	RSH (7409)	0-4-0ST	1948
—	44	RSH (7760)	0-6-0ST	1953

Above:
Tuesday 15 August was the formal opening date of the Tanfield Railway's extension to Causey Arch. The first train called the 'Causey Rambler' is seen leaving Marley Hill carrying civic dignitaries and invited guests hauled by *Sir Cecil A. Cochrane*. *T. J. Gregg*

Name	*No*	*Builder*	*Type*	*Built*
—	38	RSH (7763)	0-6-0ST	1954
—	21	RSH (7796)	0-4-0ST	1954
—		47 RSH (7800)	0-6-0ST	1954
—	1	RSH (7901)	0-4-0DM	1958
—	16	RSH (7944)	0-6-0ST	1957
FGF	—	Barclay (D592)	0-4-0DH	1969
—	2	A/Whitworth (D22)	0-4-0DE	1933
Escucha	11	B/Hawthorn (748)	0-4-0ST	1883*

*600mm gauge

Stock
19 4-wheel carriages; 3 6-wheel carriages; 1 6-wheel van; 14 hopper wagons; 9 contractors bogies; 3 brake vans; 3 steam cranes; 7 covered wagons; 4 open wagons; 4 black wagons; 4 flat wagons

Catering facilities: Basic refreshment facilities available on operating days
On site facilities: Shop and toilets
Length of line: 2-miles with 1-mile extension possibly open during 1992
Public opening: Marley Hill Engine Shed open daily for viewing, except Christmas and New Years day. Trains run every Sunday Easter-December. Also bank holiday Mondays and Thursdays and Saturdays in mid-summer. Santa trains in December
Special events: Please see press for details
Facilities for disabled: Good access to stations and coaches
Special notes: The railway is extending its line back to East Tanfield, and also features the Tyneside Locomotive Collection.
Membership details: Miss E. Martin, 33 Stocksfield Avenue, Fenham, Newcastle-upon-Tyne NE5 2DX
Membership journal: *Tanfield Railway News* — 6 times/year

Telford Horsehay Steam Trust SC

Location: Horsehay, Telford, Shropshire
OS reference: SJ 675073
Operating society/organisation: Telford Horsehay Steam Trust, The Old Loco Shed, Horsehay, Telford, TF4 2LT
Public opening: Please contact for details

Locomotives

Name	*No*	*Origin*	*Class*	*Type*	*Built*
—	5619*	GWR	5600	0-6-2T	1925

*On loan to Gloucestershire Warwickshire Railway

Industrial locomotives

Name	*No*	*Builder*	*Type*	*Built*
Peter	—	Barclay (782)	0-6-0ST	1896
Tom	—	N/British (27414)	0-4-0DH	1954
Ironbridge No 3	—	Peckett (1990)	0-4-0ST	1940
—	—	Sentinel (9535)	4wVBT	1952
—	D2959	R/Hornsby (382824)	4wDM	1955
Thomas	—*	Kierstead	4wVBT	1979
—	1*	Skinner	4wPM	1975

*2ft gauge

Stock
1 ex-BR Mk 1 coach; 1 ex-GWR auto-trailer; 1 ex-GWR Toad brake van; 1 ex-GWR 3-ton hand crane; 1 Wickham trolley; Various wagons

Tiverton Museum

M

he Museum, dominated by No 442, affectionately known as the 'ivvy Bumper', houses a large ɔllection of railway relics

ocation: Tiverton, Devon

S reference: SS 955124

perating society/organisation: iverton Museum Society, St ndrew Street, Tiverton, Devon X16 6PH

elephone: Tiverton (0884) 256295

Locomotives

Name	*No*	*Origin*	*Class*	*Type*	*Built*
—	1442	GWR	1400	0-4-2T	1935

Car park: Adjoining access by public transport: Rail to Tiverton Parkway, then by bus, or bus from Exeter

On site facilities: Museum, shop and toilets

Public opening: Daily 10.30-16.30; except Sundays and from 24 December to 31 January

Special notes: Limited facilities for disabled

Vintage Carriage Museum

M

unique collection of elderly ilway carriages. These include a lly restored and prize-winning 376-built Manchester, Sheffield & ncolnshire Railway tricomposite ɔach (in Great Central Railway very), together with fully-restored etropolitan Railway and South astern & Chatham Railway coaches nd other coaches in various stages restoration.

Audio presentations ('Travellers' ales') and access to coach interiors ing the collection to life and allow ose examination of the restoration ork, completed and in progress. ther railway items on display clude a fine collection of Frank ewbould and other railway osters. A veteran small steam comotive is usually also present, ith access to the footplate

cation: Vintage Carriage Museum, grow Station Yard, South Street, eighley, West Yorkshire

perations Manager: Michael Cape, on Secretary, VCT

perating society/organisation: ntage Carriages Trust (a egistered Charity), c/o The Railway ation, Haworth, Keighley, West orkshire BD22 8NJ

lephone: Keighley (0535) 680425

ar Park: Yes. Also limited coach rking at Ingrow station

ccess by public transport: By Rail Keighley (one mile), or by Worth alley Railway train to Ingrow West (adjacent): good bus service from Keighley town centre

Stock

Railway	*Number*	*BR or previous owner type*	*Date built*	*Seats*	*Weight*	*Length*
MS&LR	176	4-wheel 1st/2nd/3rd/ luggage	1876	34	12T	28ft 0in
GNR	?	6-wheel 3rd brake	1888	40	14T	34ft 11in
MR	358	6-wheel 1st/3rd/ luggage	1886	32	15T	34ft 0in
Met	427	BS	1910	84	30T	54ft 0in
Met	465	S	1919	108	30T	54ft 0in
Met	509	F	1923	84	30T	54ft 0in
SR (SECR)	S3554S	BSK	1924	42	33T	65ft 3in
BR (SR)	S1469S	TSO	1951	64	32T	67ft 1in

(also two oil tank wagons: MR, c1890, and Esso, 1939)

Industrial locomotives

Name	*No*	*Builder*	*Type*	*Built*
Bellerophon	—	Haydock Foundry (C)	0-6-0WT	1874
Sir Berkeley	—	M/Wardle (1210)	0-6-0ST	1891
Lord Mayor	—	H/Clarke (402)	0-4-0ST	1893

On site facilities: Toilets, small sales stall

Public opening: 12.00-16.00 whenever Worth Valley Railway trains are running. Special openings outside these times and dates, and school and other party bookings, are welcome: telephone 0535 680425 or 0535 646472

Facilities for the disabled: Limited wheelchair access

Special notes: Most, but not all, of the collection is displayed in the Museum at any one time. One or more of the carriages (and also the locomotives *Bellerophon* and *Sir Berkeley*) are occasionally in passenger use on the Worth Valley Railway or elsewhere

Membership details: Membership Secretary c/o above address (Haworth station)

Marketing names: Vintage Carriages Trust or VCT

Wells & Walsingham Light Railway

One man's railway, the life and love of retired naval commander, Roy Francis, this delightful line which is totally uncommercialised runs along the old Wells branch to Walsingham where the old station has been transformed into a Russian Orthodox Church by the addition of an onion-shaped dome to its roof. A must if you find yourself nearby

Location: On A149, Stiffkey Road, Wells next the Sea, Norfolk
General Manager: Lt-Cdr R. W. Francis
Operating organisation: Wells & Walsingham Light Railway, Wells Next The Sea, Norfolk NR23 1RB
Car park: Yes
Access by public transport: Eastern Counties buses
On site facilities: Souvenir and tea shop
Length of line: 4 miles, 10¼in gauge
Public opening: Daily Easter to the end September

Special notes: Journey may be commenced at either end, believec to be world's longest 10¼in gauge line. Built on the old Wells & Fakenham Railway trackbed. Old Swainsthorpe signalbox on site at Wells. Motive power is provided b a Garratt locomotive
Membership details: Wells & Walsingham Light Railway Suppo. Group, Mr. Crofts Esq, 49 Ditton Hill Road, Ditton Hill, Surrey
Membership journal: Newsletter - quarterly

West Lancashire Light Railway SC

Location: Alty's Brickworks. Station Road, Hesketh Bank, near Preston, Lancashire
OS reference: SD 448229
Operating society/organisation: The West Lancashire Light Railway Association, Secretary, 790 Ormskirk Road, Pemberton, Wigan WN5 8AX
Telephone: (0942) 218078 (Secretary)
Car parks: On site
Access by public transport: BR to Preston or Southport. Bus route 100 and 102. Between Preston and Southport
On site facilities: Gift shop, light refreshments, 2ft gauge line
Public opening: Easter weekend (not Saturday); May Day Bank Holiday Sunday and Monday; Spring Bank Holiday, then every Sunday until end of October. Opening times 12.30-17.00
Special events: Enthusiast's Day 12 July; Santa Specials 6, 13 20 December

Industrial locomotives

Name	*No*	*Builder*	*Type*	*Bui*
Clwyd	1	R/Hornsby (264251)	4wDM	195
Tawd	2	R/Hornsby (222074)	4wDM	194
Irish Mail	3	Hunslet (823)	0-4-0ST	190
—	4	Hibberd (1777)	4wPM	193
—	5	R/Hornsby (200478)	4wDM	194
—	7	M/Rail (8992)	4wDM	194
—	8	H/Hunslet (4480)	4wDM	195
—	9	K/Stuart (2405)	0-6-0T	191
—	10	Hibberd (2555)	4wDM	194
—	16	R/Hornsby (202036)	4wDM	194
Trent	18	R/Hornsby (283057)	4wDM	194
—	19	Lister (10805)	4wPM	193
—	20	Baguley (3002)	4wPM	193
—	21	H/Hunslet (1963)	4wDM	193
—	25	R/Hornsby (297054)	4wDM	195
—	26	M/Rail (11223)	4wDM	196
Mill Reef	27	M/Rail (7371)	4wDM	193
Red Rum	29	M/Rail (7105)	4wDM	193
—	30	M/Rail (11258)	4wDM	196
Montalban	34	O&K (6641)	0-4-0WT	191
Utrillas	35	O&K (2378)	0-4-0WT	190
—	36	R/Hornsby (339105)	4wDM	195
—	38	Hudswell (D750)	0-4-0DM	194
*Jonathan**	—	Hunslet (678)	0-4-0ST	189

*On loan from The Lytham Creek Motive Power Museum

Note: 30 M/Rail (11258) is presently on loan to Steamport Southport

Stock
Toastrack coach built 1986 by WLLR
Brake van built 1987 by WLLR
Large collection various wagons

West Somerset Railway

ınning for 20 miles, this is
itain's longest preserved railway
.d evokes all the atmosphere of a
untry railway from a more
.sured age. The line is host to
veral societies and groups, and
veral stations have their own
ıseum, such as the Somerset and
ɔrset Trust; at Washford. There are
me idyllic country stations in the
ıantock Hills and Dunster station
rved for many years as the model
r Hornby Dublo's branch line
ıtion

anaging Director: Mark L. Smith
eadquarters: West Somerset
ilway, The Railway Station,
inehead, Somerset
lephone: Minehead (0643)
4996. Talking timetable: 0643
7650
ain station: Minehead
her public stations: Dunster, Blue
ıchor, Washford, Watchet,
illiton, Doniford Beach Halt,
ogumber, Crowcombe, Bishop's
'deard
S reference: Minehead SS 975463,
illiton ST 085416, Bishops
'deard ST 164290
ır parks: Minehead, Williton,
shops Lydeard. Some parking at
l stations except Washford and
ɔniford Beach
:cess by public transport: Nearest
R station, Taunton
freshment facilities: Minehead,
shop's Lydeard (limited opening),
illiton (limited opening). Wine
.d Dine trains. Buffet car on most
eam trains
uvenir shops: Minehead, Bishop's
'deard
useum: Somerset & Dorset
ilway Museum Trust, Washford.
WR Museum at Blue Anchor
epots: Bishop's Lydeard, Williton,
ashford, Minehead
ngth of line: 20 miles
ssenger trains: Steam and diesel
ains to Bishops Lydeard
riod of public operation: SAE for
tails
ecial events: Gala Week,
ptember
cilities for disabled: Parking
ace level with entrance. No steps

Locomotives

Name	*No*	*Origin*	*Class*	*Type*	*Built*
—	53808	S&DJR	7F	2-8-0	1925
—	3205	GWR	2251	0-6-0	1946
—	3850	GWR	2884	2-8-0	1942
—	4160	GWR	5101	2-6-2T	1948
—	4561	GWR	4500	2-6-2T	1924
—	5542*	GWR	4575	2-6-2T	1928
—	6412	GWR	6400	0-6-0PT	1934
Dinmore Manor	7820†	GWR	'Manor'	4-6-0	1950
Western Yeoman	D1035	BR	52	C-C	1962
—	D2271	BR	04	0-6-0DM	1952
—	D2994	BR	07	0-6-0DE	1962
—	D7017	BR	35	B-B	1962
—	D7018	BR	35	B-B	1964
—	D9500	BR	14	0-6-0DH	1964
—	D9502	BR	14	0-6-0DH	1964
—	D9526	BR	14	0-6-0DH	1964
—	D9551	BR	14	0-6-0DH	1965

*Undergoing restoration at Taunton
†Undergoing restoration at Birmingham Railway Museum, Tyseley

Industrial locomotives

Name	*No*	*Builder*	*Type*	*Built*
Portbury	S3	Avonside (1764)	0-6-0ST	1917
—	—	Bagnall (2473)	0-4-0ST	1932
*Jennifer**	20	H/Clarke (1731)	0-6-0T	1942
Isabel	—	H/Leslie (3437)	0-6-0ST	1919
Kilmersdon	—	Peckett (1788)	0-4-0ST	1929
—	24	Ruston (210479)	4wDM	1941
—	—	Ruston (183062)	4wDM	1937
—	57	Sentinel (10214)	0-6-0DM	1964

*May not be on site for all of 1992 season

Stock

20 ex-BR Mk 1 coaches; 1 ex-BR Mk 2 coach; 2 ex-BR Restaurant cars; 7 ex-GWR camping coaches; 1 ex-BR Mk 1 Sleeper; 1 ex-GWR Sleeping Coach; 1 ex-SR 'Ironclad' coach; 2 Park Royal 2-car diesel multiple-units (50415, 50414, 56168, 56169); 1 Cravens 2-car diesel multiple-unit (51485, 56121); 1 ex-GWR Hawksworth coach; 1 ex-GWR 5-ton hand crane; more than 40 freight vehicles

Owners

53808, S3, *Isabel, Kilmersdon* and Bagnall 2473 (the Somerset & Dorset Museum Trust)
D7017 and D9526 (the Diesel and Electric Group)
5542 (the 5542 Fund)
3205 (the 2251 Class Fund)
3850 and 7820 (the 3850 Preservation Society)
4160 (4160 Ltd)
D1035 (Foster Yeoman Ltd — actually D1010)

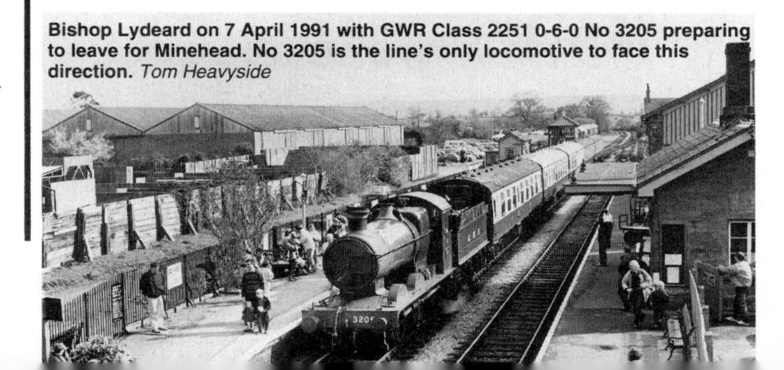

Bishop Lydeard on 7 April 1991 with GWR Class 2251 0-6-0 No 3205 preparing to leave for Minehead. No 3205 is the line's only locomotive to face this direction. *Tom Heavyside*

to shop or booking office, level access to toilets (disabled toilets at Minehead 100yd from station). Special saloon *Lorna Doone* accommodates 12 wheel chairs and has disabled toilet. Advanced booking essential. Catering facilities can be reached without difficulties. Groups can be catered for.
Membership details: West Somers Railway Association, c/o above address
Membership journal: *WSR Journal* — quarterly

West Yorkshire Transport Museum M

The West Yorkshire Transport Museum's collection consists of some 70 items, of which 13 are rail or tramway vehicles. It is hoped to progressively reopen the Spen Valley Railway, commencing at Low Moor. The railway would be all electric, traction being by integral battery, or overhead electric supply.

Two locomotives and five trams are to be seen at the Ludlam Street Depot. Also stored at Ludlam Street are about 50 road vehicles, mostly motorbuses, but including five trolleybuses and service vehicles.

Recently approved plans will see the opening of the West Yorkshire Transport Centre at Low Moor, Bradford, in the spring of 1994. Proposed attractions include the operation of trams, trolleybuses and rail vehicles backed by extensive interpretation of the West Yorkshire Transport story

Location: Ludlam Street Depot, Mill Lane, off Manchester Road, Bradford, 400yd south of Bradford Interchange, just off A641
OS reference: SE 164322
Chief Executive: Michael Haynes
Operating society/organisation: West Yorkshire Transport Museum Trust Ltd, Ludlam Street Depot, Mill Lane, off Manchester Road
Telephone: Bradford (0274) 736006
Car park: Yes, free
Access by public transport: Rail/road: 10min walk from Bradford Interchange station, 2min walk from nearest Manchester Road bus stops
On site facilities: Viewing of motorbuses, trolleybuses and trams at Ludlam Street; rides on preserved motorbuses are available; souvenir shop and light refreshments available. Special events as advertised
Public opening: Ludlam Street is open every Sunday, from 11.00-17.00. Parties welcome at other times by prior arrangement. Detail of special events, etc, may be obtained by telephoning the museum.
Facilities for disabled: No special toilet facilities, but all parts of museum accessible by wheelchair
Membership details: The Secretar The West Yorkshire Transport Museum Society, c/o above addres The Society provides volunteers who support the project in many ways, including the restoration of Trust-owned exhibits. Telephone the museum for details
Membership Journal: *Newsline*

Locomotives

Name	*No*	*Origin*	*Class*	*Type*	*Buil*
Electra	27000*	BR	EM2	Co-Co	195

*Not on site

Industrial locomotives (all electric)

Name	*No*	*Builder*	*Type*	*Buil*
—	10	Siemens	Bo	191
—	1	E/Electric	Bo	193

Stock
Derby 'Lightweight' Battery Electric unit Sc79998/9 (on loan to East Lancashire Railway); Class 506 Electric Unit — 59404/504/604 (on loan to Midland Railway Centre); 1 Blackpool tram 663; 1 Rotterdam tram 408; 2 Budapest trams 2576/2577; 1 Brussels tram 96; Various tram bodies

Winchcombe Railway Museum M

Three miles from the Gloucestershire-Warwickshire railway, the diverse collection includes signalling equipment, lineside fixtures, horse-drawn road vehicles, tickets, lamps, etc. Indoor and outdoor displays set in ½ acre of traditional Victorian Cotswold Garden. Visitors are encouraged to touch exhibits
Location: 23 Gloucester Street, Winchcombe, Gloucestershire
OS reference: SP 023283
Operating society/organisation: Winchcombe Railway Museum Association, 23 Gloucester Street, Winchcombe, Gloucestershire
Telephone: Winchcombe (0242) 602257/620641
Car Park: On street at entrance
Access by public transport: Bus service from Cheltenham operated by Castleways Ltd
On site facilities: Relic, refreshments and souvenir shop
Public opening: Daily Easter to October 13.30-18.00. Weekends an holidays only November to March 13.30-dusk
Facilities for disabled: Access to a parts except toilets
Special notes: Many visitor-operated exhibits

Scotland

Bo'ness & Kinneil Railway SC

few miles west of Edinburgh, this
ilway has won several awards,
rticularly for its recreated station
ildings — the entire railway has
en constructed on a 'green field
e'. Achieved in 1989 was the
tension of the operating line
land to Birkhill where the railway
ovides access to a new attraction,
e Birkhill Clay Mine
cation: Scottish Railway
eservation Society, Bo'ness
ation, Union Street, Bo'ness, West
thian, EH51 0AD
cess by public transport: Nearest
R stations — Falkirk Grahamston,
nlithgow, Dalmeny
S reference: NT 003817
lephone: Bo'ness (0506) 822298
ain station: Bo'ness
r park: At the site (free)
freshment facilities: Bo'ness
ufferstop' cafe with snacks,
licensed
uvenir shop: Bo'ness and
condhand sale first Sunday
roughout the year
pot: Bo'ness
ngth of line: 3½ miles
ssenger trains: Please contact for
tails
riod of public operation: Please
ntact for details
ecial events: Please contact for
tails
cilities for disabled: At Bo'ness
r shop and cafeteria

Locomotives

Name	No	Origin	Class	Type	Built
Sovereign	44871	LMS	5MT	4-6-0	1945
—	419	CR	439	0-4-4T	1908
—	1313	SJ	B	4-6-0	1917
Morayshire	246	LNER	D49	4-4-0	1928
Maude	673	NBR	—	0-6-0	1891
—	80105	BR	4MT	2-6-4T	1955
—	8 (D9524)	BR	14	0-6-0DH	1964
—	D8020	BR	20	Bo-Bo	1959
—	25235 (D7585)	BR	25	Bo-Bo	1965
—	D5351	BR	27	Bo-Bo	1961

Industrial locomotives

Name	No	Builder	Type	Built
Clydesmill	3	Barclay (1937)	0-4-0ST	1928
—	3	Barclay (2046)	0-4-0ST	1937
—	24	Barclay (2335)	0-6-0T	1953
Texaco	—	Fowler (4210140)	0-4-0DM	1958
Lord King	—	H/Leslie (3640)	0-4-0ST	1926
—	19	Hunslet (3818)	0-6-0ST	1954
DS3	—	R/Hornsby (275883)	4wDM	1949
DS4	P6687	R/Hornsby (312984)	0-4-0DE	1951
(Ranald)	—	Sentinel (9627)	4wVBT	1957
—	970214	Wickham (6050)	2w-2PMR	c1951
—	—	Matisa (48626)	—	—
—	5	Hunslet (3837)	0-6-0ST	1955
—	(7)	Bagnall (2777)	0-6-0ST	1945
Borrowstounness	—*	Barclay (840)	0-4-0T	1899
—	—*	M/Rail (110U082)	4wDH	1970
—	—	Wickham (10482)	2w-2PMR	1970
—	(17)	Hunslet (2880)	0-6-0ST	1943
—	970213	Wickham (6049)	2w-2PMR	c1951

ght:
) 2392 was a visitor from the NYMR ring 1991. It is seen here on the June whilst heading the last train of e day to Birkhill. *Melvyn Hopwood*

Name	No	Builder	Type	Built
—	17	Barclay (2296)	0-4-0ST	1952
Lady Victoria	3	Barclay (1458)	0-6-0ST	1916
The Wemyss Coal Co Ltd	20	Barclay (2068)	0-6-0T	1939
—	(6)	Barclay (2127)	0-4-0CT	1942
No 1	—	Barclay (343)	0-6-0DM	1941
City of Aberdeen	—	B/Hawthorn (912)	0-4-0ST	1887
F82 (Fairfield)	—	E/Electric (1131)	4wBE	1940
(Ellesmere) (244)	—	Hawthorns (Leith)	0-4-0WT	1861
Kelton Fell	13	Neilson (2203)	0-4-0ST	1876
— (5710)	(1)	Neilson Reid	0-6-0T	1902
—	—	N/British (27415)	0-4-0DH	1954
Kilbagie	DS2	R/Hornsby (262998)	4wDM	1949
DS6	(1)	R/Hornsby (421439)	0-4-0DE	1958
St Mirren	(3)	R/Hornsby 423658)	0-4-0DE	1958
—	D88/003	R/Hornsby (506500)	4wDM	1965
—	(DS5)	R/Hornsby (423662)	0-4-0DE	1958
—	—	BTH	4wE	1908
(Denis)	—	Sentinel (9631)	4wVBT	1958
—	—	Arrols (Glasgow)	2w-2DM	c196

*3ft 0in gauge

Stock
A large selection of coaching stock, many built by Scottish pre-Grouping companies, and an appropriate collection of early freight vehicles

Owners
80105 and (*Denis*) (owned by Scottish Locomotive Owners Group)
246 and 24 (owned by Royal Museum of Scotland)

Caledonian Railway (Brechin) SC

Information enquiries: Iain A. H. Smith, Publicity Director, c/o 30 Moathill East, Cupar, Fife KY15 4DT
Headquarters: Caledonian Railway (Brechin) Ltd, The Station, 2 Park Road, Brechin, Angus DD9 7AF
Telephone: (0334) 55965, after 4.30pm Mon-Fri or George Mitchell (03562) 4562 after 4.30pm
Main station: Brechin
Other public stations: Bridge of Dun
OS reference: NO 603603
Car park: Brechin, Bridge of Dun
Access by public transport: Nearest BR station — Montrose, 9 miles. Local bus operator, Strathtay Scottish
Refreshment facilities: Light refreshments available during steamdays at Brechin

Locomotives

Name	No	Origin	Class	Type	Built
—	46464	LMS	2MT	2-6-0	195
—	D2866	BR	02	0-4-0DM	196
Brechin City	D3059	BR	08	0-6-0DE	195
—	D8056	BR	20	Bo-Bo	196
—	27001	BR	27	Bo-Bo	196

Industrial locomotives

Name	No	Builder	Type	Built
—	6	Bagnall (2749)	0-6-0ST	194
Bon Accord	2	Barclay (807)	0-4-0ST	189
—	1	Barclay (1863)	0-4-0ST	192
Diana	1	Hunslet (2897)	0-6-0ST	194
Yard No DY326	—	Hibberd (3743)	4wDM	195
—	2/88	R/Hornsby (275880)	4wDM	194
—	6	R/Hornsby (421700)	4wDM	195

Stock
3-car Class 126 diesel multiple-unit, Nos 51017, 51043, 59404; 3 ex-BR Mk 1 TSOs; 1 ex-BR Mk 1 BSK; 1 ex-BR Suburban; 1 ex-BR Engineers Inspection Saloon; 1 ex-BR Mk 1 sleeping car; 1 ex-BR Full Kitchen Car; Various items of freight stock

ouvenir shop: Brechin
useum: Brechin
ength of line: 4 miles
epot: Brechin
assenger trains: Please contact for etails
eriod of public operation: Please ontact for details
pecial events: Please contact for etails
acilities for disabled: Easy access both stations, access to toilets and op, passengers can be assisted on nd off trains by railway staff

Owners
Bon Accord (Aberdeen Town Council)
Class 126 DMU (the Swindon Preservation Society)
27001 (the Class 27 Locomotive Group)

Disclaimer: The Caledonian Railway (Brechin) Ltd, reserve the right to amend, cancel or add to these events. And whilst every effort will be made to maintain the above services, the company does not guarantee that trains will depart or arrive at the time stated and reserves the right to suspend or alter any train without notice and will not accept any liability for loss, inconvenience or delay thereby caused
Membership details: Murray D. Duncan, 2 Binghill Crescent, Milltimber, Aberdeen

Glasgow Museum of Transport M

lasgow's magnificent railway ollection represents one of the best forts by a municipal authority to reserve a representative collection items appropriate to the ocomotive builders to the Empire'. 1989 the collection opened to ew once again in its new setting at e former Kelvin Hall
ccess by public transport: trathclyde PTE Underground elvinhall: Strathclyde Buses 6, 6A, 8A, 9, 9A, 16, 42, 42A, 44A, 57, 7A, 62, 62A, 62B, 64; Kelvin cottish Buses 5, 5A; Clydeside cottish Buses 17
perating society/organisation: lasgow City Council, Museums & rt Galleries Department
ocation: Museum of Transport, elvin Hall, 1 Bunhouse Road, lasgow G3 8DP
elephone: 041-357-3929
ar park: Opposite Museum ntrance

Locomotives

Name	*No*	*Origin*	*Class*	*Type*	*Built*
—	123	CR	123	4-2-2	1886
—	9	G&SWR	5	0-6-0T	1917
—	103	HR	—	4-6-0	1894
Glen Douglas	256	NBR	K	4-4-0	1913
Gordon Highlander	49	GNSR	F	4-4-0	1920

Industrial locomotives

Name	*No*	*Builder*	*Type*	*Built*
—	1	Barclay (1571)	0-6-0F	1917
—	—	Chaplin (2368)	0-4-0TG	1888
—	—	BEV (583)	B	1927

Stock
Glasgow District Subway car 39T; Glasgow Corporation Underground cars 1 and 4; LMS King George VI's saloon 498 of 1941

On site facilities: Toilets, cafeteria, shop and public telephone
Public opening: Monday-Saturday 10.00-17.00; Sunday 14.00-17.00. Closed 1 January and 25 December only
Facilities for disabled: Access to all areas but entry via separate entrance — enquire at main door

Lochty Railway SC

eadquarters: 23 Millfield, Cupar, ife KY15 5UT
S reference: NO 522080
elephone: 0334 54815 (Mon-Sat nly)
lain station: Lochty
ar park: Lochty
ccess by public transport: 10 iles from Cupar, 7 miles from rail (B940). BR 10 miles from upar, then taxi; Kirkcaldy 18 iles, bus to Crail, then taxi
ouvenir shop: Lochty

Locomotives

Name	*No*	*Origin*	*Class*	*Type*	*Built*
Union of South Africa	60009	LNER	A4	4-6-2	1937

Industrial locomotives

Name	*No*	*Builder*	*Type*	*Built*
—	1	Peckett (1376)	0-4-0ST	1915
—	LPR No 16	Bagnall (2759)	0-6-0ST	1944
North British	LPR No 4	R/Hornsby (421415)	4wDM	1958
—	NCB 21	Barclay (2292)	0-4-0ST	1951
Forth	SGB 10	Barclay (1890)	0-4-0ST	1926
—	NCB 10	N/British (27591)	0-6-0DH	1957
—	LPR 34	R/Hornsby (506399)	0-4-0DH	1964
River Eden	RAF 400	N/British (27421)	0-4-0DH	1955
River Tay	RAF 405	N/British (27426)	0-4-0DH	1955

Passenger trains: Steam-hauled from Lochty through the estate of J. B. Cameron (1½ miles)
Period of public operation: Please contact for details
Special notes: This line was opened as Scotland's first preserved railway in 1967. No statutory authority was required to open the line, now in its 25th year
Membership details: c/o above address

Locomotive notes: SGB 10 is the usual service locomotive.

Note: No 60009 *Union of South Africa* is stored at Markinch station for main line use on railtours.

Stock
3 ex-BR Mk 1 coaches; 1 ex-BR Shark ballast brake van; 1 LNER observation coach; 1 ex-NBR 8-ton box van (built 1901); 13 assorted private owner wagons; 1 flat wagon

Mull Rail

General Manager: Graham E. Ellis
Operations Manager: Roger Nichols
Operating society/organisation: Mull & West Highland (NG) Railway Co Ltd, Old Pier Station, Craignure, Isle of Mull PA65 6AY
Telephone: 06802 494 (during operating period); 0680 300389 (out of season
OS reference: Sheet 49, 725369
Car park: At Craigmure, free
Access by public transport: Caledonian Macbrayne ferry from Oban (40min sail)
On site facilities: Gift shop
Length of line: 1¼ miles/10¼ in gauge

Locomotives

Name	*No*	*Builder*	*Type*	*Buil*
Lady of the Isles	—	Marsh	2-6-2T	198
Waverley	—	Curwen	4-4-2	194
—	—	Alcock	4w-4PM	197
Glen Auldyn	—	Davies	8wDH	198

Rolling stock
11 coaches (two with wheelchair accommodation); 3 bogie wagons; 1 4-wheel wagon

Public opening: Easter, then daily 12 April-10 October
Facilities for disabled: No steps on railway, two compartments for wheelchairs

Membership details: Friends of Mull Rail, M. R. Oliver, Kilmory Drive, Lochgilphead, Argyll
Membership journal: *Crankpin Journal* — annual

Paddle Steamer Preservation Society

The PS *Waverley* was built to the order of the London & North Eastern Railway in 1946; she replaced a vessel of the same name which was sunk off Dunkirk during May 1940. Sold to the PSPS in 1974 she now offers cruises around the coast of the United Kingdom in company with MV *Balmoral*. Also in the 'fleet' is PS *Kingswear Castle* which cruises on the Thames and Medway

General Manager: D. K. Duncanson
Headquarters: Waverley Excursions Ltd, Waverley Terminal, Anderston Quay, Glasgow G3 8HA
Telephone: 041 221 8162
On ship facilities: All vessels have catering facilities, bars, toilets (disabled only on Waverley)
Membership details: Paddle Steamer Preservation Society, PO Box 385, Hazlemere, High Wycombe HP11 1AE
Membership journal: *Paddlewheels* — quarterly

Details of all the cruises operated b the three vessels can be obtained from the above headquarters

Scottish Industrial Railway Centre SC

'he Scottish Industrial Railway
:entre is based on part of the former
)almellington Iron Co railway
ystem which was one of the best
nown industrial railway networks
n Britain. Steam worked up until
978 when the system closed and it
s the aim of the centre to recreate
art of the railway. The Ayrshire
:ailway Preservation Group also
wn the former G&SWR station at
Vaterside, 2 miles from the centre,
nd have access to the former NCB
ocomotive shed and wagon
vorkshops at Waterside. These
ocations are not yet open to the
eneral public. Working in
onjunction with the Dalmellington
: District Conservation Trust it is
oped to create an industrial
eritage centre at Waterside based
n the iron, coal and brick making
ndustries

ocation: Scottish Industrial
:ailway Centre, Minnivey Colliery,
)almellington, Ayrshire

)S reference: NS 476074

)perating society/organisation:
yrshire Railway Preservation
iroup

'elephone: The Secretary (0292)
13579

ength of line: ¼-mile

ccess by public transport: Nearest
R station, Ayr (14 miles). Western
cottish bus service from Ayr, Nos
2/53. Tel: (0292) 264643

)n site facilities: Steam-hauled
rake van rides. Guided tours of
entre, museum of railway relics
nd photographs, souvenir shop,
uffet and locomotive shed

'ublic opening: Open for static
isplay with limited facilities every
aturday, June to end September

pecial events: Steam Open Days
1992: 31 May; 27/28* June; 5,12, 19, 25/26* July; 9, 29/30* August; 27 September. *Fireless locomotive expected to be in steam. Opening times: 11.00-16.00

Membership details: Mr Frank Beattie, 1 McKnight Avenue, Waterside, Fenwick, Kilmarnock, Ayrshire

Special notes: For further information and details of special events, telephone the Doon Valley Heritage Office (0292) 531144 daytime, (0292) 313579 evenings and weekends, or write to Gordon Thomson, 8 Burnside Place, Troon, Ayrshire KA10 6LZ (SAE appreciated)

Locomotives

Name	No	Origin	Class	Type	Built
—	MP228 (12052)	BR	11	0-6-0DE	1949
—	MP229 (12093)	BR	11	0-6-0DE	1951

Industrial locomotives

Name	No	Builder	Type	Built
—	16	A/Barclay (1116)	0-4-0ST	1910
—	8	A/Barclay (1296)	0-6-0T	1912
—	19	A/Barclay (1614)	0-4-0ST	1918
Aberdeen Corporation Gas Works	3	A/Barclay (1889)	0-4-0ST	1926
—	8	A/Barclay (1952)	0-4-0F	1928
—	10	A/Barclay (2244)	0-4-0ST	1947
NCB No 23	—	A/Barclay (2260)	0-4-0ST	1949
—	25	A/Barclay (2358)	0-6-0ST	1954
—	1	A/Barclay (2368)	0-4-0ST	1955
—	118	A/Barclay (366)	0-4-0DM	1940
—	7	A/Barclay (399)	0-4-0DM	1956
Lily of the Valley	—	Fowler (22888)	0-4-0DM	1943
—	—	R/Hornsby (224352)	4wDM	1943
Blinkin Bess	—	R/Hornsby (284839)	4wDM	1950
Johnnie Walker	—	R/Hornsby (417890)	4wDM	1959
—	—	R/Hornsby (421697)	0-4-0DM	1959
—	107	Hunslet (3132)	0-4-0DM	1944
—	—	Sentinel (10012)	4wDM	1959
—	—	Donnelli (163)	4wDMR	1979
(3ft gauge)				
—	—	R/Hornsby(256273)	4wDM	1949
—	—	Hunslet(8816)	4wDH	1981
(2ft 6in gauge)				
—	2	R/Hornsby (183749)	4wDM	1937
—	3	R/Hornsby (210959)	4wDM	1941
—	1	R/Hornsby (211681)	4wDM	1942

Note: Not all vehicles on public display

Stock

2 Wickham trolleys; 1 steam crane; various other items

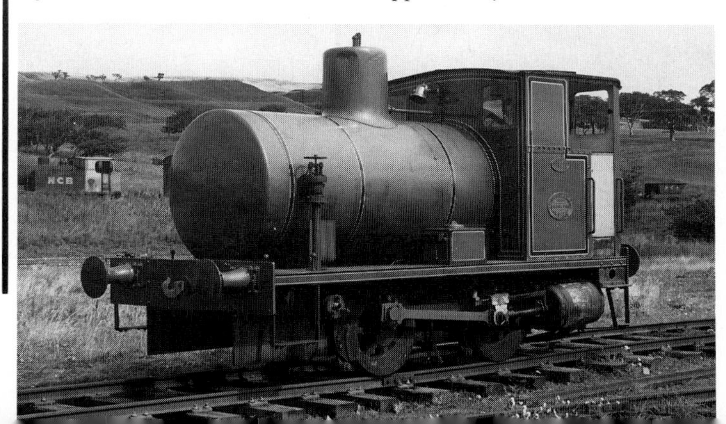

?ight:
'his unusual looking locomotive is an -4-0 fireless example. Worked by high ressure steam from an external ource this type was used in situations 'here a stray spark from the fire could ause severe problems. This Barclay-uilt example previously worked at the hell Refinery at Ardrossan.
ndrew R. Smith

Scottish Mining Museum — Prestongrange SC

Location: On the B1348 between Musselburgh and Prestonpans.
OS reference: NT 734737
Operating society/organisation: Scottish Mining Museum Trust, Lady Victoria Colliery, Newtongrange, Midlothian EH22 4QN
Telephone: 031-663-7519
Car park: On site
On site facilities: Visitor Centre — 'The Scottish Collieries', a photographic exhibition and a display of mining equipment. Machine Exhibition Hall, Cornish Beam Pumping Engine installed in 1874. In the David Spence Gallery, the former Power House, 'Cutting the Coal', an exhibition which traces the changing methods of cutting coal. There is an underground gallery, a coalface, a reconstruction of a colliery workshop and a magnificent collection of coal cutting machines and equipment
Toilets: Visitor Centre
Refreshment facilities: Available at Visitor Centre

Industrial locomotives

Name	*No*	*Builder*	*Type*	*Built*
—	6	A/Barclay (2043)	0-4-0ST	1937
—	17	A/Barclay (2219)	0-4-0ST	1946
Prestongrange	7	G/Ritchie (536)	0-4-2ST	1914
Tomatin	1	M/Rail (9925)	4wDM	1963
—	—*	Hunslet (4440)	4wDM	1952
—	32	R/Hornsby	4wDM	
—	33	R/Hornsby	4wDM	

*2ft gauge

Rolling stock
Steam crane, Whittaker No 30, c1890, occasionally in steam

Locomotive notes: *Prestongrange* is expected to be out of service during 1992, 6 to be available for passenger trains

Public opening: 1 April to the end of September, 11.00-16.00, last tour at 15.00
Length of line: 400m (standard gauge) extension in progress
Facilities for disabled: Access and toilet at Visitor Centre. Access to 'Cutting the Coal' exhibition, and footpaths along the site
Special events: Steam during summer months — date to be confirmed
Special notes: Locomotive in steam first Sunday of month April-September, passenger rides available. Advance notice is required for large parties
Membership details: Friends of the Scottish Mining Museum, Elaine Carmichael c/o above address
Contact: Charles Young, The Prestongrange Society, The Smiddy Middleton, Midlothian

Strathspey Railway

Scotland's steam railway in the highlands connects the busy tourist resort at Aviemore to the more traditional highland village of Boat of Garten, famed as one of the few nesting places of the osprey (viewing site 3 miles from station). A feature of the railway is the special evening dinner and Sunday lunch trains. The former operating during June/August, the latter throughout the season
General Manager: Colin Houston
Enquiries: Aviemore Speyside Station, Dalfaber Road, Aviemore, Inverness-shire PH22 1PM
Telephone: (0479) 810725
Main station: Aviemore (Speyside)
Other public stations: Boat of Garten
OS reference: Aviemore NH 898131, Boat of Garten NH 943789

Locomotives

Name	*No*	*Origin*	*Class*	*Type*	*Built*
—	5025	LMS	5MT	4-6-0	1934
—	46512	LMS	2MT	2-6-0	1952
—	828	CR	812	0-6-0	1899
—	08490	BR	08	0-6-0DE	1958
—	D5394	BR	27	Bo-Bo	1962

Locomotive notes: In service 5025, D5394. Under restoration 46512, 828. Under repair 08490.

Industrial locomotives

Name	*No*	*Builder*	*Type*	*Built*
—	48	Hunslet (2864)	0-6-0ST	1943
Cairngorm	9	RSH (7097)	0-6-0ST	1943
—	60	Hunslet (3686)	0-6-0ST	1948
Victor	2996	Bagnall (2996)	0-6-0ST	1951
Niddrie	6	Barclay (1833)	0-6-0ST	1924
*Forth**	10	Barclay (1890)	0-4-0ST	1926
Dailuaine	1	Barclay (2073)	0-4-0ST	1939
Balmenach	2	Barclay (2020)	0-4-0ST	1936
—	17	Barclay (2017)	0-6-0T	1935
Inveresk	14	R/Hornsby (260756)	0-4-0DM	1950
Inverdon	15	Simplex (5763)	4wDM	1957
—	16	North British (27549)	0-4-0DM	1951
Queen Anne	20	R/Hornsby (265618)	4wDM	1948

*Not on site

Car parks: Aviemore and Boat of Garten
Access by public transport: BR services and express bus to Aviemore. Highland buses local service to Boat of Garten
Refreshment facilities: On train buffet car or facilities on many trains. Evening and Sunday lunch time diner trains — booking essential — Tel: 047 983 258 for details/bookings
Souvenir shop: Boat of Garten and Aviemore (Speyside)
Museum: Small relics display at Boat of Garten
Depot: Aviemore (not open to public)
Length of line: 5 miles
Journey time: 17min, return within the hour possible on most services
Passenger trains: Steam- and some diesel-hauled services. Boat of Garten-Aviemore
Period of public operation: 28/29 March; Wednesdays 1 April-28 October; Sundays 5 April-25 October; Mondays 4, 25 May, 28 September; Daily 23 May-4 September and 21-27 September; Mondays-Fridays 7-30 September. Santa Specials 19/20, 26/27 31 December.
Special events: 28 March — Members' Day; 29 March — Mad March Fares; 23/34 May — Boat of Garten Beer Festival; 26/27 September — Friends of Thomas the Tank Engine Weekend (check for details
Facilities for disabled: Access possible at Boat of Garten and Aviemore (Speyside). Please contact in advance for directions and if a party involved
Special notes: First and third class travel available on most trains. Family fares available for third class travel. Special rates/arrangements for parties.
Membership details: Strathspey Railway Association at above address
Membership journal: *Speyside Express* — quarterly

Locomotive notes: In service 60, 2996.

Stock
18 ex-BR coaches; 5 ex-LMS coaches; 1 Pullman coach; 3 ex-LMS sleeping cars; 1 ex-LNER sleeping car; 1 ex-LNWR coach; 1 ex-HR coach; 1 ex-NBR coach; 1 ex-GNSR coach; Numerous examples of rolling stock

Owners
6, 17 and 46512 (the Highland Locomotive Co Ltd)
828 (the Scottish Locomotive Preservation Trust Fund)

Summerlee Heritage Centre M

Social and industrial history museum, interprets the communities in the west of Scotland in the 19th and 20th centuries. Working machinery in reconstructed workshops
General Manager: Stephen Kay
Operating society/organisation: Summerlee Heritage Trust, West Canal Street, Coatbridge, ML5 1QD
Telephone: 0236 31261
Public opening: Daily 10.00-17.00, except 25/26 December and 1/2 January
Access by public transport: BR Coatbridge Central and Coatbridge Sunnyside. Local buses
Car park: Opposite site
On site facilities: Tearoom, gift shop. Working electric tramway with cars from Motherwell, Brussels and Graz
Special events: Organised events from April-October, details on request
Facilities for disabled: Toilets, wheelchair available

Locomotives

Name	*No*	*Origin*	*Class*	*Type*	*Built*
Springbok (3ft 6in gauge)	4112	SAR	GMAM	4-8-2+2-8-4	1956

Industrial locomotives

Name	*No*	*Builder*	*Type*	*Built*
—	—	H/Clarke(895)	0-6-0T	1909
—	—	G/Hogg	0-4-0T	1898

Stock
2 rail mounted steam cranes

Below:
An ex-Brussels tram is seen alongside the Marshall Fleming steam crane which was overhauled at Summerlee. *Summerlee Heritage Trust*

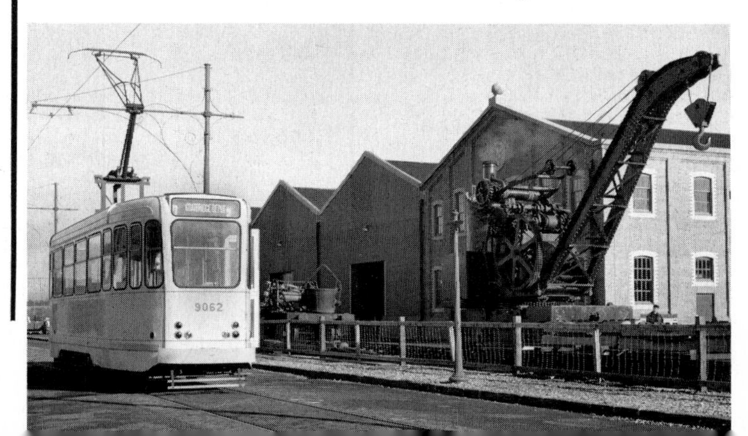

Bala Lake Railway (Rheilffordd Llyn Tegid)

Although narrow gauge, this railway is built over the old standard gauge branch to Bala, which is the line's north-eastern terminus. The railway's headquarters are to be found in the fine old station building at Llanuwchllyn at the other end of the line. Do not be deterred by the fact that the railway runs down the opposite shore of the lake to the main road — it is well worth the detour

General Manager: Roy Hardiman
Headquarters: Rheilffordd Llyn Tegid (Bala Lake Railway) Llanuwchllyn, Bala, Gwynedd LL23 7DD
Telephone: Llanuwchllyn (067 84) 666
Main station: Llanuwchllyn
Other public stations: Llangower, Bala
OS reference: Llanuwchllyn SH 880300, Bala SH 929350
Car parks: Llanuwchllyn, Llangower and Bala town centre
Access by public transport: Bus Gwynedd service No 94 to both Bala and Llanuwchllyn (from Wrexham or Barmouth)

Industrial locomotives

Name	No	Builder	Type	Built
Holy War	—	Hunslet (779)	0-4-0ST	1902
Maid Marian	—	Hunslet (822)	0-4-0ST	1903
Meirionnydd	—	Severn Lamb (7322)	Bo-Bo	1973
Chilmark	—	R/Hornsby (194771)	4wDM	1939
Indian Runner	—	R/Hornsby (200744)	4wDM	1940
—	—	Lister (34025)	4wDM	1949
—	—	Hudson (38384)	4wDM	1930
—	—	Motorail (5821)	4wDM	1934
—	—	R/Hornsby (209430)	4wDM	1942
—	—	R/Hornsby (189972)	4wDM	1938
—	—	Hibberd (FH2544)	4wDM	1941
—	—	Hunslet (1974)	4wDM	1939
Cernyw	—	R/Hornsby (200748)	4wDM	1940

Locomotive notes: *Holy War* and *Maid Marian* are in regular use, remainder are on static display

Road access: Off the A494 Bala-Dolgellau road
Refreshment facilities: Llanuwchllyn. Large picnic site with toilet facilities by lake at Llangower
Souvenir shop: Llanuwchllyn
Museum: Large collection of antique railway equipment
Depot: Llanuwchllyn
Length of line: 4½ miles, 1ft 11⅝in gauge
Passenger trains: Llanuwchllyn-Bala. Journey takes 25min in each direction
Period of public operation: 11 April-4 October
Facilities for disabled: Facilities available on most trains
Special notes: Small parties (10/12) may just turn up, but a day's notice for large parties would be helpful
Membership details: P. Briddon, 140 Earl Marshal Road, Sheffield S4 8LB
Membership journal: *Llanuwchllyn News* — approx 4 times a year

Brecon Mountain Railway

A narrow gauge passenger carrying railway close to Merthyr Tydfil built on part of the trackbed of the former Brecon & Merthyr Railway. Gradually being extended

Locomotives

Name	No	Builder	Type	Built
—	—	Baldwin (61269)	4-6-2	1930
Sybil	—	Hunslet (827)	0-4-0ST	1903
San Justo	4	H/Clarke (639)	0-4-2ST	1903
Santa Ana	—	H/Clarke (640)	0-4-2ST	1903
Graf Schwerin-Lörwitz	99.3353	Arn Jung (1261)	0-6-2WT	1908
—	—	O&K (12722)	0-4-0WT	1936
Pendyffryn	—	de Winton	0-4-0VBT	1894

ırthward, the railway has some
teresting narrow gauge steam
comotives imported from East and
est Germany and South Africa
neral Manager: A. S. Hills
adquarters: Brecon Mountain
ailway, Pant Station, Dowlais,
erthyr Tydfil, Mid Glamorgan
'48 2UP
lephone: Merthyr Tydfil (0685)
4854
ain station: Pant
ır park: Pant station
S reference: SO 063120
ccess by public transport:
mnibus to Pant Cemetery — ½
ourly frequency from Merthyr bus
ation. BR rail service to Merthyr
om Cardiff Central
epot: Pant

Redstone —		Redstone	0-4-0VBT	1905
Rhydychen —		Simplex (11177)	4wDM	1961
—	77	Hanomag (10629)	2-6-2+2-6-2	1928
—	—	Brecon MR (001)	0-6-0DH	1987
—	—	Brecon MR (003)	0-6-0DH	1987

Stock
9 bogie wagons; 2 balcony end 39-seat coaches; 2 balcony end 40-seat coaches; 1 20-seat Caboose' Miscellaneous rail carrying and ballast wagons; South African Railways Box Car; Diesel-hydraulic crane; Wickham petrol trolley

Length of line: 2 miles, 1ft 11¾in gauge
Period of public operation: Easter weekend; daily 1 May-mid-September
Refreshment facilities: Licensed restaurant at Pant, snackbar at Pontsticill
Special events: Santa Specials 5/6, 12/13, 19/20 December
Facilities for disabled: Toilets and ramps

Caerphilly Railway Society SC

n unusual collection in the
storic surroundings of the old
hymney Railway locomotive
orks, comprising a rare selection
locomotives and rolling stock
om both main line railways and
outh Wales industry.
The restored Brecon & Merthyr
ailway signalbox, with its unique
erlocking Saxby & Farmer lever
ame, is worth seeing
ompany secretary: John May
perating society: Caerphilly
ailway Society Ltd
ocation: Harold Wilson Industrial
state, Van Road, Caerphilly, Mid
amorgan
S reference: ST 163865
lephone: 0222 461414 (office
ours)
ır parking: Ample car parking
ailable at the depot
ublic transport: Approximately 1
ile from Caerphilly rail and bus
ations
n site facilities: Light snacks,
freshments and souvenirs
ailable on steam days
acilities for the disabled: No steps
e involved in gaining access to the
epot. Facilities are limited, but
elp readily given
ngth of line: ¾-mile
ublic opening: Static display every
unday 14.00-17.00

Locomotives

name	*No*	*Origin*	*Class*	*Type*	*Built*
—	41312	LMS	2MT	2-6-2T	1952
—	28	TVR	01	0-6-2T	1897
—	D2178	BR	03	0-6-0DM	1962

Industrial locomotives

Name	*No*	*Builder*	*Type*	*Built*
Victory	—	Barclay (2201)	0-4-0ST	1945
Forester	—	Barclay (1260)	0-4-0ST	1911
Desmond	—	Avonside (1498)	0-4-0ST	1906
Haulwen	—	V/Foundry (5272)	0-6-0ST	1945
—	—	Hunslet	0-6-0DM	1962
Deighton	—	YEC (2731)	0-4-0DE	1959

Locomotive notes: Locomotives operating from the 1992 season are expected to be *Victory* and D2178. Locomotives currently under repair are TVR 0-6-2T No 28, 41312 and *Deighton*. All others currently static/in store pending restoration.

Stock
GWR 6-ton hand crane and flat runner wagon; GWR 14-ton ballast wagon 60501; 3 wooden 7-plank mineral wagons;. 2 steel-framed oil tank wagons; BR Mk 1 BSK E34460 (internally converted to buffet facility); GWR 20-ton Toad goods brake van 35267; SR 4-wheel PMV 1168 (latterly mess and tool van); GWR/BR Fruit D W92040; LMS 12-ton boxvan 304986; GWR Mink D 28804 (latterly mess and tool van); Swansea Harbour Trust 4-wheel saloon carriage; TVR coach No 153; Pooley van

Owners
28 (the National Railway Museum, on loan from the Museum of Wales)
D2178 and Hunslet (on loan from National Smokeless Fuels)

Special events: For 1992 steam days please see railway press
Membership: Mr N. Radley, 3 Warwick Place, Cardiff, South Glamorgan

Conwy Valley Railway Museum

M

Conveniently situated alongside British Rail's Betws-y-Coed station, the Museum presents some well-displayed distractions to pass the time including model train layouts to delight both adult and child
Location: Adjacent to Betws-y-Coed station
OS reference: SH 796565
General Manager: Mr C. M. Cartwright
Operating society/organisation: Conwy Valley Railway Museum, The Old Goods Yard, Betws-y-Coed, Gwynedd
Telephone: (06902) 568
Car park: On site

Locomotives

Name	No	Builder	Type	Built
Britannia	70000	TMA Engineering (1ft 3in gauge)	4-6-2	1988
*Old Rube**	—	S/Lamb	2-8-0	—
*Katie**	—	S/Lamb	0-4-0ST	—

*7¼in gauge

Stock
1 GWR fitter's van; 1 LMS 6-wheel van; 1 LNER CCT van; 1 BR Mk 1 coach; 2 SR luggage vans; 1 Pullman coach

Access by public transport: Betws-y-Coed BR station
On site facilities: Refreshments in buffet car. Bookshop and model/gift shop in museum foyer, operating train layouts, miniature railway (1¼-miles, 7¼ in gauge) steam-hauled. Picnic area
Public opening: Daily Easter-end of October, 10.30-17.30
Facilities for disabled: Access to museum and toilets

Corris Railway Museum

M

This rather remote Museum merits a detour if only because of the unusual treatment of and detailed research into local history with some fascinating film and photographs that can be seen in the old stone building that houses the Museum
Location: Off A487, opposite Braichgoch Hotel, five miles north of Machynlleth
OS reference: SH 755078
Operating society: The Corris Railway Society, Corris Station Yard, Gwynedd (postal address: Corris, Machynlleth, Powys SY20 9SH)
Car park: Adjacent
Access by public transport: Bus Gwynedd services 34 & 35 (Machynlleth-Aberllefeni and Machynlleth-Dolgellau-Blaenau Ffestiniog respectively) and 'Trawscambria' (stop at Braichgoch Hotel)
Catering facilities: None, but light teas available nearby in village

Locomotives

Name	No	Builder	Type	Built
Alan Meaden	5	M/rail (22258)	4wDM	1965
—	6	R/Hornsby (51849)	4wDM	1966

Locomotive notes: 5 operational and on works trains, 6 currently under repair

Stock
Small number of representative and works wagons, one manriding carriage, with a second currently having a replica body added

On site facilities: Souvenir shop, toilets and children's playground
Length of line: ¾-mile, 2ft 3in gauge construction line, being upgraded to passenger carrying standard
Public opening: Please contact for details
Special events: Please contact for details
Facilities for disabled: Limited
Membership details: A. H. Lawson, 165 Gynsill Lane, Anstey, Leicester LE7 7AN

Fairbourne & Barmouth Railway

nce 1983 this railway has now ›en regauged from 15in to 12¼in ıt has been transformed by the troduction of new locomotives ıd rolling stock, a tunnel through e sand dunes, miniaturised ations and signalboxes, new orkshops, a creperie overlooking e Barmouth estuary
eadquarters: North Wales Narrow auge Railway Co Ltd, Fairbourne & ırmouth Leisure Park, Beach Road, ıirbourne, Gwynedd, LL38 2EX
elephone: 0341-250362 or 250083
ain station: Gorsaf Newydd, ıirbourne
ther public stations: orsafawddacháqidraigddanhed-ogleddolonpenrhynareudraeth-redigion, Porth Penrhyn
S reference: SH 616128
ar parks: Gorsaf Newydd, orsafawddach
ccess by public transport: ıirbourne BR station. Bus wynedd service
efreshment facilities: Celtic ıvillion at Porth Penrhyn. Porth Penrhyn restaurant specialises in Welsh Lamb and Breton Pancakes, with 'Sundowner' evening service for dinner and entertainment (main season) (phone for details)
Souvenir shop: Gorsaf Newydd and Penrhyn Pavillion
Depot: Fairbourne
Length of line: 2¾ miles, 12¼in gauge
Passenger trains: A 2¾ mile journey connecting with ferry at Porth Penrhyn to Barmouth. 20min single journey. Through tickets to Barmouth at reduced price
Period of public operation: Daily Good Friday-1 November (closed Saturdays except at peak season)
Facilities for disabled: Full disabled facilities with Ro-Ro coach
Membership details: Friends of Fairbourne — contact Hon Sec A. de Frayssinet at above address
Special notes: During inclement weather the service may be restricted or cancelled. Extra trains and special parties by arrangement with the manager

Locomotives

Name	No	Builder	Type	Built
Beddgelert	—	Curwen	0-6-4T	1979
Yeo	—	Curwen	2-6-2T	1978
Sherpa	—	Milner	0-4-0STT	1978
Russell	—	FLW	2-6-2T	1985
Lilian Walter	—	FLW	A1-1AD	1985
Gwril	—	FLW	4wBE	1987

FLW — Fairbourne Locomotive Works

Stock
12¼in gauge — 28 coaches (1st, 2nd class); 16 freight

Note: At the time of compilation, the line was 'for sale' with no purchaser announced. Please see press for details or contact before visit

Ffestiniog Railway

ı many ways, evocative of the early wiss mountain railways as it imbs high above Porthmadog with ome breathtaking views, the ilway still operates an interesting ıriety of locomotives including ome unusual Victorian survivors. ıssengers have replaced slate as e principal traffic over this former ıarry line
eneral Manager: Gordon Rushton
eadquarters: Ffestiniog Railway o, Harbour Station, Porthmadog, wynedd, LL49 9NF
elephone: Porthmadog (0766) 12340 or 831654
ain stations: Porthmadog arbour, Blaenau Ffestiniog

Locomotives

Name	No	Builder	Type	Built
Princess	1	G/England (199/200)	0-4-0STT	1863
Prince	2	G/England	0-4-0STT	1863
Welsh Pony	—	G/England (234)	0-4-0STT	1867
Earl of Merioneth	—	FR	0-4-4-0T	1979
Merddin Emrys	10	FR	0-4-4-0T	1879
Moelwyn	—	Baldwin (49604)	2-4-0DM	1918
Blanche	—	Hunslet (589)	2-4-0STT	1893
Linda	—	Hunslet (590)	2-4-0STT	1893
*Britomart**	—	Hunslet (707)	0-4-0ST	1899
Mountaineer	—	Alco (57156)	2-6-2T	1917
Livingston Thompson†	3	FR	0-4-4-0T	1886
—†	K1	B/Peacock (5292)	0-4-0+0-4-0	1909
Harlech Castle	—	Baguley-Drewry (3767)	0-6-0-DH	1983
Upnor Castle	—	Hibberd (3687)	4wDM	1954
Conway Castle	—	Hibberd (3831)	4wDM	1958
Moel Hebog	—	Hunslet (4113)	0-4-0DM	1955
Mary Ann	—	M/Rail (596)	4wDM	1917

7 other 4wDM units
*Privately owned
†On loan to National Railway Museum

Other public stations: Minffordd, Penrhyn, Tan-y-Bwlch, Tanygrisiau
OS reference: SH 571384
Car parks: Porthmadog, Tan-y-Bwlch, Tanygrisiau, Blaenau Ffestiniog
Access by public transport: Minffordd and Blaenau Ffestiniog BR stations. Porthmadog, Minffordd, Tanygrisiau and Blaenau Ffestiniog served by local buses
Refreshment facilities: Licensed restaurant at Porthmadog, buffet at Tan-y-Bwlch (summer only), also on most trains
Souvenir shops: Porthmadog, Tan-y-Bwlch, Blaenau Ffestiniog
Museum: Porthmadog
Depot: Boston Lodge
Length of line: 13½ miles, 1ft 11½in gauge
Passenger trains: Porthmadog-Blaenau Ffestiniog
Period of public operation: Daily March-November, limited winter service
Special events: Santa Specials — please enquire for details
Facilities for disabled: Porthmadog and Blaenau Ffestiniog easily accessible for wheelchairs. Facilities on trains for disabled in wheelchairs by prior arrangement

Above:
A special train was run on the Ffestiniog Railway on 24 April 1991 in conjunction with a visit from the Secretary of State for Wales. The train is seen passing Boston Lodge with EEC and Welsh symbols on the headboard. *FR Co*

Stock
27 bogie coaches; 4 4-wheel coaches; 2 brake vans, plus numerous service vehicles

Special notes: Reduced return rates available for journeys beginning on diesel services, shown in timetable
Membership details: Ffestiniog Railway Society (see above address)
Membership journal: *Ffestiniog Railway Magazine* — quarterly

Great Orme Tramway

A cable-hauled street tramway to the summit of the Great Orme is operated as two sections involving a change half-way. Opened throughout in July 1903, it involves gradients as steep as 1 in 10.3
Location: Great Orme Tramway, Victoria station, Church Walks, Llandudno
OS reference: SH 7781
Operating society/organisation: Griwp Aberconwy, Maesdu, Llandudno LL30 1HF
Telephone: Llandudno (0492) 870870
Car park: Approximately 100yd from Lower Terminal. Adjacent to Summit Terminal
Access by public transport: Good on site facilities: Shop
Period of public operation: Easter to end of September (daily)
Special notes: Cable tramway to summit of Great Orme, approximately 1-mile rising to 650ft (3ft 6in gauge)
Stock: 4 tramcars each seating 48, built 1902/3

Gwili Railway (Rheilffordd Gwili)

South Wales' first standard gauge passenger-carrying railway extended services back to Llwyfan Cerrig during 1987

Industrial locomotives

Name	No	Builder	Type	Built
—	1	H/Clarke (1885)	0-6-0ST	1955
Little Lady	1903	Peckett (1903)	0-4-0ST	1936
Idris	—	R/Hornsby (207103)	4wDM	1941
Trecatty	—	R/Hornsby (421702)	0-6-0DM	1959
Olwen	7058	RSH (7058)	0-4-0ST	1942
—	71516	RSH (7170)	0-6-0ST	1944

eadquarters: Gwili Railway Co
d, Bronwydd Arms station,
:onwydd Arms, Carmarthen,
yfed
elephone: Carmarthen (0267)
30666
S reference: Bronwydd Arms SN
17239
wyfan Cerrig SN 405258,
onwil SN 386263
ain station: Bronwydd Arms
ther public stations: Llwyfan
errig, also Conwil under
storation
ar park: Bronwydd Arms
ccess by public transport:
armarthen BR station, then
rosville bus service No 400 (not
undays).
efreshment facilities: Bronwydd
rms, Llwyfan Cerrig (picnic site).
ar on train
ouvenir shop: Bronwydd Arms
epot: Llwyfan Cerrig, stock also

Nellie	D2875	YEC(2779)	0-4-0DE	1960
Rosyth No 1	1	A/Barclay (1385)	0-4-0ST	1914*
Swansea Vale No 1	1	Sentinel (9622)	4wVBTG	1958*
Swansea Jack	—	R/Hornsby (393302)	4wDM	1955*
Dylan Thomas	—	N/British (27654)	0-4-0DH	1956*
—	—	R/Hornsby (3307)	4wDM	1938

Stock
1 ex-BR diesel unit trailer car; 4 ex-BR Mk 1 coaches; 2 ex-BR suburban coaches; 1 ex-BR griddle car; 1 ex-TVR coach (built 1891); Coles diesel rail crane; 1 ex-GWR Mink van; 1 ex-GWR Fruit D; 1 ex-GWR Monster; 1 ex-GWR Crocodile; 1 ex-GWR Loriot D; 1 tank wagon; 2 GWR Toad brake vans; 1 GWR Tube C; 1 GWR Tunnel Toad; 14 open wagons

Owners
*The Railway Club of Wales

kept at Bronwydd Arms, Conwil and 'Ironrails', Carmarthen
Length of line: 1¾ miles
Passenger trains: Bronwydd Arms-Llwyfan Cerrig, regular hourly service
Period of public operation: Please contact for details
Public opening: 11.00-17.15 on all operating days
Special events: See press for details

Llanberis Lake Railway (Rheilffordd Lyn Padarn)

narrow gauge passenger carrying
ilway starting at the historic
inorwic Quarry workshops (now
art of the National Museum of
Vales) and running along the
ores of the Llanberis lake using
e trackbed of the former slate
ilway line to Port Dinorwic.
xcellent views of Snowdonia and
ood picnic spots along the line
eneral Manager and Secretary:
Ir V. Bailey
eadquarters: Llanberis Lake
ailway, Gilfach Ddu, Llanberis,
wynedd LL55 4TY
elephone: Llanberis (0286) 870549
Iain station: Llanberis (Padarn
ation/Gilfachddu)
ther public stations: Cei Llydan
S reference: SH 586603
ar park: Llanberis (Padarn station)
efreshment facilities: Padarn
ation
ouvenir shop: Padarn Station
ength of line: 2 miles, 1ft 11½in
auge

Industrial locomotives

Name	No	Builder	Type	Built
Elidir	1	Hunslet (493)	0-4-0ST	1889
Thomas Bach/Wild Aster	2	Hunslet (849)	0-4-0ST	1904
Dolbadarn	3	Hunslet (1430)	0-4-0ST	1922
—	7	R/Hornsby (441427)	4wDM	1961
Twll Coed	8	R/Hornsby (268878)	4wDM	1956
Dolgarrog	9	M/Rail (22154)	4wDM	1962
—	—	R/Hornsby (425796)	4wDM	1958
Garrett	11	R/Hornsby (198286)	4wDM	1939
Braich	10	R/Hornsby (203031)	4wDM	1942
—	18	M/Rail (7927)	4wDM	1941
Llanell	19	R/Hornsby (451901)	4wDM	1961
*Una**	—	Hunslet (873)	0-4-0ST	1905

*Not part of the railway's motive power stock. Housed at the adjacent slate museum and can sometimes be seen working demonstration freight trains

Stock
13 bogie coaches; 20 wagons

Passenger trains: Llanberis-Penllyn-Llanberis
Journey time: 40min round trip
Period of public operation: Mondays to Thursdays in March and October. Monday to Friday in April and May. Sundays to Fridays, June through September, Saturdays July and August
Facilities for disabled: Level approaches throughout shop, cafe and to train. Special toilet facilities provided. All disabled visitors welcomed
Marketing names: Rheillfordd Llyn Padarn Cyfyngedig (Padarn Lake Railway Ltd); Llanberis Lake Railway

Llangollen Railway

The line, which is presently 3½ miles long, is the only preserved standard gauge line in North Wales. Situated in the Dee Valley, it follows the course of the River Dee for much of its route, and affords good views of the surrounding countryside between Llangollen and Deeside Loop. It is the eventual aim to reach Corwen, some 9 miles from Llangollen where a terminus will be re-established

Location: Llangollen station, A542 from Ruabon, A5 from Shrewsbury, A5 from Betws y Coed

General Manager: Mr G. Roughsedge

Locomotives

Name	No	Origin	Class	Type	Built
—	2859	GWR	2800	2-8-0	1918
Kinlet Hall	4936†	GWR	'Hall'	4-6-0	1929
—	5199	GWR	5101	2-6-2T	1934
—	5538	GWR	4575	2-6-2T	1928
Cogan Hall	5952	GWR	'Hall'	4-6-0	1935
—	6430†	GWR	6400'	4-6-0PT	1937
—	7754	GWR	5700	0-6-0PT	1930
Ditcheat Manor	7821	GWR	'Manor'	4-6-0	1950
Foxcote Manor	7822	GWR	'Manor'	4-6-0	1950
—	03162	BR	03	0-6-0DM	1960
—	D3265 (08195)	BR	08	0-6-0DE	1956
—	D7629	BR	25	Bo-Bo	1965
—	25313	BR	25	Bo-Bo	1966
—	D9500*	BR	14	0-6-0DH	1964
—	D9502	BR	14	0-6-0DH	1964

Also ex-BR Class 127 No M51618 and Class 105 No 54456 DMUs
•Undergoing restoration at West Somerset Railway
†Not on site

Industrial locomotives

Name	No	Builder	Type	Built
Darfield No 1	—	Hunslet (3783)	0-6-0ST	1953
Eliseg	—	Fowler (22753)	0-4-0DM	1939
—	—	Fowler (400007)	0-4-0DM	1947
Richboro	—	H/Clarke (1243)	0-6-0T	1917
Burtonwood Brewer	—	Kitson (5459)	0-6-0ST	1932
—	14	H/Clarke (D1012)	0-4-0DM	1956
—	—	North British (27734)	0-4-0DH	1958
—	1	YEC/BTH	0-4-0D	c1950
—	—	YEC	0-6-0DE	—
—	—	R/Hornsby (416213)	0-4-0DE	1957

Below:
A visitor to the Llangollen Railway for a short period during 1991 was the Severn Valley Railway's Ivatt Mogul. No 46443 is seen at Llangollen having worked the 16.15 service from Deeside on 26 May. The period of loan was cut short following boiler trouble which resulted in the locomotive returning to the SVR. *Melvyn Hopwood*

affic Manager: Mr C. Wilson
erating society/organisation: ingollen Railway Society Ltd, ingollen station, Abbey Road, ingollen, Clwyd LL20 8SN
lephone: Answerphone (24hr): ingollen (0978) 860951. Other quiries: (0978) 860979 (office urs only)
ain station: Llangollen
her stations: Berwyn, Deeside op
reference: SJ 214422
r park: Llangollen (Market Street)
cess by public transport: Nearest tion: Ruabon (2hr service), then osville bus service No D1 to ingollen or Nos D93/D94
freshment facilities: Llangollen d Berwyn
uvenir shop: Llangollen
ngth of line: 3½ miles
ssenger trains: Llangollen-eside Loop
riod of public operation: turdays and Sundays Easter-July; ily July-mid-September; turdays and Sundays mid-ptember-mid-October. Special event days during winter as advertised. Please see timetable for details of services to Deeside Loop
Special events: Please refer to timetable or event leaflet
Facilities for disabled: Special passenger coach for wheelchairs, also shop and refreshment rooms at Llangollen. Toilet available at Berwyn station. Advance notice required for special coach
Membership details: Mr J. Short, 'Bryn Aber', Llangollen Road, Trevor, Nr Llangollen, Clwyd
Membership journal: *Steam at Llangollen* — quarterly

Stock — *coaches*
17 Mk 1 coaches; 2 Mk 1 sleepers; 4 GWR coaches
Stock-wagons — 4 wagons; 1 Bolster wagon; 1 LNWR tool van; 2 GWR brake vans; 1 GWR Mink D wagon; 1 SR 'BY' parcels van; 3 tank wagons; 1 LNER parcels van; 2 BR Fruit vans; 1 ex-LNWR brake van; 1 Matisa track tamper; 1 BR ballast wagon; 1 Coles diesel/electric 5-ton crane; 1 BR generator van; 1 LMS Inspection saloon; 1 GWR Siphon G coach; 1 LMS box van; 1 GWR Mink A van; 1 BR Presflow bulk cement wagon; 1 BR CCT
Stock-maintenance — 1 Matisa Track Recording Machine; 1 BR Bridge/Viaduct Inspection Unit; 1 steam crane

Owners
5199, 5952 and 7821 (the GW Steam Locomotive Group)
7822 (the Foxcote Manor Society)
7754 (the National Museum of Wales)
Richboro (the National Coal Board)
Burtonwood Brewer (the Burtonwood Brewery)
03162 (the Wirral Borough Council)

Narrow Gauge Railway Centre — M

very extensive collection of rrow gauge railway equipment m the British Isles mainly housed a purpose-built exhibition hall at oddfa Grand Slate Mine, a major urist attraction. Close to other urist attractions in Blaenau estiniog, principally the echwedd Slate Caverns and the estiniog Railway
cation: Off the A470 Blaenau estiniog road ½-mile north of the wn, turn at the locomotive
OS reference: SH 693470
General Manager: Eryl Roberts
Operating society/organisation: Gloddfa Ganol Slate Mine, Blaenau Ffestiniog, Gwynedd, North Wales LL41 3NB
Telephone: (0766 830) 664
Car park: On site
Access by public transport: Blaenau Ffestiniog BR/FR station, bus connection to mine
On site facilities: Licensed restaurant, snack bar and grill. Toilets, children's playground and playroom, slate works, craftshops, mining museum, preserved quarrymen's cottages. Extensive underground workings, Land Rover tours and rail ride
Public opening: Easter-October
Length of line: ½-mile to mine entrance
Facilities for disabled: Toilets, shops, museums, restaurant and section of mine suitable. No advance notice required. Special party rates available

Penrhyn Castle Industrial Railway Museum — M

collection of historic industrial eam locomotives, both standard d narrow gauge, displayed in nrhyn Castle, a well known ational Trust property in the area gularly open to visitors

Industrial locomotives

Name	No	Builder	Type	Built
Kettering Furnaces No 3	—	B/Hawthorn (859)	0-4-0ST	1885*
Watkin	—	de Winton	0-4-0VBT	1893*
Fire Queen	—	Horlock	0-4-0	1848†
Hawarden	—	H/Clarke (526)	0-4-0ST	1899
Vesta	—	H/Clarke (1223)	0-6-0T	1916
Charles	—	Hunslet (283)	0-4-0ST	1882§
Hugh Napier	—	Hunslet (855)	0-4-0ST	1904§
—	1	Neilson (1561)	0-4-0WT	1870

Location: Llandegai, near Bangor. One mile east of Bangor on the A5
OS reference: SH 603720
Operating society/organisation: National Trust, Penrhyn Castle, Industrial Railway Museum, Llandegai, near Bangor, Gwynedd
Telephone: Bangor (0248) 353084
Car park: Within castle grounds
Access by public transport: Nearest BR station, Bangor
On site facilities: The castle is open to the public, and contains a gift shop. Light refreshments are available
Public opening: Daily 1 April-1 November

Name	No	Builder	Type	Built
Haydock	—	Stephenson (2309)	0-6-0T	1879
Acorn	—	R/Hornsby (327904)	0-4-0DM	1948

*3ft gauge
†4ft gauge
§1ft 10¾in gauge

Stock
10 narrow gauge rolling stock exhibits from the Padarn/Penrhyn system. The small relics section includes a comprehensive display of railway signs and model locomotives.

Facilities for disabled: Access to castle and museum
Special notes: For those interested in stately homes the castle is well worth a visit. The entrance fee covers both the castle and the railway exhibits housed in the castle courtyard

Pontypool & Blaenavon Railway SC

The historic Blaenavon site, complete with its railway installations and locomotives can easily be included in a visit to Big Pit Mining Museum
Location: Near Big Pit, Blaenavon, Gwent
OS reference: SO 237093
Operating society/organisation: Pontypool & Blaenavon Railway Co (1983) Ltd, Council Offices, Lion Street, Blaenavon, Gwent
Telephone: (0495) 772726 (evenings only)
Car park: Adjacent to railway terminus
On site facilities: Light refreshments and souvenir shop
Public opening: 1 March; Sundays and bank holidays 19 April-30 August;
Special events: 4/5 July — Thomas the Tank; Santa Specials 5/6, 12/13, 19/20 December
Special notes: The railway incorporates the former mineral/LNWR passenger lines running through Big Pit. Both north and southbound extensions are being considered. Service currently operates between Furnace Sidings platform and Whistle Inn platform
Membership details: c/o above address

Locomotives

Name	No	Origin	Class	Type	Built
—	2874	GWR	2800	2-8-0	1918
—	3855	GWR	2884	2-8-0	1942
—	4253	GWR	4200	2-8-0T	1917
—	5668	GWR	5600	0-6-2T	1926
Bickmarsh Hall	5967	GWR	'Hall'	4-6-0	1937

Industrial locomotives

Name	No	Builder	Type	Built
Brookfield	—	Bagnall (2613)	0-6-0PT	1940
Nora	5	Barclay (1680)	0-4-0ST	1920
Menelaus	—	Peckett (1889)	0-6-0ST	1935
—	8	RSH (7139)	0-6-0ST	1944
—	104	E/Electric (D1249)	0-6-0DH	1968
—	106	E/Electric (D1226)	0-6-0DH	1971
—	1	Fowler (22497)	0-6-0DM	1938
—	—	Drewry (2252)	0-6-0DH	1948
—	170	Hunslet (7063)	0-8-0DH	1971
—	10083	R/Royce (10083)	0-4-0DH	1961

Stock
1 brake van; 5 BR Mk 1 coaches; Several vans, china clay, coke and tank wagons

Snowdon Mountain Railway

The only public rack and pinion railway in the British Isles, this bustling line climbs up the slopes of Snowdon, often through the clouds, to the hotel at the top. The trip should not be missed
General Manager: D. Rogerson
Engineering Manager: N. A. Massey
Headquarters: Snowdon Mountain Railway, Llanberis, Gwynedd LL55 4TY
Telephone: Llanberis (0286) 87022
Main station: Llanberis
Other public stations: Summit

OS reference: SH 582597
Car park: Llanberis
Access by public transport: Bangor BR station then by Crosville bus to Caernarfon and there change to local bus to Llanberis
Refreshment facilities: Llanberis, Summit
Souvenir shops: Llanberis, Summit
Depot: Llanberis
Length of line: 4¾ miles, 80cm gauge
Passenger trains: Llanberis-Summit. Journey time 60 minutes. Departures from Llanberis at 30 minute intervals during peak periods
Period of public operation: Daily 15 March-1 November
Special notes: All trains are subject to weather and traffic restrictions, especially before mid-May and during October. Parties welcome by prior arrangement

Locomotives

Name	No	Builder	Type	Built
Enid	2	SLM (924)	0-4-2T	1895
Yr Wyddfa	3	SLM (925)	0-4-2T	1895
Snowdon	4	SLM (988)	0-4-2T	1896
Moel Siabod	5	SLM (989)	0-4-2T	1896
Padarn	6	SLM (2838)	0-4-2T	1922
Ralph	7	SLM (2869)	0-4-2T	1923
Eryri	8	SLM (2870)	0-4-2T	1923
Ninian	9	Hunslet (9249)	0-4-0DH	1986
Yeti	10	Hunslet (9250)	0-4-0DH	1986
—	11	Hunslet (9305)	0-4-0DH	1990

All steam locomotives were built by Swiss Locomotive Works, Winterthur

Stock
8 closed bogie coaches; 1 bogie works car; 1 4-wheel open wagon

Swansea Maritime & Industrial Museum M

This Museum houses a number of relics from Swansea's industrial and maritime past and includes some railway exhibits, some of which are operated on the former dock sidings adjacent to the Museum. The new Tramshed Annexe houses a restored Swansea City double-deck tram (Brush Electrical Engineering 1923/24 model), and a replica of the early Mumbles railway carriage, in addition to the sole surviving example of the Mumbles Railway rolling stock, the front section of the tramcar, manufactured by the Brush Electrical Engineering Co in 1928.

Artifacts from the Mumbles Railway are also displayed within a graphic presentation, as are examples of Brunels 'GWR' broad gauge rail track.

Industrial locomotives

Name	No	Builder	Type	Built
Sir Charles	—	A/Barclay (1473)	0-4-0F	1919
—	—	Peckett (1426)	0-6-0ST	1916

Location: On the south side of the town between the shopping centre and the sea in the newly created Maritime Quarter
OS reference: SS 659927
Operating society/organisation: City of Swansea Museum Services. Maritime & Industrial Museum, Museum Square, Maritime Quarter, Swansea SA1 1SN
Telephone: Swansea (0792) 650351
Car park: Public car parks close by
Access by public transport: Reached on foot from shopping centre, central bus depot or by car
On site facilities: No refreshments in the Museum but several cafes close by. Museum shop selling souvenirs and produce of the Woollen Mill which operates in the Museum throughout the year. Education Service available on request to Education Officer
Public opening: 10.30-17.30 seven days a week, closed 25/26/27 December and New Year's Day
Facilities for disabled: Available
Membership details: Museum's Friends Organisation c/o above address

Talyllyn Railway

The very first railway in the country to be rescued and operated by enthusiasts, the line climbs from Tywyn through the wooded Welsh hills past Dolgoch Falls to Nant Gwernol. The trains are hauled by a variety of veteran tank engines all immaculately maintained by the railway's own workshops at Tywyn Pendre
General Manager: D. Woodhouse
Headquarters: Talyllyn Railway Co, Wharf station, Tywyn, Gwynedd LL36 9EY
Telephone: Tywyn (0654) 710472
Main station: Tywyn Wharf
Other public stations: Tywyn Pendre, Rhydyronen, Brynglas, Dolgoch Falls, Abergynolwyn, Nant Gwernol
OS reference: SH 586005 (Tywyn Wharf)
Car parks: Tywyn Wharf, Dolgoch, Abergynolwyn

Access by public transport: Tywyn BR station. Bus Gwynedd services to Tywyn
Refreshment facilities: Tywyn Wharf, Abergynolwyn hot and cold snacks available
Souvenir shops: Tywyn Wharf, Abergynolwyn
Museum: Tywyn Wharf
Depot: Tywyn Pendre
Length of line: 7½ miles, 2ft 3in gauge
Passenger trains: Tywyn-Nant Gwernol
Period of public operation: Daily April to end of October, Christmas and New Year.
Journey times: Tywyn-Nant Gwernol — single 51min, return 1hr 10/20min
Special events: 15 August — annual 'Race the Train' event (with Tywyn Rotary Club); 19 December — Santa Specials
Facilities for disabled: No problem for casual visitors, advanced notice preferred for groups. Access to shop and cafeteria possible at Tywyn and Abergynolwyn. Disabled toilet facilities at Tywyn and Abergynolwyn. Access possible to lower floor of museum. Limited capacity for wheelchairs on trains. New vehicle for wheel chairs now in operation on selected trains
Special notes: Special parties and private charter trains by arrangement. Children under 5 years of age free. Narrow gauge 'Wanderer' four- and eight-day tickets accepted

Locomotives

Name	*No*	*Builder*	*Type*	*Built*
Talyllyn	1	F/Jennings (42)	0-4-2ST	1865
Dolgoch	2	F/Jennings (63)	0-4-0WT	1866
Sir Haydn	3	Hughes (323)	0-4-2ST	1878
Edward Thomas	4	K/Stuart (4047)	0-4-2ST	1921
Midlander	5	R/Hornsby (200792)	4wDM	1940
Douglas	6	Barclay (1431)	0-4-0WT	1918
*Tom Rolt**	7	Barclay (2263)	0-4-2T	1949
Merseysider	8	R/Hornsby (476108)	4wDH	1964
Alf	9	Hunslet (4136)	0-4-0DM	1950

Locomotive notes: In service — 1, 2, 4 and 7; limited use — 6
*Virtually a new locomotive rebuilt from the original at Pendre Works

Stock
13 4-wheel coaches/vans; 10 bogie coaches; 45 wagons

Narrow Gauge Museum, Tywyn

Name	*No*	*Builder*	*Type*	*Built*
Dot	—	B/Peacock (2817)	0-4-0ST 1887	
*Pet**	—	LNWR	0-4-0ST	1865
Rough Pup	—	Hunslet (541)	0-4-0ST	1891
—	2	K/Stuart (721)	0-4-0WT	1902
Jubilee 1897	—	M/Wardle (1382)	0-4-0ST	1897
George Henry	—	de Winton	0-4-0T	1877
—	13	Spence	0-4-0T	1895
*Nutty**	—	Sentinel (7701)	0-4-0VB	1929

*Not currently on site

Stock
Various wagons and miscellaneous equipment

Membership details: Mr A. Johnston, 9 Reynolds Way, Croydon, Surrey CR0 5JW
Membership journal: *Talyllyn News* — quarterly
Marketing names: One of the Great Little Trains

Teifi Valley Railway

Operating Society/organisation: Teifi Valley Railway, Henllan Station, Llandysul, Dyfed SA44 5TD
Operations Manager: Mr Alan G. White
Telephone: 0559 371077
Main Station: Henllan
Other public stations: Forest Halt, Pontprenshitw, Llandyfriog
Car Park: Henllan
OS reference: SN 358407
Access by public transport: BR station — Carmarthen (20 miles). Bus service 461 to Henllan
Refreshments: Henllan
Souvenirs: Henllan

Industrial locomotives

Name	*No*	*Builder*	*Type*	*Built*
Alan George	—	Hunslet (606)	0-4-0ST	1894
Sholto	—	Hunslet (2433)	4wDM	1941
Simon	—	M/Rail (7126)	4wDM	1936
—	—	M/Rail (7215)	4wDM	1938
—	—	M/Rail (8683)	4wDM	1941
Neath Abbey	—	R/Hornsby (476106)	4wDM	1964
Cilgwyn	—	R/Hornsby (175414)	4wDM	1936

On site facilities: Children's playground, nature trail, crazy golf
Depot: Henllan, engine shed open to public
Facilities for disabled: Portable steps and wide door for wheelchairs in one coach
Period of public operation: Good Friday to last Sunday in October
Special events: Easter Sunday fair, Dragon day (mid August), Victorian Day (late August)
Membership details: Vale of Teifi Narrow Gauge Railway Society, c/o Henllan station
Membership journal: *Right Away* — quarterly

Vale of Rheidol Railway

This narrow gauge railway offers a 23-mile round trip from Aberystwyth to Devils Bridge providing spectacular views which cannot be enjoyed by road. At Devils Bridge there are walks to the Mynach Falls and Devils Punch Bowl. Many artists have been inspired by the magnificence of Devils Bridge and the Rheidol Valley

General Manager: A. S. Hills
Headquarters: Vale of Rheidol Railway, The Locomotive Shed, Park Avenue, Aberystwyth, Dyfed SY23 1PG
Telephone: 0970 615993 (before 17 April, after 4 October) 0970 625819 (17 April to 4 October)
Main station: Aberystwyth (adjacent to BR station)
Other public stations: Devil's Bridge, Rhiwfron, Rheidol Falls, Aberffrwd, Nantyronen, Capel Bangor, Glanrafon, Llanbadarn
OS reference: SN 587812
Car parks: Aberystwyth, Devil's Bridge
Access by public transport: Aberystwyth BR station: and bus services to Aberystwyth
Refreshment facilities: Aberystwyth (not railway-owned), Devils Bridge (not railway operated)
Souvenir shop: Aberystwyth
Depot: Aberystwyth (not open to the public)
Length of line: 11¾ miles, 1ft 11½in gauge
Passenger trains: Aberystwyth-Devil's Bridge
Period of public operation: Daily 17 April-4 October

Locomotives

Name	No	Origin	Ex-BR Class	Type	Built
Owain Glyndwr	7	GWR	98	2-6-2T	1923
Llywelyn	8	GWR	98	2-6-2T	1923
Prince of Wales	9	GWR	98	2-6-2T	1924
—	10	Brecon MR (002)	98/1	0-6-0DH	1987

Stock

16 bogie coaches including one Vista coach; 1 4-wheel baggage van; 12 wagons for maintenance use; 1 inspection trolley

Wales Railway Centre

SC

The world's first steam locomotive ran in Wales in 1804 and the aim of the Wales Railway Centre is to show the history of railways in Wales and their impact on the country. It is situated at Bute Road station which was once the headquarters of the Taff Vale Railway; the first main line company in Wales. The station building houses the Railway Gallery of the Welsh Industrial & Maritime Museum, while outside, work has started on the restoration of 10 ex-Barry locomotives, all of which are representatives of locomotives which worked in different parts of the Principality. It is hoped that ex-Mountain Ash Colliery 0-6-0ST *Sir Gomer* will be working in 1992

Location: Bute Road Railway station, Cardiff
Operating society: The Butetown Historic Railway Society
Car park: On site
Access by public transport: Frequent train services from Cardiff (Queen Street) station (not Sundays). Frequent bus services from the city centre
On site facilities: Shop and light refreshments at weekends
Public opening: Daily (except Mondays), 10.00-16.30; Sunday 14.30-16.30
Membership journal: *Wrth Ddwr a Thân* — twice yearly
Further inforation: Mr D. J. Morgan, 34 Bryngwyn Road, Cyncoed, Cardiff DF2 6PQ

Locomotives

Name	No	Origin	Class	Type	Built
—	2861	GWR	2800	2-8-0	1918
—	4115	GWR	4101	2-6-2T	1936
—	5227	GWR	5205	2-8-0T	1924
—	5539	GWR	4575	2-6-2T	1928
—	6686	GWR	5600	0-6-2T	1928
Willington Hall	7927	BR	'Hall'	4-6-0	1950
—	44901	LMS	5MT	4-6-0	1945
—	48518	LMS	8F	2-8-0	1944
—	80150	BR	4MT	2-6-4T	1956
—	92245	BR	9F	2-10-0	1958

Industrial locomotives

Name	No	Builder	Type	Built
Sir Gomer	—	Pecket (1859)	0-6-0ST	1932
—	52/001	Barclay (1966)	0-4-0F	1929
—	107	North British (27932)	0-6-0DM	1959
—	D1198	English Electric (D1198)	0-6-0DH	1967

Stock

Various freight vehicles

Welsh Highland Railway

SC

The 1964 company operates services over a short section at the south-western end of the old Welsh Highland line which linked the North Wales line with the Cambrian Coast. Negotiations are in hand to extend the line northward through the more spectacular scenery that attracted passengers from far and wide in the early part of the century. In the meantime, you have the compensation of low fares
Location: Porthmadog, Gwynedd, adjacent to BR station
OS reference: SH 571393
General Manager: Stuart Weatherby
Operating society/organisation: Welsh Highland Light Railway (1964) Ltd, Gelert's Farm Works, Madoc Street West, Porthmadog, Gwynedd LL49 9DY
Telephone: Porthmadog (0766) 513402 (weekends and operating days) or 051-327 3576 (evenings) or 051-608 1950 (day)
Car park: At terminus
Catering facilities: Station buffet — 'Russells' supplying hot meals, cold buffet, sandwiches and light refreshments
Access by public transport: Rail service to Porthmadog BR station. Festiniog Railway Harbour station. Bws Gwynedd service 1 and 3 to Porthmadog
On site facilities: Souvenir shop, information boards, taped commentary on coaches, shed tours on each journey
Length of line: ¾-mile, 1ft 11½in gauge
Passenger trains: Porthmadog-Pen-y-Mount. Return journey time 30 minutes approximately, steam hauled bank holidays, every weekend during high season and every day (except Fridays) in August
Period of public operation: Easter, then May-October

Locomotives

Name	*No*	*Builder*	*Type*	*Built*
Moel Tryfan	—	Bagnall (2875)	0-4-2T	1948
Gelert	—	Bagnall (3050)	0-4-2T	1953
Russell	—	Hunslet (901)	2-6-2T	1906
Pedemoura	—	O&K (10808)	0-6-0WT	1924
Karen	—	Peckett (2024)	0-4-2T	1942
Glaslyn	1	R/Hornsby (297030)	4wDM	1952
Kinnerley	2	R/Hornsby (354068)	4wDM	1953
Cnicht	36	M/Rail (8703)	4wDM	1941
Katherine	9	M/Rail (60S363)	4wDM	1968
—	4	M/Rail (60S333)	4wDM	1969
—	5	Hunslet (6285)	4wDM	1968
—	3	R/Hornsby (370555)	4wDM	1953
Jonathon	6	M/Rail (11102)	4wDM	1959
—	7	Hunslet (7353)	4wDM	1977
—	10	R/Hornsby (481552)	4wDM	1962
—	11	Hunslet (3510)	4wDM	1947

Locomotive notes: 1991 steam service will be worked jointly by *Russell* and *Gelert, Karen* will be the stand-by engine. Diesel service will be worked by *Glaslyn* with *Kinnerley* on stand-by.

Stock
A collection of rolling stock including bogie coaches and numerous service construction vehicles including Vale of Rheidol brake van (1902). Original coaches under restoration inlcude the Gladstone Car, built 1892 and due to re-enter service in late 1992. This will be followed by rebuilding another original vehicle — the buffet car — rescued recently from a field near Caernafon.

Special events: Please contact for details
Facilities for disabled: Disabled passengers can be accommodated without prior notice — except in parties
Membership details: Membership Secretary, c/o above address
Membership journal: *The Journal* — quarterly

Right:
Whilst preparing to work the day's service, *Karen* hauls the empty stock out of the carriage shed. *D. W. Allan*

Welshpool & Llanfair Light Railway

'here is a decidedly foreign tmosphere to the trains over this ine. The steam locomotive ollection embraces examples from hree continents, and the coaches re turn-of-the-century balcony aloons from Austria or 1960s ogies from Africa. The line follows steeply graded route (maximum 1 n 24) through very attractive olling countryside, and is rather a em in an area too often missed by he traveller heading for further hores

;eneral Manager: Andy Carey
Ieadquarters: Welshpool & Llanfair ,ight Railway Preservation Co Ltd, 'he Station, Llanfair Caereinion, 'owys SY21 0SF
'elephone: Llanfair Caereinion 0938) 810441
/Iain station: Llanfair Caereinion
)ther public stations: Castle ;aereinion, Sylfaen, Welshpool Raven Square)
)S reference: SJ 107069
;ar park: Llanfair Caereinion, Velshpool (both free)
ccess by public transport: BR tation at Welshpool, one mile from Raven Square. Crosville buses from ;hrewsbury, Oswestry and Jewtown
tefreshment facilities: Light efreshments at Llanfair Caereinion
'ouvenir shops: Llanfair Caereinion
)epot: Llanfair Caereinion

Locomotives

Name	*No*	*Builder*	*Type*	*Built*
The Earl	1	B/Peacock (3496)	0-6-0T	1902
The Countess	2	B/Peacock (3497)	0-6-0T	1902
Monarch	6	Bagnall (3024)	0-4-4-0T	1953
Chattenden	7	Drewry (2263)	0-6-0DM	1949
Dougal	8	Barclay (2207)	0-4-0T	1946
Sir Drefaldwyn	10	Franco-Belge (2855)	0-8-0T	1944
Ferret	11	Hunslet (2251)	0-4-0DM	1940
Joan	12	K/Stuart (4404)	0-6-2T	1927
SLR 85	14	Hunslet (3815)	2-6-2T	1954
Orion	15	Tubize (2369)	2-6-2T	1948

Locomotive notes: Locomotives expected in service 1992 — *Countess, Joan, Sir Drefaldwyn, Dougal,* SLR No 85. The remainder can be seen at Llanfair station, 15 is displayed with access to the footplate.

Stock
1 Wickham trolley; 6 W&LLR wagons; 8 ex-Admiralty wagons; 2 ex-Bowater wagons; 5 ex-Zillertalbahn coaches; 4 ex-Sierra Leone coaches

Length of line: 8 miles, 2ft 6in gauge
Passenger trains: Welshpool-Llanfair Caereinion
Period of public operation: Weekends and Bank Holidays Easter to early October. Daily mid-July-mid-September
Special events: Santa trains on three weekends before Christmas; 20/21 June — Friends of Thomas the Tank; 5/6 September — narrow gauge steam gala
Facilities for disabled: Specially adapted coach for wheelchairs now available. Easy access to shop, but no special toilet arrangements
Membership details: John Parkinson, 124 London Road, Long Sutton, Spalding, Lincolnshire PE12 9EE
Membership journal: *The Journal* — quarterly
Marketing name: Llanfair Railway
Special notes: New buildings at Raven Square will open for 1992 — largely a reconstruction of the 1863 station from Eardisley in Herefordshire

Below:
Franco-Belge built this rather chunky-looking 0-8-0T in 1944 as part of the German war effort. Now residing at Welshpool it is seen at on 31 August 1991 during the line's gala weekend. *Alan C. Butcher*

Channel Islands, Ireland and Isle of Man

Alderney Railway

Location: Alderney, Channel Islands
Operating society/organisation: Alderney Railway Society, PO Box 75, Alderney, Channel Islands
Telephone: 0481-823580
Car park: Yes
Access by public transport: Aurigny Air Services from Southampton and Bournemouth
On site facilities: Shop at Braye Road, refreshments (Sundays)
Public opening: Weekends and Bank Holidays, Easter to October
Special events: Alderney Week 3-10 August. Easter Egg Specials on Easter Saturday. Santa Specials, Saturday before Christmas
Length of line: 2 miles
Facilities for disabled: Yes
President: Roger Warren
Chairman: Bruce Nightingale
Engineer: Ross McAllister
Membership journal: Issued infrequently

Industrial locomotives

Name	*No*	*Builder*	*Type*	*Buil*
J. T. Daly	3	Bagnall (2450)	0-4-0ST	193
Elizabeth	—	Vulcan (D2271)	0-4-0DM	194

Stock
4 Wickham trolleys
2 Goods wagons
2 ex-London Underground 1938 Stock tube cars, Nos 10177/11177 (locomotive-hauled)
2 Wickham Flats
NB: some items privately-owned

Downpatrick Railway Project

Location: Downpatrick Station, Market Street, Downpatrick, Co Down BT30 6LZ
OS reference: J483444
Operating society/organisation: Downpatrick & Ardglass Railway Co Ltd, with the support of the Downpatrick Railway Society
Telephone: (0396) 830141 or (0396) 615779
Car park: Available adjacent to station in Downpatrick
Access by public transport: A regular service is operated by Ulsterbus from Belfast Tel: (0232) 320011
Refreshment facilities: Buffet carriage open on operating days
On site facilities: Souvenir shop, toilets

Locomotives

Name	*No*	*Origin*	*Class*	*Type*	*Buil*
—	E421	CIE	421	C	196
—	E432	CIE	421	C	196
—	G613	CIE	611	B	196

Industrial locomotives

Name	*No*	*Builder*	*Type*	*Buil*
Guinness	3BG	H/Clarke (1152	0-4-0ST	191
—	1	O&K (12475)	0-4-0T	193
—	3	O&K (12662)	0-4-0T	193

Rolling stock
1 CIE Brake open standard; 1 CIE Brake open standard generating steam van; 1 CIE Buffet open standard; 2 NCC parcels vans; 1 NR brake open standard; 1 NR brake open standard driving trailer; 1 NCC open wagon; 1 GNR(I) brake van; 1 CIE closed van; 1 GS&WR ballast hopper; 1 GSR ballast hopper; Belfast & County Down Railway 'Royal Saloon' No 153; 1 B&CDR 1st/2nd composite (No 152); 1 B&CDR 3rd open (ex-railmotor); 1 B&CDR 6 wheeled brake 3rd (No 39); 1 B&CDR 6 wheeled 2nd (No 154); 1 GS&WR 3rd open (No 836); 1 GS&WR ballast plough van (on loan from Westrail [Tuam] Ltd); 1 GNR(I) 6 wheeled saloon (No unknown)

ɜngth of line: ¾-mile
ıblic opening: St Patricks Day (17 arch); Easter Monday and ıesday; Sundays in July; 'eekends and 31 August and ı October; 5/6, 12/13, ı/20 December — Santa Specials
ɜriod of public operation: 14.00-.00
urney time: 30min return journey Quoile marshes
ɔecial events: 25 May — ıthusiast's Day; 25 August — Gala ay; 27 October — Ghost Trains; Easter Egg and Santa Specials
Facilities for disabled: All station facilities at Downpatrick have facilities for disabled
Membership details: The Secretary, Downpatrick Railway Society, The Railway Station, Market Street, Downpatrick, Co Down BT30 6LZ

Owners
1 and 3 (the Irish Sugar Locomotive Group)
3BG (on loan from the Railway Preservation Society of Ireland)

Irish Steam Preservation Society — M

ɔcation: Stradbally Hall, eight iles from Athy, six miles from ɔrtlaoise.
elephone: (0502) 25136
ccess by public transport: Irish ail train to Athy or Portlaoise. avanagh's Bus Portlaoise-radbally-Athy (daily Monday-ıturday)
n site facilities: 3ft gauge railway
atering facilities: None on site but wn centre ¼-mile away
ɜngth of line: 1km

Industrial locomotives

Name	*No*	*Builder*	*Type*	*Built*
—	2	Barclay (2264)	0-4-0WT	1949
—	—	Hunslet (2281)	4wDM	1941
Nippy	—	Planet (2014)	4wDM	1936
—	4	R/Hornsby (326052)	4wDM	1952

Stock
1 Passenger coach; 1 Ballast wagon; 1 Brake van

Public opening: Public open days 19/20 April — Easter; 7/8 June — June Bank Holiday; 25 July — Open Day and Flower Festival; 2/3 August — National Steam Rally; 20 September; 25/26 October. 14.30-17.00 each day (noon-18.30, 2/3 August only)

Railway Preservation Society of Ireland — SC

he RPSI is more famed for its ctivities elsewhere in Ireland than ır its line based at Whitehead and ullingar. The Society enjoys xcellent co-operation from the two ational railway systems of both arts of Ireland and its spring 'hree-Day Railtour' (which ormally provides up to five days of ctivities) has become renowned orld-wide and regularly sells out ell in advance. Numerous other ay excursions are operated ıroughout the year for those unable ı participate in the spring weekend ɔur. Short steam train rides are also

Locomotives

Name	*No*	*Origin*	*Class*	*Type*	*Built*
Merlin	85*	GNR (I)	V	4-4-0	1932
Slieve Gullion	171	GNR (I)	S	4-4-0	1913
—	4	LMS (NCC)	WT	2-6-4T	1947
—	184†	GS&WR	J15	0-6-0	1880
—	186	GS&WR	J15	0-6-0	1879
—	461	D&SER	K2	2-6-0	1922
Lough Erne	27	SL&NCR	Z	0-6-4T	1949

Industrial locomotives

Name	*No*	*Builder*	*Type*	*Built*
Guinness	3§	H/Clarke (1152)	0-4-0ST	1919
R. H. Smyth	3	Avonside (2021)	0-6-0ST	1928
—	23	Planet (3509)	0-4-0DM	1951
—	4	R/Hornsby	0-4-0DM	1954

*On loan from Ulster Folk & Transport Museum
†Normally based in the Republic of Ireland
§On loan to Downpatrick & Ardglass Railway Society

provided on certain dates at the main depot at Whitehead which is well worth a visit to view the Society's extensive collection. Visits by organised groups are welcome if advanced notification is given in writing to Whitehead Operations Manager at RPSI Whitehead BT38 9NA
Location: Whitehead Excursion station N. Ireland
Operating society: Railway Preservation Society of Ireland, Whitehead Excursion Station, Castleview Road, Whitehead, Co Antrim BT38 9NA
Telephone: Whitehead (09603) 53567 (for N Ireland trains only)
Car park: At the station
Access by public transport: Northern Ireland Railways services from Belfast (York Road) or Larne Harbour: Ulster Bus service from Belfast
On site facilities: Souvenir shop and dining car, open on public operating days
Public opening: Easter Sunday, Monday and Tuesday, and for Santa services on December Sundays before 25 December
Special notes: The RPSI is noted for its main line railtours operated each year using primarily its own rolling stock. For details telephone above number or write enclosing SAE.
Special events: 19-21 April — Easter Bunny rides at Whitehead; 9-11 May — Grainne Vaile International Railtour (Dublin-Westport-Taum-Galway-Dublin-Belfast-Whitehead (Nos 171 and 461); 20 June — The Hills of Donegal rail/coach tour (Belfast-Londonderry and return — steam coach tour of Co Donegal from Londonderry); 18 July/1, 15 August — The Portrush Flyer (Belfast-Portrush and return); 31 August — The Banfor Belle (Belfast*-Bangor and return); 5, 19 Septeber — The Steam Enterprise (Belfast*-Dublin and return). Special steam trains will also operate on certain dates from Dublin. Please contact Publicity & Marketing Department (South) at 33 Torquay Wood, Foxrock. Dublin 12 for details. All operations are subject to confirmation
Note: Belfast departures from York Road station unless otherwise indicated*, as Central. Locomotive availability and building of Cross Harbour rail link and New Yorkgate station may dictate changes. Telephone 09603 53567 for details.

Other day drips often arranged at short notice — contact RPSI, 33 Torquay Wood, Dublin 18 for Republic of Ireland trips and RPSI, Castleview Road, Whitehead BT38 9NA for Northern Ireland trips
Operations Officer: Michael McMahon
Membership details: Membership Secretary, 148 Church Road, Newtonabbey BT36 6HJ
Future developments: A new workshop and carriage shed is being built at Whitehead. Costing almost £460,000 this development will result in temporary relocation of certain items of rolling stock during the construction phase

Stock
The Society also owns some 20 operational coaches, normally resident at Whitehead and Mullingar. A small number of freight wagons are also preserved, as are a number of coaches awating restoration

Shanes Castle Railway

SC

A 3ft gauge line runs from the Lodge Gates to the Old Castle ruins through the park and along the shore of Loch Neagh and runs through Lord O'Neill's nature reserve
General manager: The Lord O'Neill
Headquarters: Antrim station, Shanes Castle Estate, Co Antrim, Northern Ireland
Telephone: Antrim (084 94) 63380/62216
Main station: Antrim (SCR)
Car parks: Shanes Castle Estate, Antrim
Access by public transport: By Ulsterbus from several centres. By NI Railways to Antrim station
Refreshment facilities: Shanes Castle station
Length of line: 1½ miles, 3ft gauge
Souvenir shop: Antrim station

Locomotives

Name	*No*	*Builder*	*Type*	*Built*
Tyrone	1	Peckett (1026)	0-4-0T	1904
Shane	3	Barclay (2265)	0-4-0WT	1949
Blue Circle	4	Simplex (102T016)	0-4-0DH	1976
Nancy	5	Avonside (1547)	0-6-0T	1908
Rory	6	Simplex (102TO07)	0-4-0DH	1974

Stock
12 4-wheel carriages; 3 4-wheel Tram cars; 1 ex-Londonderry & Lough Swilly Railway wagons

Passenger trains: Steam and diesel-hauled trains from Antrim station through the Shanes Castle estate.
Period of public operation: Sundays and Bank Holidays April; Saturdays, Sundays and Bank Holidays in May; Sundays, Wednesday and Bank Holidays in June; Tuesday, Wednesday, Thursdays and weekends and bank holidays in July-August; Sundays in September. Opening times 12.00-18.30
Special events: May Day (steam working) 4 May; Car Rally 14 June; Steam Rally 17/18 July; August Fairground Event 30/31 August
Facilities for disabled: Limited, no toilets, ramps available
Special notes: Railway serves visitors to the Shanes Castle estate of Lord O'Neill which includes an extensive nature reserve.

Diesel service only, Wednesdays in June, Tuesdays and Thursdays in July and August

Ulster Folk & Transport Museum

M

This former weaving machinery manufacturer's premises has all the atmosphere of an early Victorian railway terminus with the trains waiting in the platforms. A real Aladdin's cave and alone would justify a visit to the province
Location: Witham Street, Belfast
Operating organisation: Ulster Folk & Transport Museum, Cultra Manor, Holywood, Co Down
Telephone: Belfast (0232) 451519
Access by public transport: Citybus routes 16, 21, 24, 25, 76 and 77 to Rope Works
Car park: No facilities
On site facilities: Shop, toilets. 7¼in line (at Cultra)
Public opening: Daily (except Sunday) 10.00 to 17.00

Locomotives (5ft 3in)

Name	No	Origin	Class	Type	Built
—	93	GNR(I)	JT	2-4-2T	1895
—	30	BCDR	I	4-4-2T	1901
Dunluce Caste	74	LMS(NCC)	U2	4-4-0	1924
Maeve	800	GSR	B1A	4-6-0	1939
—	1	R/Stephenson (2738)	—	0-6-0T	1891
Merlin	85*	GNR(I)	V	4-4-0	1932

Locomotives (narrow gauge)

Name	No	Origin	Class	Type	Built
Kathleen	2	CLR	—	4-4-0T	1887
Blanche	2†	CDJRC	—	2-6-4T	1912
Phoenix	11	CVR	—	4wD	1928
—	2	Industrial	—	0-4-0	1956
—	20	Industrial	—	0-4-0	1905

*On loan to RPSI for operational use
†On loan to Derry Railway Heritage Centre

Stock
1 Dublin, Wicklow & Wexford Railway coach; 1 Dundalk, Newry & Greenore Railway coach; 1 Midland & Great Western Railway director's saloon (ex-private vehicle); 1 Electric tramcar of Bessbrook-Newry Tramway; 1 Covered 'toastrack' of Giant's Causeway, Portrush and Bush Valley Railway & Tramway Co; 1 Cavan-Leitrim Railway coach; 1 County Donegal Railway railcar (plus 1 on loan to DRHC); 1 County Donegal Railway director's coach; 1 County Donegal Railway trailer coach (bodywork ex-Dublin & Lucan Railway coach)

Westrail

Location: Tuam, Co Galway, Ireland
OS Reference: Lat 42, Long 52
Operating society/organisation: Westrail (Tuam) Ltd, The Railway Station, Vicar Street, Tuam, Co Galway
Telephone: (093) 24200, (091) 91039, (091) 65269. Fax: (091) 65384
Car park: On site
Access by public transport: Irish Rail — Athenry. Bus Eireann — Tuam
Catering facilities: On train, licensed snack bar. Platform shops at Athenry
Length of line: Athenry-Tuam, 15 miles
Period of public operation: Weekends June-August — please check for specific details

Locomotives

Name	No	Origin	Class	Type	Built
—	90	GSWR	J30	0-6-0T	1875
—	E428	CIE	421	C	1962
—	3	CSET	—	0-4-0DM	1960
—	B104	CIE	101	A1A-A1A	1956
—	B113	CIE	113	Bo-Bo	1951

Rolling stock
3 ex-CIE coaches

Journey time: 1-3hr return (see timetable for details)
Memberships details: Contact above address for details

Note: At the end of 1991 it was reported that CIE had lifted the track for re-use. Prospective visitors are advised to check before their visit.

Right:
Westrail's ex CIE shunter No E428 is seen restored to its former livery at the head of a train bound for Athenry.
Shane G. McQuillan

Groudle Glen Railway

SC

Location: Groudle Glen Railway, Isle of Man
Officer in charge: Tony Beard
Operating company: Groudle Glen Railway Ltd (managed by the Isle of Man Steam Railway Supporters' Association) of 19 Ballabrooie Grove, Douglas, Isle of Man
Telephone: 0624 622138 (evenings)
car park: Yes
Access by public transport: Manx Electric Railway
On site facilities: Sales shop
Length of line: ¾-mile, 2ft gauge
Public opening: Sundays and Bank Holidays May to September with some Wednesday evening services in July and August; Santa Trains in December
Facilities for disabled: Due to the line's location, those who are disabled will have some difficulty. It is suggested that they telephone for advice
Further information and membership details: From above address
Membership journal: *Manx Steam Railway News* — quarterly

Locomotives

Name	No	Builder	Type	Built
Dolphin	1	H/Hunslet (4394)	4wDM	1952
Walrus	2	H/Hunslet (4395)	4wDM	1952
Sea Lion	—	Bagnall (1484)	2-4-0T	1896

Isle of Man Railway

The 3ft gauge Isle of Man Railway is a survivor of a system which covered the whole island. Almost continuous operation since 1874 makes it one of the oldest preserved railways in the British Isles. The railway has changed little since the turn of the century and retains much of its Edwardian atmosphere. It runs for 15 miles between Douglas and Port Erin through the island's rolling southern countryside. One of the original locomotives built in 1874 is still in daily service making it one of the oldest operational steam locomotives in the British Isles
Operations Superintendent: M. G. Warhurst
Headquarters: Isle of Man Railways, Strathallan Crescent, Douglas, Isle of Man
Telephone: Douglas (0624) 663366
Main station: Douglas
Other public stations: Port Soderick, Santon, Castletown, Port Erin, Ballasalla, Port St Mary
Car parks: Douglas, Ballasalla, Castletown, Port Erin
Access by public transport: Isle of Man Transport buses to main centres
Refreshment facilities: Port Erin and Douglas

Locomotives

Name	No	Builder	Type	Built
Loch	4*	B/Peacock (1416)	2-4-0T	1874
Peveril	6	B/Peacock (1524)	2-4-0T	1875
G.H. Wood	10	B/Peacock (4662)	2-4-0T	1905
Maitland	11*	B/Peacock (4663)	2-4-0T	1905
Hutchinson	12*	B/Peacock (5126)	2-4-0T	1908
Kissack	13*	B/Peacock (5382)	2-4-0T	1910
—	19*	Walker (GNR (I))	diesel railcar	1950
—	20*	Walker (GNR (I))	diesel railcar	1951

*Operational, Nos 6 and 10 stored out of use, not on display.

On display in museum at Port Erin

Name	No	Builder	Type	Built
Sutherland	1	B/Peacock (1253)	2-4-0T	1873
Caledonia	15	Dubs & Co (2178)	0-6-0T	1885
Mannin	16	B/Peacock (6296)	2-4-0T	1926

Owned by Isle of Man Railway Society (not on display)

Name	No	Builder	Type	Built
Mona	5	B/Peacock (1417)	2-4-0T	1874
*Tynwald**	7	B/Peacock (2038)	2-4-0T	1880
Fenella†	8	B/Peacock (3610)	2-4-0T	1894
Douglas	9	B/Peacock (3815)	2-4-0T	1896

*Chassis only
†Undergoing restoration to working order.

Souvenir shops: Douglas and Port Erin
Museum: Port Erin
Depot: Douglas
Length of line: 15¼ miles, 3ft gauge
Passenger trains: Douglas-Port Erin
Period of public operation: Daily 17 April-27 September
Facilities for disabled: Level access throughout Douglas and Port Erin stations including snack bar. Carriages able to carry wheelchairs, ramps provided. Advance notice helpful

Manx Electric Railway

The 3ft gauge Manx Electric Railway is a unique survivor of Victorian high technology. A mixture of railway and tramway practice, it was built in 1893 and was a pioneer in the use of electric traction. Two of the original cars are still in service making them the oldest tramcars still in operation in the British Isles. After leaving Douglas, the railway passes the newly opened Groudle Glen Railway before reaching the charming village of Laxey, home of the Snaefell Mountain Railway. The line continues over some of the most breathtaking coastal scenery in the island before reaching its terminus at Ramsey nearly 18 miles from Douglas

Operations Superintendent: M. G. Warhurst
Headquarters: Isle of Man Railways, Strathallan Crescent, Douglas, Isle of Man
Telephone: Douglas (0624) 663366
Main station: Douglas (Derby Castle)
Other public stations: Laxey, Ramsey
Car parks: Douglas, Laxey, Ramsey nearby

Motor Cars

Nos	*Type*	*Seats*	*Body*	*Built*
1, 2	Unvestibuled saloon	34	Milnes	1893
5, 6, 7, 9	Vestibuled saloon	32	Milnes	1894
14, 15, 17, 18	Cross-bench open	56	Milnes	1898
16	Cross-bench open	56	Milnes	1898
19-22*	Winter saloon	48	Milnes	1899
23	Centre-cab locomotive	—	IOMT & EP	1900
25-27	Cross-bench open	56	Milnes	1898
28-31	Cross-bench open	56	ERTCW	1904
32, 33	Cross-bench open	56	UEC	1906

*21 re-bodied 1991, McArd/MER

Trailers

Nos	*Type*	*Seats*	*Body*	*Built*
13	Cross-bench open	44	Milnes	1893
36, 37	Cross-bench open	44	Milnes	1894
40, 41, 44	Cross-bench open	44	EE Co	1930
42, 43	Cross-bench open	44	Milnes	1903
45-48	Cross-bench open	44	Milnes	1899
49-50, 53, 54	Cross-bench open	44	Milnes	1893
52	pw flatcar (ex trailer)	—	Milnes	1893
55, 56	Cross-bench open	44	ERTCW	1904
57, 58	Saloon	32	ERTCW	1904
59	Special Saloon	18	Milnes	1895
60	Cross-bench open	44	Milnes	1896
61, 62	Cross-bench open	44	UEC	1906

Access by public transport: Isle of Man Transport buses to main centres
Depots: Douglas, Laxey, Ramsey
Refreshment facilities: Laxey
Museum and souvenirs: Ramsey
Length of line: 17 miles, 3ft gauge

Passenger service: Douglas-Ramsey
Period of public operations: Daily 13 April-27 September
Special notes: Folded wheelchairs can be carried. Please notify in advance

Ramsey Electric Railway Museum

M

Location: Manx Electric Railway Station, Parsonage Road, Ramsey, Isle of Man
Operating society/organisation: (General enquiries) Isle of Man Railway Society, 4 Clifton Road, Rugby, Warwickshire (applications for special opening) c/o Isle of Man Railways, Douglas, IoM
Telephone: (General enquiries) 0788 543026
Car parks: Locally in nearby street
Access by public transport: Manx Electric Railway station adjoins museum; Douglas-Laxey-Ramsey buses pass within a few yards, alight at Parsonage Road

No	*Origin/Type*	*Built*
	Manx Electric Railway	
23	MER Bo-Bo electric loco	1900
26	MER Bogie freight car	1895
	Douglas Horse Tramway	
11	Douglas, open toastrack	1886
47	Douglas, bulkhead car	1911
49	Douglas, convertible car	1935
—	Horse tram transporter wagon	c1930
	Queens Pier Tramway	
—	Hibberd 'Planet' 4WPM (2037)	1937
—	Hibberd-PRV bogie trailer (2038)	1937
—	4w Skip, ex-Ballajora Quarry	
—	4w Skip, ex-Poortown Quarry	

On site facilities: Museum shop, toilets in MER station

Public opening: Monday to Friday only; late May to mid-September 11.00-15.45

Special notes: For parties travellin by MER, opening outside normal hours may sometimes be possible

Snaefell Mountain Railway

The 3ft 6in gauge Snaefell Mountain Railway is unique. It is the only electrically-driven mountain railway in the British Isles. Almost all the rolling stock is original and dates back to 1895. The railway begins its journey at the picturesque village of Laxey where its terminus is shared with the Manx Electric Railway. The climb to the summit of Snaefell (2,036ft) is a steep one and the cars travel unassisted up gradients as steep as 1 in 12. From the summit, the views extend to Wales, Scotland, England and Ireland

Operations Superintendent: M. G. Warhurst

Headquarters: Isle of Man Railways, Strathallan Crescent, Douglas, Isle of Man

Telephone: Douglas (0624) 663366

Main station: Laxey

Nos	*Type*	*Seats*	*Body*	*Buil*
1-4, 6	Vestibuled saloon	48	Milnes	189
5 (rebuild)	Vestibuled saloon	48	MER/ Kinnin	197

Other public stations: Bungalow, Summit

Car parks: Laxey, Bungalow (nearby)

Access by public transport: Manx Electric Railway or Isle of Man Transport bus to Laxey

Refreshment facilities: Laxey, Summit

Museum: Ramsey

Souvenirs: Summit

Length of line: 5 miles, 3ft 6in gauge passenger service: Laxey-Snaefell summit

Period of public operation: Daily 2 May-27 September

Special notes: No special facilities for disabled

Below:
Although not a recent photograph the Snaefell Mountain Railway is unique in that each winter it dismantles part of its overhead catenary to save it from the ravages of the weather. No 4 pushes the wire trolley past the site of 'The Bungalow'. *R. E. Ruffell*

Miniature Railways

udley End Railway
udley End, Saffron Walden, Essex. Tel: (0799) 41354
: 41956
eneral Manager: Donald Saggers
pening details: Daily — Easter week, summer half-
rm, summer school holidays; Saturdays, Sundays
nd bank holidays April-October (from 14.00)
)¼in gauge; 1½-miles long; 3 steam, 3 diesel
comotives
ublic access: BR Audley End (1 mile), free car park
ite facilities: Light refreshments, toilets
ote: (Postal address) Audley End Estate Office,
runketts, Wendens Ambo, Saffron Walden, Essex
B11 4JL

reat Cockcrow Railway
ardwick Lane, Lyne, Chertsey, Surrey. Tel: Mon-Fri
932) 228950; Sun (0932) 565474
pening details: Every Sunday May to October
clusive, 14.15-17.30
¼in gauge; normal run ⅞-mile; 14 steam
comotives, 1 electric, 1 petrol (nine normally in
rvice)
ublic access: BR Chertsey (1 ¼ miles); London
uslines 561, 586 Holloway Hill (½-mile), free car
ark
ite facilities: Toilet; light refreshments

ightwater Valley Theme Park
orth Stainley, Nr Ripon, North Yorkshire. Tel: (0765)
35368 (24 hours), 6355321 (office)
pening details: 11 April-25 October (NOT daily,
lephone for details)
hief Engineer: Chris Bulmer
5in gauge; 1-mile long; 6 steam, 1 diesel, 1 petrol
comotives
ublic access: BR Harrogate (12 miles), BR Thirsk (9
iles), free car park
ite facilities: Self service restaurant, coffee shop,
st foods, theatre, toilets (including disabled),
hops, selection of rollercoaster rides and other
ttractions

Ioors Valley Railway
*larogauge Ltd, Moors Valley Country Park, Horton
oad, Ashley Heath, Nr Ringwood, Dorset.* Tel: (0425)
71415
eneral Manager: Mr J. A. W. Haylock
pening details: Open every weekend throughout
ne year, plus half-term holidays and daily from
pring Bank Holiday to end September. Santa
pecials in December
¼ in gauge; 1-mile long; 6 steam locomotives
ublic access: BR Christchurch, free car park
ite facilities: Toilets (including disabled), shop

Above:
Head on view of a Curwen-built 10.25 inch gauge 2-8-2. Based on a Denver & Rio Grande Rail Road prototype, this locomotive runs at Audley End. *R. E. Ruffell*

LHJC
5

Marketing Names

A number of lines make use of a marketing name in addition to their usual title. This list has been included as a guide to those that may be used.

Airfield Line — Coventry Steam Centre
Battlefield Line — Battlefield Steam Railway
Battlefield Steam Railway — Battlefield Line
Britain's International Steam Railway — Nene Valley Railway
Butterley Park Miniature Railway - Midland Railway Centre
Coventry Steam Centre — Airfield Line
Dean Forest Railway — Friendly Forest Line
East Lancashire Railway — East Lancs
East Lancs — East Lancashire Railway
East Somerset Railway — Strawberry Line
England's Friendly Little Line — Leighton Buzzard Railway
England's Highest Narrow Gauge Railway — South Tynedale Railway
Friendly Forest Line — Dean Forest Railway
Golden Valley Light Railway — Midland Railway Centre
Harboro Line — Northampton Steam Railway
Keighley & Worth Valley Railway — Worth Valley
Leighton Buzzard Railway — England's Friendly Little Line
Llanberis Lake Railway — Rheilffordd Llyn Padarn
Llanfair Railway — Welshpool & Llanfair Light Railway
Mid-Hants Railway — Watercress Line
Midland Railway Centre — Butterley Park Miniature Railway
Midland Railway Centre — Golden Valley Light Railway
Midland Railway Centre — More than just a railway
More than just a railway — Midland Railway Centre
Nene Valley Railway — Britain's International Steam Railway
North Norfolk Railway — Poppy Line
Northampton Steam Railway — Harboro Line
One of the Great Little Trains — Talyllyn Railway
Plym Valley Railway — Woodland Line
Poppy Line — North Norfolk Railway
Primrose Line — South Devon Railway
Purbeck Line — Swanage Railway
Ratty — Ravenglass & Eskdale Railway
Ravenglass & Eskdale Railway — Ratty
Ravenglass & Eskdale Railway — T' laal Ratty
Rheilffordd Llyn Padarn — Llanberis Lake Railway
Sittingbourne & Kemsley Light Railway — Sittingbourne Steam Railway
Sittingbourne Steam Railway — Sittingbourne & Kemsley Light Railway
South Devon Railway — Primrose Line
South Tynedale Railway — England's Highest Narrow Gauge Railway
Strawberry Line — East Somerset Railway
Swanage Railway— Purbeck Line
Swindon & Cricklade Railway — Tiddlydyke
T' laal Ratty — Ravenglass & Eskdale Railway
Talyllyn Railway — One of the Great Little Trains
Tiddlydyke — Swindon & Cricklade Railway
VCT — Vintage Carriages Trust
Vintage Carriages Trust — VCT
Watercress Line — Mid-Hants Railway
Welshpool & Llanfair Light Railway — Llanfair Railway
Woodland Line — Plym Valley Railway
Worth Valley — Keighley & Worth Valley Railway

Late Information

Transfers

No 27001 has been transferred form the Caledonian Railway to the Bo'ness & Kinneil line, No 25057 has been transferred from the Buckinghamshire Railway Centre to the North Norfolk Railway.

The Nene Valley-based DB Class 80, 80.014 has been transferred to The Netherlands for a full overhaul.

No 4144 has been transferred from a private site at Swindon to the Crewe Heritage Centre along with 4121 and 4953 from the Dean Forest.

Glasgow Museum of Transport's No 256 *Glen Douglas* has been transferred to Bo'ness for restoration to working order.

Peckett 1722 and Manning Wardle 2015 have left the Birmingham Railway Museum, both for private sites.

Loans

Severn Valley-based 2857 is going to the Gloucestershire Warwickshire Railway until the end of the year.

Birmingham Railway Museum is to lend 7752 to the South Devon Railway, and not as stated elsewhere.

The Royal Corps of Transport have loaned Hunslet 3798/1953 No 198 *Royal Engineer* and a Barclay 0-4-0DH to the Isle of Wight Railway, both locomotives are eventually destined for a museum at Chatham.

Didcot Railway Centre is lending 3822 to the West Somerset Railway for the summer.

Left:
Former Lambton Hetton & Joicey Collieries No 5 is now preserved on the North Yorkshire Moors, it is seen on 19 May 1991 pounding towards Goathland assisted in the rear by No 2398. *Robin Stewart-Smith*

Association of Railway preservation Societies Ltd

Company Limited by Guarantee and not having a share capital.

Registered in England No 1222717

(Registered Office: 21 Market Place, Wednesbury, West Midlands WS10 7AY)

Administrative Office: 3 Orchard Close, Watford, Hertfordshire WD1 3DU. Tel: (0923) 221280. Fax: (0923) 241023 (ARPS).

President: Dame Margaret Weston DBE

Vice President: Capt Peter F. Manisty MBE, Royal Navy (Retd) (also Member of Council), 2 Cleaver Square, London SE11 5DW. Tel: 071-735 5012.

Directors/Council of Management

Chairman and Legal Advisor:
David Morgan, 7 Cheyne Place, London SW3 4HH. Tel: 01-352 6077

Vice Chairman and Meetings Officer:
Peter Ovenstone, 33 Palmerston Place, Edinburgh EH12 5AU. Tel: 031-225 1486 (answerphone).

Company Secretary:
Robert Yates FCA, 21 Market Place, Wednesbury, West Midlands WS10 7AY. Tel: (Office) 021-556 1084.

General Administrator:
Raymond Williams, 16 Woodbrook, Charing, Ashford, Kent TN27 0DN. Tel: 023-371 2130.

Treasurer:
Reg Palk, 5 Bradene Close, Wootton Bassett, Swindon, Wilts SN4 8DG. Tel: 0793 853166 (ansaphone).

Technical Officer:
David Madden, The Station, Sheringham, Norfolk NR26 8RA. Tel: (0263) 822045.

Press Officer:
John Jeffery, 42 North Street, Oundle, Peterborough PE8 4AL. Tel: (Office) (0733) 67474, ext 2129, (Home) (0832) 73010.

Annual Award:
John Ransom, Woodside, Craggan, Lochearnhead, Perthshire FK19 8QD.

Coaching Stock:
Chris Smyth, 7 Woodside, Knutsford, Cheshire WA16 8BX. Tel: 0565 51241.

Narrow Gauge:
David Woodhouse MBE, c/o Talyllyn Railway, Wharf Station, Tywyn, Gwynedd LL36 9EY. Tel: 0654 710472.

Minutes Secretary and Overseas Liaison:
Richard Tapper, 39 Grange Court, Boundary Road, Newbury, Berkshire RG14 7PH. Tel: (0635) 30464.

Membership Secretary (Corporate):
David Woodhouse MBE, c/o Talyllyn Railway, Wharf Station, Tywyn, Gwynedd LL36 9EY. Tel: (0654) 710472.

Membership Secretary (Private and Membership Records):
Arthur Harding, 6 Ullswater Grove, Alresford, Hants SO24 9RP. Tel: (0962) 733327.

Journal Editor:
Rodney Pitt, 1 Queen's Drive, Newport, Shropshire TF10 7EU. Tel/Fax: 0952 811444.

Association Officers

Chairman of ARPS
John Lockett, 21 Knollwood Road, Branbridge, County Down BT32 4PE. Tel: 08206 22018

European Co-ordinator:
Livius Kooy, Prins Bernhardstraat 25, 7481 GX Haaksbergen, The Netherlands. Tel: 31 (5427) 17357.

Sales:
Frank Sheppard, Sobbyns, St Lucians Lane, Wallingford, OX10 9ER. Tel: 0491 36983

Information Papers:
John Crane, 7 Robert Close, Potters Bar, Herts EN6 2DR. Tel: 0707 43568.

Magazine Competition Organiser:
David Wilson, 19 Manor Close, Rothwell, Leeds, West Yorkshire LS26 0RF. Tel: 0532 824147.

Museum Liaison:
Stephen Dyke, Darlington Railway Museum, North Road Station, Darlington DL3 6ST. Tel: 03255 460532 (office), 091-548 2163 (home).

Railway Castings:
Adrian Crafer, 36 Parklands Road, Swindon, Wiltshire SN3 1EG.

Railway Heritage Awards (enquiries):
Gordon Biddle, The Crossings, Levens, Kendal, Cumbria. Tel: (05395) 60993.

Railway Heritage Awards (entry forms): Arthur Harding, 6 Ullswater Grove, Alresford, Hants SO24 9NP. Tel: (0962) 733327

Society Archivist:
Susan Youell, 5 North Grange Mount, Leeds LS6 2BY. Tel: 0532 786441.

Asscoiation Advisors

Diesel/Electrical Adviser:
John Crane, 7 Robert Close, Potters Bar, Herts. Tel: (0707) 43568.

Historical Adviser:
Dick Riley, 115 Albemarle Road, Beckenham, Kent BR3 2HS.

Publications Adviser:
Roger Cromblehome, 140 New Road, Netherton, Dudley, West Midlands DY2 6AY.

Railway Catering:
David Williams, The Station, Sheringham, Norfolk NR26 8RA. Tel: 0263 822045.

Railway Operating Adviser:
Allan Garraway MBE, Coedwig, Nethybridge Road, Boat of Garten, Invernesshire PH24 3BQ. Tel: 047-983 303.

Rating:
David Smith, 5 Svenskaby, Orton Wistoe, Peterborough PE2 0ZY. Tel: 0733 239866.

Railtours Adviser:
Malcolm Burton, 85 Balmoral Road, Gillingham, Kent.

Special Projects Adviser:
Andrew Roberts, 2 Litchfield Close, Frog Hall, Brixworth, Northampton NN6 9BP.

Technical Adviser:
John Snell, RH&DR Head Office, New Romney, Kent TN28 8PL.

embers of the Association of Railway Preservation Societies

re no address is given, it can be found the Society's entry within the alphabetical gs.

Members

amas Locomotive Society: Mr K. J. Tait, 73 y Road, Heaton Moor, Stockport, shire SK4 4NG

n Railway Co Ltd (Avon Valley Railway)

bell Railway Preservation Society

es Railway Co Ltd

Bulleid Society Ltd: Mr D. A. Foale, ron', South Chailey, Lewes, East Sussex 4AD

brian Railways Society Ltd

rphilly Railway Society Ltd

sewater Light Railway & Museum Co

sey & Wallingford RPS

e Valley Railway Co Ltd

is Railway Society

ington Railway Preservation Society

Valley Railway Association (South Devon way)

n Forest Railway Co Ltd

Lancashire Railway Preservation Society

Somerset Railway Co Ltd

iniog Railway Society Ltd

ield Light Railway Society Ltd

nds of the National Railway Museum

at Central Railway Co

at Western Society Ltd (Didcot Railway tre)

li Railway Co Ltd

lass Trust: Mr E. R. C. Oades, 5 Senlac , St Leonards-on-Sea, Sussex

Steam Preservation Society Ltd

hley & Worth Valley Preservation Society

eside Railway Society

hton Buzzard Narrow Gauge Railway iety Ltd

gollen Railway Society

omotive Club of Great Britain: Mr R. L. ick, 8 Wolviston Avenue, Bishopgate, York 3DD

omotive Owners Group (Scotland) Ltd: Mr Stevenson, 4 Queens Road, Blackhall, burgh EH4 2BY

d Marian Locomotive Fund: Mr H. Jones, lden', 139 Stoops Lane, Bessacar, caster DN4 7RG

n Line Steam Trust Ltd (Great Central way)

chant Navy Locomotive Preservation iety Ltd: Mr R. Abercrombie, 12 Inglewood nue, Heatherside, Camberley, Surrey

-Hants Railway Preservation Society

dleton Railway Trust Ltd

land & Great Northern Joint Railway iety Ltd (North Norfolk Railway)

land 4F Preservation Society: Mr I. nson, 13 Shepley Close, Hazel Grove, ckport, Cheshire SK7 6JJ

land Railway Trust Ltd

ne Valley International Steam Railway

th Eastern Locomotive Preservation Group: D. F. Martin, 21 Grassington Avenue, thallerton, North Yorkshire DL7 8SY

North Gloucestershire Railway Co Ltd: Mr R. H. Wales, 'Wellesbourne', Oakfield Street, Tivoli, Cheltenham, Gloucestershire GL33 8HR

North York Moors Historical Railway Trust

Quainton Railway Society (Buckinghamshire Railway Centre)

Railway Preservation Society of Ireland

Ravenglass & Eskdale Railway Preservation Society Ltd

Ruislip Lido Railway Society

Scottish Railway Preservation Society (Bo'ness & Kinneil Railway)

Severn Valley Railway Holdings PLC

Shackerstone Railway Society Ltd (The Battlefield Line)

Sittingbourne & Kemsley Light Railway Ltd

South Tynedale Railway Preservation Society

Southern Electric Group: Mr P. Stavely, 247 Davidson Road, Croydon CR0 6DR

Stanier 8F Locomotive Society Ltd: Mr D. R. McIntosh, 296 Lower Hillmorton Road, Rugby, Warwickshire CV21 4AE

Steam in Hereford Ltd (6000 Locomotive Association): Mr B. R. Wallis, 8 Little Birch Croft, Whitchurch, Bristol BS14 0JB

Stour Valley Railway Preservation Society (East Anglian Railway Museum)

Strathspey Railway Association

Talyllyn Railway Preservation Society

Tenterden Railway Co Ltd (Kent & East Sussex Railway)

Vintage Carriages Trust

Wainwright 'C' Preservation Society: Mr I. Demaid, 69 Bromley Gardens, Bromley, Kent BR2 0ES

Welshpool & Llanfair Light Railway Preservation Co Ltd

Wight Locomotive Society (Isle of Wight Steam Railway)

Yorkshire Dales Railway Museum Trust (Embsay Steam Railway)

1247 Society: Capt W. G. Smith, 1 Church Road, Willington, Bedford MK44 3QD

1708 Locomotive Preservation Trust Ltd: Mr G. W. Kingham, Registered Office, 106 Stanford Road, Luton, Beds LU2 0QA

6201 Princess Elizabeth Society Ltd: E. J. Whitlock, 4 Lypiatt View, Bussage, Stroud, Gloucestershire LG6 8DA

Associate Members

A4 Locomotive Society Ltd: Mr G. R. Pope, Secretary, Keeper's Cottage, Muntham Farm, North End, Findon, Worthing BN14 0RQ

Avonside Steam Preservation Society: B. Barham, The Buffers, High Street, Hinxton, Saffron Walden, Essex

Ayrshire Railway Preservation Group (Scottish Industrial Railway Centre

Battle of Britain Locomotive Preservation Society: Mr R. J. Tanner, 317 Cardington Road, Bedford MK42 0DU

Bodmin & Wenford Railway plc

BRC&W Type 3 Preservation Group: Mr R. Hodgkinson, Flat 6, 4 Briarswood, Winchester Road, Shirley, Southampton, Hants SO24 5QX

Brechin Railway Preservation Society (Caledonian Railway)

Brecon Mountain Railway Cod Ltd

Bressingham Steam Preservation Co Ltd

Britannia Locomotive Society: Mr A. A. Lawson, Gaylands, 9 Bennett Drive, Myton Grange, Warwick CV34 6QJ

Butetown Historic Railway Society Ltd (Wales Railway Centre)

Cadeby Light Railway

Camelot Locomotive Society: Mr P. W. Gibbs, 3 Garden Close, Northolt, Middx UB5 5ND

Conwy Valley Railway Museum Ltd

Cornish Steam Locomotive Preservation Society Ltd: Mr M. Orme, 3 Jubilee Terrace, Goonhavern, Truro, Cornwall TR4 9JY

Cotswold Steam Preservation Ltd: Mr J. M. Colley, Birchwood Farm, Bridgnorth Road, Shatterford, Nr Bewdley, Worcs DX12 1TP

Derwent Railway Society: Mr S. Buck, Owsen Place, Lamplough, Workington CA14 4SO

Diesel and Electric Group: Mr R. E. Tiller, 40 Newbarn Park Road, Taunton, Somerset TA1 4NP

Downpatrick & Ardglass Railway Co Ltd: Mr M. Collins, 29 Glenco Park, Antrim Road, Belfast BT36 7PT

Dyfed Railway Co Ltd (Teifi Valley Railway)

Eastleigh Railway Preservation Society: Mr D. B. Smith, 17 Twiggs End Close, Locksheath, Southampton, Hants SO3 6ET

Errol Station Museum Trust: David Tough, 48 Mayness Park Drive, Blairgowrie, Perthshire PH10 6LX

Fairbourne & Barmouth Railway

Forest Pannier Tank Fund: Mr J. S. Metherall, 15 Sudbrook Way, Gloucester GL4 9QP

Forest Prairie Fund: Mrs H. Davies, 55 Victoria Street, Cinderford, Glos GL14 2ET

Foxcote Manor Society: Mr I. N. Travers, 5 Harlow Avenue, Upton-by-Chester, Cheshire CH2 1NQ

Foyle Valley Railway: Arthur Thompson, 44 Peeten Park, Londonderry, N Ireland BT47 2PA

Friends of Swindon Railway Museum Ltd

Gloucestershire Warwickshire Steam Railway PLC

Gravesend Railway Enthusiasts Society: Mr D. Hanger, 47 Lower Range Road, Gravesend, Kent DA12 2QL

Great Central Railway Coach Group: Mr K. H. Brooker, Manor Road, Sulgrave, Banbury, Oxon OX17 2RY

Great Western Preservations Ltd: Mr A. R. Machon, 15 Calder Close, Maidenhead, Berkshire SL6 7RS

The Gresley Society: Mr G. Goslin, 8 Pevensey Grove, Flitwick, Bedford MK45 1SD

GWR 813 Preservation Fund: Mr P. Goss, 23 Hatchmere, Thornbury, Bristol BS12 3EU

Hastings Diesels Ltd: Mr N. Carter, 40 Westwood Park, Forest Hill, London SE23 3QH

Hull & Barnsley Railway Stock Fund: Mr A. Halman, 6 Chequerfield Court, Chequerfield Avenue, Pontefract, West Yorkshire WP8 2TQ

Irchester Narrow Gauge Railway Trust: Mr R. Hingston, 'Lysander', 5 Merchants Lane, Cranfield, Bedfordshire MK43 0DA

Ivatt Locomotive Trust: Mr R. B. Miller, 'Ducal', 25 Loudham Road, Little Chalfont, Amersham, Buckinghamshire

Lambton No 29 Syndicate: Mr J. M. Richardson, 5 Ravine Hill, Filey, North Yorkshire YO14 9EU

Lancashire County Fire Brigade Railway Society: Mr K. A. Bridge, 93 Ainslie Road, Fulwood, Preston PR2 3DE

Lancashire & Yorkshire Railway Preservation Society: Mr R. J. Rouse, c/o Keighley & Worth Valley Railway

Leicester Industrial Locomotive Group: Mr J. P. Bailey, 414 Hinckley Road, Leicester LE3 0WA

Lincolnshire Coast Light Railway Historical Vehicles Trust: Mr H. L. Goy, 12 Giles Street, Cleethorpes DN35 8AE

Liverpool Locomotive Preservation Group: Mr K. Soper, 90 Brick Kiln Lane, Rufford, Lancs L40 1SY

Lloyds Railway Society: Hon Secretary, Lloyds, Lime Street, London EC3

LM 2MT 46464 Trust: Mr I. N. Fraser, Palace Gates, Viewfield Road, Arbroath, Angus DD11 2BS

London & North Western Society: Mr J. C. James, 'Solaby', 4 Longview Drive, Huyton, Liverpool L36 6EE

Lowthers Railway Society Ltd: Mr D. Lappin, 44 Lednock Road, Stepps, Glasgow G33 6LU

Manchester Rail Travel Society: Mr F. G. Cronin, 12 Chiltern Road, Ramsbottom, Bury BL0 9LF

Manston Locomotive Preservation Society: T. L. Mann, 41 Crow Hill Road, Garlinge, Margate, Kent CT19 5PF

Maunsell Locomotive Society: Mr R. Packham, Chairman, 132 Church Road, Swanscombe, Kent DA10 0PH

North London Locomotive Preservation Society: Mr R. T. Moore, 2 Woodbine Grove, Enfield, Middlesex EN2 0EA

North Staffordshire Railway Co Ltd (Cheddleton Railway Centre)

North Tyneside Steam Railway Association (Stephenson Railway Museum)

Peak Rail PLC

Plym Valley Railway Association

Pontypool & Blaenavon Railway Society

Railway Club of Wales: Mr N. Wessell, Aberlogin Cottage, Llanmorlais, Swansea SA4 3TY

Redditch Steam Locomotive Preservation Society: Mr A. Marsden, 72 Longhurst Croft, West Heath, Birmingham B31 4SQ

Rheilffordd Llyn Tegid Ltd (Bala Lake Railway)

Romney, Hythe & Dymchurch Railway Association

Rutland Railway Museum

Salisbury Steam Locomotive Preservation Trust: Mr E. J. Roper, 33 Victoria Road, Wilton, Salisbury, Wiltshire SP2 0OZ

The Cutty Sark Maritime Trust: Janet Hales, 2 Greenwich Church Street, Greenwich, London SW10 9BG

Somerset & Dorset Railway Trust: M. J. Palmer, The Haven, Chandlers Lane, Edington, Bridgwater, Somerset TA7 9JY

Southern Steam Trust (Swanage Railway)

South Yorkshire Railway Preservation Society

Stanier Black Five Locomotive Preservation Society: Mr D. J. Porter, 29 High Street, Shoreham Village, Kent TN14 7TD

Steamport Southport (Southport Railway Centre)

Steam Power Trust '65: Mr K. H. Cockerill, 30 Hartburn Lane, Stockton-on-Tees TS18 3QH

Stephenson Locomotive Society: Mr B. F. Gilliam, 25 Regency Close, Chigwell, Essex IG7 5NY

Swindon & Cricklade Railway Society

Swindon Railway Workshops Ltd: Mr Bill Parker, Rodbourne Road, Swindon, Wiltshire SN2 2AA

Telford Horsehay Steam Trust Ltd

Thompson B1 Locomotive Trust: Mr J. G. Gwnett, 11 Valance End, Dunstable LU6 3LP

Tunbridge Wells & Eridge RPS: Mr F. Wallace, The Old Dairy, Snatts Lane, Uckfield, East Sussex TN22 2AL

Underground Railway Rolling Stock Trust: Mr D. C. Alexander, 13 Irvine Drive, Stoke Mandeville HP22 5UN

Urie Locomotive Society: Mr A. Ball, 'Lavenham', Adams Lane, Selbourne, Alton, Hants GU34 3LJ

Wells & Walsingham Light Railway

Welsh Highland Light Railway 1964 Ltd

Welsh Industrial and Maritime Museum (Swansea Industrial & Maritime Museum)

West Somerset Railway Co Ltd

Western Locomotive Association: Mr A. M. Clarke, 6 Greatly, Welwyn Garden City, Herts AL7 4TS

Winchcombe Railway Museum Association

Worcester Locomotive Society Ltd: Mr A. T. Dowling, 23 Belle Orchard Close, Ledbury, Herefordshire WR14 1HR

1857 Society: Mr K. R. Bowen, 18 Lochmore Close, Hollycroft, Hinckley, Leicestershire

·7 Preservation Society: Mr N. Powles, tion House, Lower Heyford, Oxon OX5 3PD

·4 Preservation Society Ltd: Mr E. F. W. ;, 63 Georges Hill, Widmer End, High combe, Buckinghamshire HP15 6BH

·2 Preservation Group: Mr W. L. Jones, 74 church Road, Bridgend, Glamorgan CF31

·28 Stanier Class Five Locomotive Society · Mr J. B. Hollingsworth, 'Creua', nfrothen, Penrhyndeudraeth, Gwynedd 8 6SH

·00 Duke of Gloucester Steam Locomotive st Ltd: Mr J. Shuttleworth, 25 Patiene Road, pham, London SW11 2PY

erseas Affiliate Members

AC: Dr J. Brenot, Boite No 1, 33034 Cedex deaux, France

PF: The Chairman, Caixa Postal 6501)51, Sao Paulo, Brazil

CFM: M J. David, President, Marcilly-sur-ulne, 37330 Chateau-la-Valliee, France

PEVA: M Jacques Pradaro, 21 Rue eneguard, 75006 Paris 6, France

sociation Bordelaise des Amis: Dr J. F. not, Boite No 1, 33034 Bordeaux Cedex, nce

sociation of Railway Enthusiasts Ltd: Wal chberg, Box 2 Yarrambat, Victoria 3091, stralia

ains Magazine: Chief Librarian, Mr G. H. ry, Kalmbach Publishing Co, 1027 North 7th eet, Milwaulkee, USA

rliner Eisenbahn Freunde: Herr Rudiger ich, Stresemanstrasse 30, 1000, Berlin, rmany

M Blonay-Chamby: Mr J. F. Andrist, PO Box 3 CH 1001, Lausanne, Switzerland

seumtramway: Herr A. Fleissner, Mariazell-aufsee, An der Museumbham 5, Postfach , A-8630 Mariazel, Austria

Museum Buurt Spoorweg: Mr H. Cats, Industrie Straat, 87/F, 7553 LS Hengelo, The Netherlands

National Federation of Rail Societies: Mr K. Henderson, PO Box 2429, Auckland, New Zealand

National Museum of Science & Technology: The Librarian, PO Box 9724, Terminal T, Ottawa, Ontario K1G 5A3, Canada

National Railway Historic Society: Mr V. A. Vaughan, 320 Wisconsin Avenue, Oak Park, Illinois 60302, USA

National Railroad Museum: Mr R. A. Sauvey, PO Box 28171, Green Bay, WI 54304, USA.

Pacific Vapeur Club: M Henri Williaume, Boite Postale 115 76303, Sotteveille-les-Rouen, France

Smalsparet Vajo-Vastervik: Philip Groves, WHVJ-Sec, Box 64 14600, Tullinge, Sweden

Stichting Brabant Rail: Mr J. E. F. L. Simons, Karel Dormanlaan 14, 4B19 BK Breda, Netherlands

Stoomscentrum Maldegem: Rik Degruyter, De Streep 19, B-B340 Damme-Sysele, Belgium

Stoompoorlijn Dendermonde-Puurs: Mr L. Blommaerts, Ten Berg 101, B 9300 AALS, Belgium

Stoomtram Goes Borsele: Mr J. P. Wytenburg, Postbus 250 4460, AR Goes, Netherlands

Stoomtram Hoon-Medemblik: Mr Peter Scholten, PO Box 137, 1620-AC Hoorn, Netherlands

UK Affiliate Members

Great Western Railway Museum

Ian Allan Group: Chairman, Mr Ian Allan, Clock House, Station Approach, Shepperton TW17 8AS

Jarrold Colour Publications: The Chairman, Barrack Street, Norwich, Norfolk NR3 1TR

Leicester University Library: Periodicals Department, University Road, Leicester LE1 7RH

London Transport Museum Library: Mrs M. A. Fletcher, 39 Wellington Street, Covent Garden, London WC2E 7BB

Monkswearmouth Station Museum: The Curator, North Bridge Street, Sunderland SR5 1AP

Narrow Gauge Railways of Wales: Mr D. Woodhouse, Wharf Station, Tywny, Gwynedd LL36 9EY

National Tramway Museum Society: The Chairman, Crich, Matlock, Derbyshire DE4 5DP

National Trust Industrial Railway Museum (Penryhn Castle)

Railway Associations in London: Mr S. J. Butler, 163 Lambpits, Hoddesdon, Herts EN11 8EF

Transport Trust: Mr D. Muirhead, c/o British Coal Corporation, Hobart Huse, Grosvenor Place, London SW1X 7AE

Ulster Folk & Transport Museum: Mr J. S. Moore, Cultra Manor, Hollywood, Co Down, Northern ireland BT18 0EU

Westinghouse Signals: Mr H. R. Preater, PO Box 79, Pew Hill, Chippenham, Wiltshire SN15 1ND

Private Members and their Societies

Alderney Railway Society

Cleethorpes Coast Light Railway

Coventry Steam Railway Centre

Glyn Valley Tramway Group: Mr B. Heatley, Cantlow House, Vicarage Lane, Burton-in-Wirral, Cheshire L64 5TJ

Great Western Preservation Group

Llanberris Lake Railway Ltd

North Downs Steam Railway

Ongar Railway Preservation Society

Paddle Steamer Preservation Society

Shanes Castle

South Down Railway Society: Mr J. Carrall, Glendile House, Brentor, Dunkineely, Co Donegal

---

To a person actively interested in nationwide railway reservation as opposed to one particular preservation scheme, PRIVATE MEMBERSHIP of the ASSOCIATION OF RAILWAY PRESERVATION OCIETIES LTD offer many advantages. Three major neetings are organised annually, often at the railway ite of a leading Member Society. Here one can meet well known personalities in the railway preservation world, and the host society invariably lays on a full day's programme which is both stimulating and enjoyable.

The ARPS Journal is sent to members, containing nostly the latest news of member societies' activities out also full of interesting titbits such as lists of steam locomotives for sale.

Railways Restored and other publications by Ian Allan in conjunction with ARPS are made available at reduced prices.

Private members receive Transport Trust Travel Back ards yearly enabling them to visit transport museums r travel on steam railways at reduced charges (and in ome cases free). Some 120 sites are covered (1992) and are listed in *Railways Restored* and *Steam Heritage Yearbook*

Private Membership Application Form (1992)

Send this form (or photostat of) to: Membership Secretary, ARPS, 6 Ullswater Grove, Alresford, Hants SO24 9NP

Name ....
(BLOCK LETTERS PLEASE)

Address ....

....

....

Post Code .... Telephone

Subscription enclosed .... Donation enclosed

Private membership costs: 1 April-31 March (UK addresses) £12, (overseas) £15; Life membership £150 (UK), £180 (overseas).

Index